Warwick University Caribbean Studies

Across the Dark Waters

Ethnicity and Indian Identity in the Caribbean

Edited by
David Dabydeen
and Brinsley Samaroo

For Jim and Sonia Jhinkoo, and for Matthew Niland, Alicia, Amanda and Andrew Latiff

First published 1996

Published by MACMILLAN EDUCATION LTD
London and Basingstoke
Associated companies and representatives in Accra, Banjul, Cairo, Dar es Salaam, Delhi, Freetown, Gaborone, Harare, Hong Kong, Johannesburg, Kampala, Lagos, Lahore, Lusaka, Mexico City, Nairobi, São Paulo, Tokyo

ISBN 0–333–53508–1

Printed in Hong Kong

A catalogue record for this book is available from the British Library.

Cover based on a painting by Aubrey Williams presented to The Centre for Caribbean Studies, University of Warwick.

Series Preface

The importation of Africans to work as slaves on the sugar plantations of the Caribbean has generated an enormous literature, fuelled by the abolitionist movement of the early nineteenth century, by a sense of guilt, by research into the relationship between slavery and European economic growth and by the writings of Africans themselves, exposing what Europeans have preferred to keep hidden. There is also a commonly-held view that the culture of the Caribbean is primarily African in origin and inspiration. Far less attention has been paid to the history and culture of those Asians who were imported under the system of indenture – a 'new form of slavery' – between 1838 and 1917. The experiences of the Asian 'Middle Passage' have gone largely unrecorded, in spite of the horrors and mortality which invite comparison with the notorious Atlantic Middle Passage. The cultural trauma and the legacies of loss of caste occurring during the voyage from India have not been adequately studied or appreciated.

Nor have the positive contributions of Asians, principally in the Guyanas and Trinidad and to a lesser extent in the French islands and Jamaica, been properly evaluated. In spite of hardship and of being wrenched from familiar surroundings, and of the prejudices shown towards them by hard-bitten planters, by a distant Colonial Office and by fervent missionaries, many Indo-Caribbeans have achieved prominence, both in the Caribbean and internationally, in culture, politics, commerce, finance, academia, cricket and in the professions. To some extent their very success has bred inter-ethnic tensions to which cultural and religious incomprehension and intolerance have been contributory factors.

This collection of essays reflects the work of a new generation of scholars, both Indo-Caribbean and others, who are now addressing issues which have attracted little outside attention. The essays here analysing the religious dimension, focusing on less well-known aspects of the Hindu and Muslim experience as well as on processes of religious syncretism, are particularly apposite as they raise problems of identity, posing questions about differing responses of Africans and Asians to creolization.

A striking contrast between the African and Asian experience in the Caribbean has been the closer interest taken by the Indian Government (both imperial and post-imperial) as well as by other Indians – Ghandi for example – in the diaspora. There is also a marked contrast between the number of indentured labourers returning to the sub-continent and the minimal numbers of Africans returning to Africa. These wider aspects are analysed here as well as the internationalist vision of Dr Jagan whose remarkable career climaxed in his eventually coming to power after a lifetime of disappointments and reverses – an event which passed almost unnoticed in the Western press.

It is to be hoped that this wide-ranging collection will make a substantial contribution to burgeoning Indo-Caribbean studies and serve to stimulate further research in this area.

Alistair Hennessy

Warwick University Caribbean Studies

Series Editor: Alistair Hennessy

Behind the Planter's Back – Lower Class Response to Marginalty in Beguia Island, St Vincent 0–333–47460–0
Neil Price

The Bloodstained Tombs – The Muharram Massacre in Trinidad, 1884
Kelvin Singh 0–333–47177–6

The Commonwealth Caribbean in the World Economy
Ramesh Ramsaran 0–333–49867–4

Europe and the Caribbean
Editor: Paul Sutton 0–333–48785–0

Explanation in Caribbean Migration – Perception and the Image: Jamaica, Barbados, St Vincent
Elizabeth M. Thomas-Hope 0–333–53503–0

Financing Development in the Commonwealth Caribbean
Editors: Delisle Worrell, Compton Bourne,
Dinesh Dodhia 0–333–55204–0

Hindu Trinidad – Religion, Ethnicity and Socio-Economic Change
Steven Vertovec 0–333–53505–7

In Miserable Slavery – Thomas Thistlewood in Jamaica, 1750–86
Douglas Hall 0–333–48030–9

Intellectuals and Society in the Twentieth Century Caribbean
Editor: Alistair Hennessy
Vol 1: Spectre of the New Class – The Commonwealth Caribbean
0–333–53509–X
Vol 2: Unity in Variety – The Hispanic and Francophone Caribbean
0–333–56939–3

The Jamaican People 1880–1902
Patrick Bryan 0–333–55125–7

Labour in the Caribbean – From Emancipation to Independence
Editors: Malcolm Cross and Gad Heuman 0–333–44729–8

Land and Development in the Caribbean
Editors: Jean Besson and Janet Momsen 0–333–45406–5

The Literate Imagination – Essays on the Novels of Wilson Harris
Editor: Michael Gilkes 0–333–49518–7

The Powerless People – The Amerindians of the Corentyne River
Andrew Sanders 0–333–45096–5

Teachers, Education and Politics in Jamaica, 1892–1972
Harry Goulbourne 0–333–47331–0

Trinidad Ethnicity
Kevin Yelvington 0–333–56601–7

The Autobiography of a Runaway Slave (Esteban Montejo)
(Miguel Barnet: Introduction: Alistair Hennessy) 0–333–53507–3

Caribbean Revolutions and Revolutionary Theory – Cuba, Nicaragua and Grenada
Brian Meeks 0–333–57759–0

Across the Dark Waters – Ethnicity and Indian Identity in the Caribbean
David Dabydeen and Brinsley Samaroo 0–333–53508–1

The Fractured Blockade – Western Europe and Cuba during the Revolution
Alistair Hennessy and George Lambie 0–333–58365–5

French and West Indian: Martinique, Guadeloupe and French Guiana Today
Richard Burton and Fred Reno 0–333–56602–5

Noises in the Blood – Orality, Gender and the 'Vulgar' Body of Jamaican Popular Culture
Carolyn Cooper 0–333–57824–4

The United States and the Caribbean
Anthony Maingot 0–333–57231–9

Woman Version – Issues in West Indian Fiction by Women Writers
Evelyn O'Callaghan 0–333–57837–6

Caribbean Economic Policy and South–South Cooperation
Ramesh F. Ramsaran 0–333–58677–8

Frontiers of Caribbean Literature in English
Editor: Frank Birbalsingh 0–333–60062–2

From Dessalines to Duvalier – Race, Colour and National Independence in Haiti (Third Edition)
David Nicholls 0–333–65026–3

Contents

Notes on the editors and contributors

The editors

David Dabydeen is Director of the Centre for Caribbean Studies at the University of Warwick. He is a poet and novelist.

Brinsley Samaroo was until recently a Cabinet Minister in the Government of Trinidad and Tobago. He teaches in the History Department at the University of the West Indies (Trinidad).

The contributors

Malcolm Cross teaches at the Europe Research Centre of Migratory and Ethnic Relations, University of Utrecht, the Netherlands.

Ralph Premdas teaches in the Department of Government, University of the West Indies (Trinidad).

Verene Shepherd teaches in the Department of History, University of the West Indies (Jamaica).

Noorkumar Mahabir and **Ashram Maharaj** teach in Trinidad and are involved in research and publication of materials relating to Indo-Caribbean culture.

Steven Vertovec is a Research Fellow in the Centre for Research in Ethnic Relations, University of Warwick.

Peter van der Veer teaches at the Caribbean Studies Institute, Leiden University, the Netherlands.

Frank Birbalsingh teaches in the Department of English, University of York, Toronto.

Basdeo Mangru lives and works in New York, having recently completed his doctorate in Indo-Guyanese history at the School of Oriental and African Studies, London University.

Marianne Ramesar, formerly a Research Fellow in the Institute of Social and Economic Research at the University of the West Indies (Trinidad), is now a Librarian at the University.

A note on nomenclature

Historical references to Guyana before independence appear as Guiana or British Guiana.

To avoid confusion, Surinam, which was known as Dutch Guiana until 1948, is herein always referred to as Surinam. The spelling Surinam, not Suriname, follows accepted British practice.

The black population of the islands are called Africans when they are newly arrived; subsequently they are usually called Creoles, though on occasion the usages Afro-Guyanese, Afro-Jamaican and Afro-Caribbean are used. They are 'black Creoles' when Mixed Race people are also mentioned.

The Indian population of the islands are referred to as Indian, East Indian or Indo-Caribbean. Amerindians are referred to only in Tables 2.1 and 2.2 and on pp. 40, 42 and 49.

Introduction

During the period 1838 to 1917 some 551 000 indentured Indians were brought to the islands of the Caribbean and to the colonies on the northern coasts of the South American continent. In the Caribbean, the labourers were assigned to various colonies depending on the demand of the various plantocracies:

British Guiana	238 909	Surinam	34 404
Trinidad	143 939	Martinique	25 404
Guadeloupe	42 326	French Guiana	8 500
Jamaica	37 027	Grenada	3 200

Smaller numbers went to Belize (3000), St Vincent (2472), St Kitts (337) and St Croix (300). These numbers formed part of a larger Indian diaspora which witnessed the migration of about 1.4 million indentured Indians to Natal, Kenya, Uganda, Mauritius, Fiji, Malaysia, Réunion and the Seychelles.[1]

Why were these labourers required in the Caribbean in the first place? After the abolition of slavery there was the large-scale abandonment of the plantations by the ex-slaves. This occurred for a number of reasons. Many left because they wished to distance themselves from the degradation of the slave system: enforced labour, the whip, the stocks and the endless hours during crop-time. The period of apprenticeship (1834–38), which was supposed to have been a transition from slavery to freedom, was even worse than slavery, in that slave-owners sought to maximise the output from their slaves whom they were going to lose shortly. When, therefore, freedom came in 1838, the ex-slaves either worked when they needed to purchase necessities or they went off to form free villages, recreating their gardens of vegetables and root crops as they had been used to doing in Africa. In addition, many fled the plantations because the planters would not pay them a fair wage for their work. To the settlements where they went, the free Africans gave names which signified their aspirations: Mon Repos, Sans Souci, Ne Plus Ultra or Good Fortune. At other times they gave to these settlements names which reminded them of home: Congo Village, Krooman settlement or Tambar. The consequence of this abandonment was serious dislocation of the sugar industry. In 1842 the Secretary of State, Lord Stanley, told the Commons that West Indian planters were undergoing 'serious and ruinous expense in the cultivation of their estates'. To the planters whose major concern was the maximization of their profits with as little investment as possible, the labour situation could be eased by the importation of other labour to replace the disaffected Africans. Even before the slave trade in the British Empire was abolished in 1807, attempts were being made to bring labourers to the region from other parts of the world. From 1806, for example, Chinese were brought, first to Trinidad and then to British Guiana, Jamaica and the smaller Islands. His Majesty's Council in Trinidad regarded this first importation of '192 Chinamen' as a bold step towards the solution of the labour problem:

> The introduction of them into this colony appears to be a measure which His Majesty's Ministers regard as an experiment of the greatest magnitude, and from the success of which they not only consider that the early degree of prosperity and rapid advancement of this island will be secured, but that the British colonies generally in the West Indies will derive the most important benefits therefrom.[2]

But these Chinese were drawn, not from the agricultural classes of inner China but rather, from the ranks of itinerant hucksters and other tradespeople and fishermen found in the coastal areas, which were frequented by Europeans. These commercial men soon drifted away from the plantations and set up retail shops close to the estates, filling a vital need in the rural Caribbean. This was, however, not the purpose for which they were brought to the Caribbean, and this plan was quickly abandoned. By the 1870s, the flow had been reduced to a trickle.

Trial was also made of Portuguese peasants from the offshore islands of Madeira, Fayal and the Azores. Between 1834 and the 1880s some 41 000 Portuguese were brought to British Guiana, Jamaica, Trinidad, St Vincent and Grenada. This experiment was also doomed to failure. The Portuguese who were brought to the region were cultivators of vine, not sugar-cane. In addition, many of them died in the steamy swamps and lowlands of the Caribbean. Those who survived abandoned the cane fields and took to trading, vegetable-growing and cocoa-cultivation in the sheltered valleys. Recourse was then made to the free Africans of North America, who were encouraged to come and settle as free labourers in the region. In August 1840, for example, Dr Thomas Rolph of Upper Canada, offered to bring three to five hundred 'coloured people' to Trinidad. This idea found great favour with the island's governor who noted that 'the demand for field labour is very great and any number of Emigrants would find instant employment on their arrival'.[3] Rolph was referred to the colony's agent in New York. A few such persons came to the island but found the place more backward than their home bases: wages were lower, good land was difficult to obtain and communications were very poor. In a further attempt to lure workers to the region, efforts were made to induce settlers from West Africa and to use Africans freed by the British from their captors after 1807. But the infrequency and insufficiency of supplies from these sources rendered these efforts undependable. What made these matters worse, was the fear of the spread of black revolution to the other colonies in the wake of the continuing San Domingue Revolution in the early nineteenth century. The Colonial Office was loath to support immigration from West Africa. Their Caribbean governor was instructed 'neither to encourage nor discourage' such movement; the people are 'free to go or to remain, exactly as they see fit'.[4]

Around the time that these unsuccessful attempts were being made to solve the labour problem, the West Indian sugar lobby learnt of the successful use of Indians as indentured labourers on the island of Mauritius. There were favourable reports of the supposedly tractable nature of the Indian labourer and of his dedication to agricultural work. Important precedents had already been put in place in that a model contract had been drawn and a recruitment network had been started, complete with a central agency in Calcutta. What was necessary now was the extension of this system to the Caribbean. This was achieved in 1838, with the arrival of two ships carrying 396 indentured immigrants to British Guiana. In this manner was the Caribbean drawn into the vortex of a much wider mass movement of people in a period of world-wide demographic change. The Industrial Revolution had greatly opened up the world, creating a vast array of European goods which needed outlets. Equally there was the increasing demand in Europe for sources of raw materials needed to cater to the increasingly sophisticated tastes of the rising middle class. The nineteenth century was a time when Australia and New Zealand received thousands of their British cousins; when continental America was peopled from all parts of Europe; when a post-Industrial revival of imperialism stimulated a considerable extension of imperial frontiers. There were then wide open spaces in the New World and in Australasia for the expansion of European enterprise. In this movement people became as important a commodity of international trade as ores, whale-oil, rice or rolling stock.

A comparison with slavery

East Indian indentureship turned out to be, as Hugh Tinker wrote, 'a new system of slavery'. In the same manner that slavery brought together Africans of different religions and linguistic affiliations, so did indentureship create a mélange out of Bhojpuri speakers and Tamils. Beefeaters were bundled together on the same ships and on the same estates with those to whom this practice was abhorrent. Low castes now became *jahagis* (shipmates) with twice-born brahmans, and Aryan-descended North Indians rubbed shoulders with Southern Dravidians with whom they had little intercourse in India. On this later re-visit to the middle passage, a melting pot was created which broke down some of the barriers existing in the homelands. In the new environment, Hindus could be found celebrating the Muslim Shia observance of Muharram in which even Afro-West Indians participated vigorously.[5] Singaravelou, the Caribbean's leading researcher on the Indians who went to the French colonies, has documented the ways in which the Indian became integrated into French Creole society and the manner in which that partial assimilation had in turn enriched that society.[6] Indentureship, like slavery, furthered the creation of a new civilization in the Americas out of the blending of disparate traditions and the interaction of many peoples.

Upon arrival in the New World, the African slave was rested and refreshed so that he would 'look nice' for the prospective purchaser; indentureship was hardly any different. In July 1858, Mrs Jane Swinton who had accompanied her husband, captain of the 'Salsette', on a voyage from Calcutta to the Caribbean, related the manner of disposal of the newly-arrived coolies:

> They made the best appearance they could when the planters came to collect them. (It looks very like slavery). They were put into boats in sixes and sevens like cattle and sent to their different destinations. I pitied them much at parting with them.[7]

On that fateful voyage, the death toll was very reminiscent of that on the previous slave ship; out of 324 persons who had embarked at Calcutta, as many as 120 had died.

What is the present role of the East Indian population in the Caribbean? In Surinam, at the far southern end, out of a population of some 400 000, East Indians constitute 35 per cent, Javanese 15 per cent and Chinese 1.7 per cent of the population. In Guyana (which is the post-independence name of what had been British Guiana), out of a population of 940 000, East Indians form 51 per cent and Chinese 0.6 per cent. In Trinidad and Tobago, out of a population of 1.2 million, East Indians and Afro-Trinidadians are almost equally balanced at 40.5 per cent and 40.8 per cent respectively, with a Chinese population of about 1 per cent. In Jamaica, with a population of 2.3 million, East Indians constitute approximately 2 per cent and Chinese 1.2 per cent. In the French *départements* of Martinique and Guadeloupe, out of a population of some 660 000, the East Indian population forms some 16 per cent of that total. In Barbados, with a population of 257 000, Indians number about 1500 or 0.5 per cent and the Chinese are included with the others who constitute about 0.2 per cent. In the other islands of the Caribbean, Asians form about 3.2 per cent of the population of Grenada and 2.6 per cent of the population of St Lucia.

Although the larger international community records the Caribbean as predominantly Afro-influenced, the East Indian presence has certainly altered the culture of the place. This can be seen in the patterns of agricultural enterprise, commerce, politics and the region's cuisine as well as in religious and cultural expression. From the 1970s, scholarship has been catching up with this social, economic, religious and cultural reality; there is an extensive body of literature, as our bibliography indicates. Let us now look briefly at the growth of that scholarly enquiry since 1975.

In June 1975 the first conference on East Indians in the Caribbean was held on the St Augustine Campus of the University of the West Indies. In the opening address, delivered by V. S. Naipaul, a plea was made for rationality with regard to the study of the Caribbean East Indian community:

> There is an ignorance of the Indian community not only from without, but also from within. Indians here know little of the many things that have made them. But we mustn't only blame; we must also examine. I think we have to consider the culture from which we have come. And this is where the subject becomes a bit more difficult and requires a bit more than a sentimental warmth.... We forget; we have no idea of our past; it is part of the trouble.... I think that this first Indian attempt at self-examination – this intellectual response to a cultural loss, this break with the past – makes the community more complex and interesting than it perhaps has been.[8]

Since that time there has been a good deal of study and research not only on the subject of East Indians in the Caribbean but, increasingly, on the larger question of the diaspora of peoples from the Indian sub-continent since 1838. Two subsequent conferences were held in Trinidad and scholars met and presented papers in New York, Toronto and at the University of Warwick. These studies emanated not only from the New World; rational enquiry has also come through collections of essays published in India.[9] There remain wide areas to be explored, as will be pointed out presently.

This collection derives mainly from a conference conducted on the general theme of East Indians in the Caribbean, held at the University of Warwick in May 1988, organized by David Dabydeen. Not all the papers from that conference are included in this collection; some have come from a 1988 conference held at the University of York in Toronto; and others have been commissioned in order to cover areas of current interest and to give a pan-Caribbean flavour to the collection. A deliberate attempt has been made to present work which addresses the modern political situation, religious practices and beliefs and to look also at the process of syncretism at work as East Indians seek to relate to the non-Indian sections of the populations among whom they came, lately, as a strange and bewildering people.

The ever-present dilemma of race relations in the Caribbean cannot be overlooked in any study of this nature. Three essays spanning the Caribbean from Jamaica to Guyana deal with this issue in the historical as well as the contemporary dimensions. These are the essays of Malcolm Cross, Ralph Premdas and Verene Shepherd. Both Cross and Premdas work from the premise that it was an economic determinant – the scarcity of resources – which formed the initial roots of ethnic antagonism.

Subsequently, it was the degree to which resources were available or unavailable which determined the extent and intensity of ethnic rivalry. In Guiana, both during and after indentureship, the scarcity of available agricultural land was always more acute than in Trinidad. In Guiana, Cross argues, the constant contest for a scarce resource led to progressively deteriorating ethnic relations whereas in Trinidad a *modus vivendi* was worked out during the last century. Premdas takes up this theme in its various current manifestations, arguing that despite overt inter-racial interaction in Guiana, the mutual antipathies persist, reflected in a variety of forms. His theoretical framework, 'the political economy approach', argues that the competition for scarce resources, which triggered off the antagonisms in the first instance, is still very present. This primary factor of scarcity of resources soon became overlaid by all kinds of other considerations: uni-ethnic patterns of occupation, residence and voluntary organizations which did much to heighten the divide. This separation has now become institutionalized in the forces which determine the direction (or mis-direction) of that sad society. Premdas concludes gloomily that the Guyana model of race and politics tells us clearly how we should *not* move if a reasonable degree of societal harmony is to be achieved.

The experience of the East Indians in Jamaica from the start of indentureship there (1845) until the year after its abolition (1921) forms the subject of Verene Shepherd's long overview. In this instance we see a different pattern of race relations from that in Trinidad or Guiana. In Jamaica, Shepherd points out, the volume of immigrants was small, just over 30 000, as compared to 239 000 who went to Guiana and 144 000 to Trinidad. Nor was it as sustained as in the two other colonies. Additionally, Jamaican society saw the indentured Indian as a transient worker who would leave upon completion of his term of bondage. Consequently, Jamaicans were generally indifferent, or else they welcomed the Indians as a potential market for the produce which they grew. Unlike their compatriots in Trinidad and Guiana/Guyana, therefore, the Jamaican East Indian was in a more benign situation and over the years has become virtually integrated into the larger Christian population. In recent times, as many New World peoples seek relation to the source of their nativity, Indo-Jamaicans have been seeking contact with the wider East Indian community in the Caribbean. They were active participants in the conferences held in Trinidad, and cultural exchanges with Trinidad and Guyana have become the norm.

Yet another manner of looking at the question of inter-ethnic relations is to focus on similar cultural practices of both the Indo- and the Afro-West Indian. Deriving from common agricultural backgrounds in Africa and in India, both groups related to the same nature-derived divinities such as sun, moon, earth, plants and animals which were the bases of their existence. Forms of worship, belief and ritual centring on the same elements were developed in the ancestral lands and brought across the water by both peoples. In the case of the Africans in the New World, every attempt was made to wean them from these 'heathen' forms of worship, even forcibly when that was considered necessary. In the case of the East Indians, the thinking of the rulers had been modified. There was now a measure of tolerance of Indian faiths. There existed, indeed, a policy of conversion of these people to Christian faiths, but active suppression of native religions was not followed as rigorously as in the days of slavery. In the atmosphere of religious freedom that now prevails, the common links in the two areas of worship are being sought and highlighted. Noorkumar Mahabir and Ashram Maharaj explore this area in their essay on Hindu elements in the Shango/Orisha cult of Trinidad. In this essay the authors trace the development of this multi-cultural common heritage, arguing that such research can lead towards a greater understanding between the two major sectors of the population.

The Warwick conference gained much from the research into Caribbean Hinduism done by Steven Vertovec and Peter van der Veer, whose familiarity with the Caribbean work on Hinduism and the European research on Caribbean Hinduism was matched by a similar familiarity with texts and commentaries from the Indian sub-continent. Both essays present new work on the Indian origins of Caribbean Hinduism and the ongoing inspiration drawn from the original roots. In each relocation of the religion, however, significant changes have taken place as upholders of such faiths sought to trim their sails according to the new winds of change in the other India. For one thing, there has been a frontal assault on the practice of caste, as everyone now tried to assert themselves in the new order of things. Although the original sources of guidance were hardly ever disputed, the resulting modifications have recreated a form of Hinduism which is becoming more and more independent of the ancient origins and more reflective of the open society of their adoption.

One biographical chapter has been included in this collection, on the writings of the veteran Guyanese politician Cheddi Jagan. The impact of this politician on Caribbean political thought is a study that cries out for the attention of our scholars. His very numerous speeches and writings, particularly during the last three decades, need to be collated for analysis. In the interim, a brief foretaste of that fare is given in this collection. Jagan is important for many reasons, but this essay makes the point that whereas the majority of the political élite was concerned principally with the consideration of race, Jagan presented an alternative frame of reference, namely, the class line. Above all, Jagan possesses a moral strength that enables him to persist in what some call a 'rigidly dogmatic belief'. It is this moral toughness, our essayist Frank Birbalsingh concludes, which enables Jagan to bring a measure of political maturity to Guyana and now propels him forward in his burning passion to remould his society nearer to the heart's desire.

The remaining three essays are mainly historical in context. Basdeo Mangru draws from his years of research and writing on Indian immigration for his engaging chapter on the campaign for the abolition of indentureship, waged from India.[10] While a good deal has been written on the Caribbean input into this campaign to end Indian bondage, we know little about the agitation from the Indian end. In the event, this essay fills an important need, indicating clearly the disgust felt by Indians against this new form of slavery. Notwithstanding the abhorrence of the system, the West Indian plantocracy did all in its power to maintain it and it was the 'uncompromising opposition' of the anti-indenture campaigners that finally won the day. Marianne Ramesar, in her study of the repatriates, demonstrates the effectiveness of oral history, properly managed. In this essay we have a first-hand account of the voyage back to India from Trinidad, so full of excitement and drama. The narrative is followed by useful commentary on the numbers who went, the conditions on board and the general inability of the repatriates to integrate themselves into the original society. They had crossed the *Kala pani* – the ocean's dark waters – and had lost caste. Brinsley Samaroo in his chapter on early African and Indian Muslims in Trinidad and Tobago challenges the belief, commonly held, that it was the Indians who brought Islam to the Caribbean. The study demonstrates that the faith arrived with African slaves but that every attempt was made by the ruling classes to suppress it. By the mid-nineteenth century, most of the traces of African Islam had been obliterated and the revival of the religion had to await the influx of Indian Muslims during the second half of that century.

There remain, however, a number of areas which urgently need to be explored and which must be the object of future work. The most basic question to be settled is the relationship of the Caribbean East Indian to the larger West Indian environment in which the East Indians are now permanently settled. There is a general fear among this minority group that in a largely non-Indian society, their culture is being eroded and being replaced by a value-system that is neither as relevant to them nor as spiritually substaining for them as their own. The clash of their Oriental norms with those of a more open society is the cause of much anxiety. Not infrequently, it has led to women in particular resorting to the deadly weedicide gramoxone – 'Indian tonic' – as a final solution to this cultural dilemma.[11]

There has emerged, therefore, a feeling of alienation among large sectors of the population resulting in withdrawal from the larger life of the society, large-scale migration to North America, application for refugee status and most recently a call for the carving-out of a West Indian East Indian enclave in the New World, to be called Bharatiyadesh, as a homeland for the East Indians of Guyana, Surinam and Trinidad and Tobago. Our thinkers must, consequently, address their minds to this problem, namely a working-out of the premises of our participation in this society. This is no easy task in a society such as the Caribbean: of very diverse origins, complex and complicated interrelationships and powerful environmental and cultural influences.

At the cultural level, there is the need to bring together the many scattered bits and pieces of research on the festivals and religious/cultural observances which Hindus and Muslims brought to the region. A number of these are now national celebrations, attracting the larger population and adding richness to the cultural diversity of the region. One has to look also at the ways in which East Indians are now participating in cultural activities that were previously regarded as Creole, as they seek to further work out a *modus vivendi* with the wider society. In fact this whole question of the direction of cultural development in the East Indian population needs to be charted, towards a better understanding of the community.

Much work needs to be done on the lives of the leaders of East Indian descent who historically and currently have been trying to chart directions for a new people in a new milieu. There is enough material in our archives, in our oral tradition and in our literature for an outpouring of writing on the women who led the agitation for better conditions, beginning in Central Trinidad during the 1930s. We now know who were the religious and political leaders in Guyana and Surinam who stood up against colonial rule and encouraged their compatriots in the spirit of resistance. Those East Indians who embraced Christianity as a means of obtaining Western education and thereby entry into the mainstream of the society need to be studied. Similarly those who entered the trade union movement and subsequently sought political office at a time when colonial society saw the East Indian's place as the cane fields; those pioneers need now to be presented as beacons for the new generation. Biographies must now be a cornerstone of the new work.

Another area which needs to be explored is the remigration of East Indians from the Caribbean to North America and Europe. Some work has been started on this aspect of the diaspora but this is only the beginning.[12] To what extent does the Caribbean remain a source of inspiration? Is this second wave a temporary phenomenon or is it a permanent feature? What are the contacts with 'home' and what new forms of social and political organization do we see in the new regions of settlement?

Finally, the most under-researched aspect of the East Indian presence is in the area of gender studies. The historiography is dominated by men, as our own book reveals. Caribbean societies have not yet matured to the point where women are adequately represented at their universities. The few women scholars that exist tend to be under-resourced, in terms of overseas travel grants, for instance. Male scholars must not only consider the particularities of female experience in their writings on the East Indian experience, but they must also campaign for resources to be redirected to female scholars so that the latter may gain access to research materials. They must also seek to alter the practices of their academies to allow for growth in numbers of female scholars. Alternative and potentially radical or original perspectives on East Indian history will not emerge without such growth.[13]

If the essays in this collection, together with the suggestions of new work, have the effect of clearing up previous areas of darkness and of stimulating ideas about additional research, then the authors' aim will have been achieved. The East Indian in the Caribbean and abroad is at a critical historical moment: pulled by an ancient ancestral culture with fixed theories on the position of the individual in time and in space and, on the other hand, tugged by the constantly changing values of a new society where variation is the only thing that is constant. On the one side there is the constant, involuntary assertion of (what some have called) the bio-genetic memory, seeking to recreate the ambience of a former, spiritual life. On the other side there is the dissonance created by the sights and sounds of a profoundly materialistic society where the norms are quite different. The longer we take to probe these fundamental issues, the longer we prolong the agony of adjustment. This collection hopes to take us one step closer towards that realization.

Notes

1 Figures drawn mainly from Steven Vertovec, *Hindu Trinidad*, Warwick University Caribbean Studies (London: Macmillan, 1992), p. 4.

2 CO 295/14. Hislop to Windham. (No. 44) Minutes of meeting of H. M. Council, 15 October 1806.

3 CO 295/131. Macleod to Russell, 14 November, 1840.

4 CO 295/133. Enclosure in Macleod to Russell, 20 May 1841.

5 Kelvin Singh, *Bloodstained Tombs: The Muharram Massacre 1884*, Warwick University Caribbean Studies (London: Macmillan, 1988), pp. 6f.
6 See, for example, *Les Indiens de Guadeloupe* (Bordeaux, 1975), pp. 149 and 179f.
7 James Carlile, *Journal of a Voyage with Coolie Emigrants* (London, 1859, p. 15).
8 V. S. Naipaul's introduction to *East Indians in the Caribbean: Colonialism and the struggle for identity* (ed.) B. Brereton and W. Dookeran (New York: Kraus International Publications, 1982), pp. 3 and 4.
9 For examples, I. J. Bahadursingh (ed.), *The Other India*. (New Delhi: Arnold-Heinemann, 1979). Also I. J. Bahadursingh (ed.), *Indians in the Caribbean* (New Delhi: Sterling Publishers, 1987).
10 Basdeo Mangru, *Benevolent Neutrality: Indian Goverment policy and labour migration to British Guiana, 1854–1884* (London: Hansib Publications, 1987).
11 Ramabai Espinet, 'The Invisible Indian Woman in Trinidad and Tobago', unpublished essay. The editors are grateful to Espinet for sight of her essay. It was our intention to include Espinet's essay in our volume but it was already promised to another publication and copyright issues prevented dual publication.
12 For example, M. Gosine, *Caribbean East Indians in America* (New York: Windsor Press, 1990).
13 Espinet, 'The Invisible Indian Woman', has argued that under the umbrella of the patriarchal structure brought from India, women were marginalized and kept under the veil of the purdah system even in the twentieth century. See also Patricia Mohammed, 'The "Creolization" of Indian Women in Trinidad', in Selwyn Ryan (ed.), *Trinidad and Tobago: The Independence Experience 1962–1987* (St Augustine: Institute of Social and Economic Research, University of the West Indies, 1988), pp. 381–97; 'The Caribbean Family Revisited', in Patricia Mohammed and Catherine Shepherd (eds), *Gender in Caribbean Development* (St Augustine: Institute of Social and Economic Research, University of the West Indies, 1988), pp. 170–82; and 'Structures of Experience: Gender, Ethnicity and Class in the Lives of Two East Indian Women', in Kevin A. Yelvington (ed.), *Trinidad Ethnicity* (London: Macmillan, 1993, pp. 208–34); Rhoda Reddock, *Women, Labour and Politics in Trinidad and Tobago: A History* (London: Zed Books, 1994).

Part I

Race relations

CHAPTER 1 East Indian–Creole relations in Trinidad and Guiana in the late nineteenth century

Malcolm Cross

> There were in effect two semi-autonomous sets of working class struggles against the domination of capital – the one conducted by the descendants of ex-slaves and the other by indentured labourers and their fellow Indians. Pursuing their legitimate aspirations, these two ethnically defined sectors of the laboring people could and did come into conflict with each other (Walter Rodney, *A History of the Guyanese Working People*, 1981, p. 179).

In his masterly study of the working class of Guiana in the late nineteenth century, Walter Rodney argues that inter-racial or inter-ethnic discord must be seen in the context of the indentureship system, and – in particular – the use of the system to repress, displace and undermine the Afro-Guianese working class. This is undoubtedly true. Rodney goes on to suggest that there were five main reasons for a 'racial contradiction' emerging in what was, in essence, a working-class struggle. These were the numbers of Indian immigrants, their separation from the Afro-Guianese population, the mutual unintelligibility of cultural traditions, the 'slow rate of diversification of the colonial economy' and the attempt to exploit racial differences by those with state power. What Rodney does not do is weigh the significance of these factors.

This chapter is an attempt to do that by looking at the indenture system in its local context in both Guiana and Trinidad.[1] Immediately this is attempted, it becomes clear that some of the issues that Rodney addresses are much less relevant than others. While it is true that relatively and absolutely more Indians were imported into Guiana than Trinidad, it is not immediately obvious why the simple demographic fact of numbers should create a sense of injustice. We can see from elsewhere that numbers of immigrants can be very low and still generate fears of 'swamping'. The issue is one of competition or the availability of resources and the degree to which differences are exploited for political ends. I argue in this chapter that the key issue of resources was not numbers but land. Second, I do not accept the 'spatial' or the 'cultural' arguments. While the question is not specifically addressed in this chapter, there is no reason to suppose that where propinquity is increased, hostilities diminish. On the contrary, the opposite is probably true. Certainly in Trinidad, where inter-ethnic hostilities were far less, it would not be true that propinquity was greater. Moreover, there is no reason to think that the cultural gap was wider in Guiana than in Trinidad which, if we accept that important relevant differences existed between these two colonies, suggests that we should not look to culture itself for an adequate explanation.

On the other hand, the remaining two arguments used by Rodney are confirmed as being of major importance. This chapter opens therefore with some comparative notes on the indenture systems in each territory and then looks at explanations for understanding the relations between newly-arrived Indians and indigenous or migrant Africans in terms of land availability, economic conditions and official policies. The argument is that in these topics lie the essential differences, and thus the key issues in accounting for patterns of inter-ethnic rivalry.

The indenture period

It is hardly surprising that the abolition of slavery should have prompted the black Creoles to try to leave the estates that were associated in their minds with such previous degradation. There is every reason to suppose that this was a common feature throughout the West Indies, but whereas Jamaica, Barbados and the smaller islands did not have land readily available, Trinidad and Guiana certainly did. In Trinidad there were plentiful supplies of fertile land in the Northern and Central ranges which, in terms of accessibility, were also suited to peaceful squatting as well as subsistence agriculture. Despite the vast size of Guiana, fertile land was confined largely to the narrow coastal strip, and was not as easy to obtain. Crown lands too required extensive and expensive preparation which made squatting more difficult, so that much of the drive for independence from the estates had to be in the form of land purchases. Although by the time of complete emancipation on 1 August 1838 there were a number of settlements already in existence, these had tended to form as trading posts at ferry-points such as on the Mahaica and Mahaicony Rivers and at Williams Town on the Essequibo Coast.[2] Individual Creoles bought front lands from some plantation owners but these were notoriously difficult to maintain with the critical problems of drainage and irrigation with which all the estates had to contend.[3]

What was particularly important during this period was the collective purchase of plantations by groups of freed Creoles. These were later to form the first real village settlements entirely independent of the plantations. The first of these was taken over in November 1839 when 83 former slaves paid 30 000 guilders for Plantation Northbrook on the Demerara East Coast. Part of its 500 acres was later to be renamed as the village of Victoria. Again, plantation New Orange Nassau (380 acres) was bought by 128 Creoles for $50 000 in April 1840 and later became Buxton. These were soon followed by plantations such as Beterverwagting, Fellowship, Dem Amstel, Plaisance, Friendship, Litchfield, Perseverance, Ithaca, Gibralter, Rosehall and Liverpool. Initially an attempt was made to run the plantation as a genuine cooperative, but this type of shareholding usually failed and the land was then divided up in accordance with the amount of initial investment. In this way the Creole villages of Guiana were formed.[4]

The effect on the sugar plantations was marked, for labour became very scarce and sporadic and wage rates doubled. In all probability the 'push' from the estates was much stronger than the 'pull' of peasant proprietorship for the treatment that the labourers could expect on the estates was almost as harsh as in the earlier period and land was very difficult to obtain. There is no doubt, however, that the plantations began to decline for lack of labour. Sometimes attempts to deter the loss of labour during slavery rebounded upon the planter after emancipation in a quite specific way. For example, a slave seeking to buy his freedom would hear his master declaring his worth, albeit exaggerated, to the court and was loath thereafter to work for anything less. This argument convinced at least one contemporary:

> In that valuation he (the planter) sought ... to impede the negro in his desire for freedom but by it *he settled on oath the future rate of wages.*[5]

Despite higher wages and the other steps taken by the planters to retain their labour, such as preventing the black Creoles obtaining land or destroying their crops, a serious alienation of labour occurred in both colonies.[6] After a number of other possible labour supplies had been unsuccessfully tried, the owner of plantations Vreeden Hoop and Vreedestein in Guiana wrote to a firm in Calcutta requesting immigrants under an indenture contract. This letter, written by John Gladstone, father of William Ewart, on 4 January 1836, really marks the first West Indian interest in labour from India.[7] It resulted in the arrival of 396 'coolies' in two ships in 1838 under five-year indenture contracts, of whom 236 were to return to India in 1843, while almost two-thirds of the remainder died – often from ill-treatment. It was reports of slave-like conditions in Guiana and Mauritius which led to the temporary cessation of Indian immigration from 11 July 1838 until it was revived under pressure from the planters in 1845. In all, over 380 000

Indians were eventually introduced into Trinidad and Guiana during the indenture period, as shown in Table 1.1.

Table 1.1 East Indians introduced into Trinidad and Guiana mainly under indenture, 1838–1918[8]

Year	*Guiana*	*Trinidad*
1838	396	–
1845–50	12 374	5 568
1851–55	9 981	5 054
1856–60	16 206	11 208
1861–65	15 654	7 474
1866–70	22 436	11 836
1871–75	24 355	11 868
1876–80	27 374	12 763
1881–85	20 500	11 551
1886–90	20 471	13 988
1891–95	21 397	13 565
1896–1900	14 780	7 414
1901–05	13 177	12 433
1906–10	10 592	12 547
1911–15	7 304	4 051
1916–18	1 912	2 619
	238 909	143 939

During the period from 1843 to 1916, 66 140 Indians returned to India from Guiana and 29 448 from Trinidad, usually with free or later with assisted passages. These returning immigrants reached their peak in 1891–95 for Guiana when 10 082 Indians left, compared with a high point of 3838 a decade later in Trinidad. Of course, long after the indenture system ended, many immigrants were entitled to return passages. Thus in 1930 the Government of Trinidad, in answer to a question from Saran Teelucksingh, estimated that 42 000 Indians were still entitled to return passages in addition to the 41 763 who had already been repatriated by 1929.[9] It was common practice to return not only those who wished to exercise their rights under the original contract but also those who were a drag upon the resources of the colony. In 1931, 56 per cent of the 1012 Indians returned to India from Trinidad were classified as 'destitutes'; a proportion far in excess of that for earlier years.[10] For example, in Guiana the total sent back who were classified as 'criminals, bad characters, habitual idlers, infirm, old, blind, lepers etc.,' was 3584 for the whole period 1838–1859.[11]

Migration from India to these West Indian colonies was not the only inflow of labour – although it was by far the most important. Guiana received far more Portugese-speaking Maderians and Chinese than Trinidad, as Table 1.2 shows.

Table 1.2 Migrants introduced into British Guiana and Trinidad, 1834–1918[12]

Origins and year of entry	*Guiana*	*Trinidad*
India (1838–1918)	238 909	143 939
Madeira (1835–81)	32 216	897
Africa (1834–67)	14 060	8 854
China (1852–84)	13 533	2 645
Europe	381	–
Other	1 868	1 333

In terms of the social characteristics of the Indian immigrants, there is no reason to suppose that there was any great variation in recruitment for each colony. Nearly all the immigrants came originally through the port of Calcutta though they were drawn from the United Provinces and Bihar.[13] A survey of the Immigration Agent-General's records in Georgetown revealed that 85 per cent of immigrants were recruited from this area and that 83 per cent fell between the ages of 10 and 30 years. The average sex-ratio worked out at slightly over two men to every woman, although in both colonies this was far more unequal when the system first started. The disparity was reduced through pressure from government sources. Because of continued trouble over infidelity on the estates, a minimum of 40 women to every 100 men were recruited, which was achieved by paying more for women to recruiting agents.[14]

In both societies the ordinances governing the introduction and treatment of the Indians were comprehensive and paternalistic. They determined in law the conditions of recruitment, housing and health of the immigrants. There were also sections on marriage, divorce and conditions of work (including a minimum wage) and the penalties which were likely to be incurred for offences (such as 'wilful indolence' or absconding) against the indenture code.[15] A government department was set up for the purpose of enforcing this code and in general supervising the welfare of the Asiatics. In Trinidad the head of this department, following the Indian precedent, was styled the 'Protector of Immigrants' while in Guiana he was known as the Immigration Agent-General, or more popularly both the office and the incumbent came to be termed the Crosby after James Crosby, a particularly sympathetic and fair-minded holder of that office from 1858 to 1880.

The societies into which the Indians came were essentially very similar, for there was not that much to discriminate between a plantation in Guiana and one in Trinidad. The graphic picture painted by Edward Jenkins could have depicted with equal accuracy a plantation along the West coast of Trinidad:

> Take a large factory in Manchester, or Birmingham, or Belfast, build a wall round it, shut in its work people from all intercourse, save at rare intervals, with the outside world, keep them in absolute heathen ignorance, and get all the work you can out of them, treat them not unkindly, leave their social habits and relations to themselves, as matters not concerning you who make the money from their labour, and you would have constituted a little community resembling, in no small degree, a sugar estate village in British Guiana.[16]

And yet a crucial difference began to emerge very early on in the post-emancipation societies, which was later to become magnified by a number of important events. This was essentially to do with the relations between the ethnic and racial groups constituting each society. In both, the intention of the planters was, apart from merely acquiring cheap labour, to offer competition to the despised black Creole labourers. Throughout much of the literature of the period runs a streak of smug retribution by the planters for what they regarded as the disloyal and ungrateful attitude of the Creoles who were no longer prepared to suffer their previous indignities. It is this which lies behind the emphasis on the 'coolies', supposed virtues of thrift and industry. And it is perhaps at this time that the familiar stereotypes of the Creole appear most frequently, for such caricatures had no real function in a system based solely on coercion but became more necessary after emancipation.

In the early years it is hard to find a voice raised against the indenture system from within the societies themselves although, as before, the Anti-Slavery Society could be relied upon to challenge what to them appeared to be merely vicarious slavery. Barrett sarcastically warned against encomiums of Indian indentureship and slavery alike:

> In the old days of slavery, every tropical tongue was eloquent in descriptions of the comfort of the slave, his abundant rations of food and rum, and his happy exception from those vulgar earth-born cares that distracted the heart of his languid master, residing in his humble Belgravian home.[17]

They, at least, saw no more reason to believe the glowing testimonials to the new system than they had for the old.

The important point is that the threat offered by the arrival of the

Indians proved to be a very real one for the Creoles of Guiana whereas it did not emerge as anywhere near such a strong force in Trinidad. As a result, relations between Indians and Creoles in the latter society fluctuated between indifference and passive hostility while for the former, competition was continually perceived as being present and overt conflict along racial lines was common. I will document the degree to which this was so before going on to account for it.

The pattern of inter-ethnic relations

The Wesleyan missionary H. V. P. Bronkhurst, who had spent his life's work among the East Indians in Guiana, was in no doubt that this conflict was real – so much so that only the cessation of immigration (a policy which he advocated) would prevent it:

> There is no denying the fact that there exists an uncalled-for, bitter feeling between the native Creole and the Indian Immigrant towards each other. The native looks upon the heathen Indian as an intruder or interloper, whilst the Indian looks down upon the native black as a being inferior to him in a social aspect. Very often in the Colony disturbances of a serious nature take place between the Asiatics and the descendants of the old slaves, which end in a free fight; and I suppose this feeling of hatred and dislike for each other will last as long as Immigration from India continues.[18]

He seemed to feel, however, that Christianity would cope eventually with those that were there, but that the fight to integrate them would never be successful if thousands more, committed to 'heathen idolatry', were admitted. In particular he singled out competition in the crucial field of employment as the area of greatest strife and another reason why immigration should cease.

> At times I have sincerely wished that Immigration from India could altogether be stopped, so as to enable the native Creole to enter the labour field without any opposition.[19]

Where there is a chance of comparing the reception given to the Indians in both colonies, the evidence again shows that a much more hostile reaction came from the Creoles of Guiana. Surgeon-Major D. W. D. Comins, the Protector of Immigrants in Calcutta, who visited both colonies at the request of the Government of India in 1891, supported the view put forward by Bronkhurst and remarked that

> There is not as yet an approach to anything like fusion between the immigrants and other sections of the population, in fact between them and the blacks there is a mutual antipathy.[20]

Indeed, it was partly on the basis of this antipathy that the gold-mines of the interior became solely a black preserve:

> In this colony Indian immigrants are not allowed to the gold diggings, where being physically weaker than the negroes, in the minority, and not overloved by the blacks, they would probably be roughly treated.[21]

But Comins was much more impressed with the position which the Indians had come to occupy in Trinidad – his next port of call on leaving Guiana. In fact he could hardly contain his enthusiasm for the lot of the immigrant, especially if he had been able to acquire his own lands in the Northern or Central Ranges after serving the initial five years of the Indenture. Beneath his usual paternalism, it is obvious that he perceived a far more rosy situation:

> Here the cooly, who in India has been accustomed to lead a life of drudgery to gain the daily pittance sufficient to keep him alive, finds himself the possessor of a comfortable homestead with an increasing farm of the richest and most fertile land around him on which he lives with his family and becomes in a small way quite an important person.[22]

At times Comins seems to become almost lyrical at the possibilities which pertained for the fortunate Indian:

> it looks very much as if they [Indians] [are] going in the course of years to take entire possession of this beautiful island, through the principal forests of which they are boring in every direction and turning what was dense jungle into a highly cultivated garden.[23]

On the other hand, Comins was not quite so keen on the condition of those still serving indenture contracts, for the ordinances in Trinidad lacked the comprehensive coverage of the new 1891 Ordinance in British Guiana.[24] He remarks that

> The immigration Ordinances of Trinidad are so little in accord which [sic] actual practice, and are so far behind what is now expected in a first class colony, that a complete revision is necessary.[25]

It was another eight years before his warning was heeded and then two revisions followed quickly on each other to bring Trinidad into line.[26]

Despite all this, when it came to the question of permanent settlement, the representative of the Indian Government was in no doubt at all as to where his fellow countrymen received the better deal:

> Of all the colonies of the West Indies, Trinidad is the favoured home of the coolie settler, where he can easily and rapidly attain comfortable independence, and even considerable wealth with corresponding social position. British Guiana, in consequence of the long continued efforts of successive generations of legislators and planters, has brought its system for the beneficial control of indentured labour to a higher pitch of perfection than any other colony, but it has no such solid advantages to offer the settler as Trinidad. If I were a coolie I should like to spend my indentured service in British Guiana, and then settle down in the hills of Trinidad.[27]

Explanations of difference

There are three reasons – or rather groups of reasons – that seem to have been important in raising the level of competition and conflict between the different ethnic groups in Guiana relative to that in Trinidad. While these are not discrete categories, I will discuss them under the headings of availability of land, the overall social and economic situation, and the attitudes and policies of the planters.

The land question

In the first place, there seems little doubt that for all the vast areas of empty land in Guiana there was little which was suitable for the type of crop that the Creoles, trying to get away from the estates, might have wished to grow. To this day the sandy loams between the alluvial coastlands and high uplands of Guiana support little but tropical forest, and they must have seemed an impenetrable barrier to the aspiring Creoles. It is true that they bought old estates and often found land on the banks of the great rivers that divide the hinterland, but even for those who were successful, life could be particularly hard. The most pressing problem was coping with the ravages of the sea on one side and the flood waters from the highlands behind – an almost insuperable task. The planters themselves were constantly demanding assistance from central revenues to help them, but the independent smallholder stood no chance of any such help – not least because he could expect nothing but unmitigated opposition from the planters themselves.

The policy of the government was not, in general, to encourage land-settlement but where it did it was only for the benefit of the Indians. In order to absolve the Colony from the costs of returning former indentured labourers to India in accord with their contracts, the Government instituted a number of land-settlement schemes. The first of any note was the old plantation at Huis t'Dieran in Essequibo which was bought in 1880 and laid out in two-acre plots for the sole use of the Indians, who were prepared to commute their return passage. After November 1882, when 49 residential plots and 69 for cultivation had been laid out, the policy of granting land in lieu of a return passage was ended and the plots had to be bought. Whether purchased or not, this settlement, and later ones at Helena, Whim and Bush Lot, all proved disastrous failures and those that had not already been inundated and ruined by water were effectively destroyed by the drought of 1899.[28] The interesting point is that all of these land-settlement schemes were for the sole benefit of the Indians and even though they never rivalled the successes achieved by the Indians on their own, it must have been a policy which aggravated the sense of frustration and bitterness felt by the 'dispossessed' Creoles.

In Trinidad events were rather different. First, there was abundant fertile land available. Much of this was taken over illegally by squatters, some of whom had extensive estates under cocoa, occasionally in excess of one thousand trees. Despite the obvious annoyance of the planters, no great attempts were made to remove such squatters and indeed a number of governors, such as J. H. T. Manners–Sutton and Lord Harris before him, had declared themselves in favour of establishing an independent peasantry. But it was during the term of Arthur Hamilton Gordon (1866–70) that this policy became firmly established. Between 1847 and 1865 only 3423 acres of Crown Land had been sold – and that at the comparatively high price of $10 (£2.08) per acre. Such were the financial and legal difficulties involved that even by the time of Gordon only 4.63 per cent of the surface of Trinidad was legally occupied.[29]

Gordon halved the price of Crown Lands and lessened the administrative burden entailed in acquiring them. Squatters with long-established holdings were normally granted legal rights while others were moved to new settlements. Gordon did pursue the same line of policy as the administrators of Guiana but with far more success:

> By the end of 1870, one-hundred and eighty time expired Indians had commuted their return passages for land and another ninety-six had bought nearly one-thousand acres between them.[30]

But apart from this, lands were not distributed along racial lines and many Creoles gained an independent economic base during this period.

Testimony to the importance of Gordon's policies comes from a number of quarters. For example, Sir William Des Voeux, Governor of St Lucia but formerly magistrate on the west coast of Demerara, and bane of the planter interest for his outspoken criticisms over the suffering of Indians, referred to Gordon as a man 'whose views in respect of coolie immigration and the subject races generally were much in accord with my own and who had already carried out in Trinidad some of the reforms which I desired for British Guiana'.[31]

So far as Crown Lands in Guiana were concerned it was not until more than twenty years later that the cost was substantially reduced. On 14 January 1890, Crown Lands, which before had cost $10 an acre, were reduced to one dollar (21p).[32] In addition, it was only at this time that the previous policy of refusing to alienate Crown Land in parcels of under 100 acres was modified; a policy which did not finally disappear until 1898. Even then the settlements which could be opened up, and the encouragement given by the Government, were almost solely for rice-growing – an occupation peculiarly suited to the Indians but one which was anathema to the Creoles.

Dr Comins too was keen to point out the important effect that Gordon's policies had had on the fortunes of, in particular, the Indians:

> How greatly the system he (Gordon) introduced has prospered is sufficiently illustrated by the fact that at the present day Indian immigrants alone own or occupy 35,844 acres of land besides 2,026 lots and 2,480 houses.[33]

It was the continuation of Gordon's policy which was of crucial significance after the sugar crisis of 1885, for this depression stimulated the exodus from the estates and thus the demand for land, which, in the case of Trinidad, could easily be met. Not only was the policy of distributing Crown lands continued by a number of Gordon's successors (notably Sir William Robinson), but they undertook the vital improvements to the road system which itself became another important source of employment:

> New facilities were given to the buying and holding of Crown Lands in places the choice of which was left to the purchaser. The extension of roads not only gave lucrative employment, but introduced the immigrants to parts of the island remote from the sugar estates.[34]

Because of the comparatively healthy state of Trinidad's economy during the slump in primary product prices after 1890, she was able to continue building up an effective communications system. In fact, it was only in Trinidad that official funds were sanctioned for such expenditure, constituting as it did only 'indirectly remunerative' investment.[35]

Where the two main racial groups were forced to remain in praedial work on the estates it appears that antipathetic feelings deepened between them. This was the case in Guiana where Africans were paid substantially more as cane-cutters than the Indians could hope to achieve as weeders.[36] This discrimination was justified in terms of the Africans' greater strength, but it is notable that this competitive situation did not enter the fields in Trinidad where all the labour on the estates, with the exception of the factory workers, was East Indian. This is not to deny that cane-cutters were paid more in Trinidad but any antagonisms this engendered were kept within the Indian group. It is also true that factory workers could expect more money but they were not viewed as competition in the same sense and, in any case, they worked much longer – averaging for the year about ten hours per day but rising in crop-time to 16–18 hours.

The availability of land for both races in Trinidad also had the effect of bringing into existence the so-called 'cane farmers', who were independent smallholders supplying cane to the central factory or *usine*. The establishing of these *usines* greatly assisted the development of the cane farmers, who were initially made up of Creoles and Indians. In 1899 they supplied 20 per cent of the cane milled and by 1908 they grew 139 422 of the 519 756 tons of cane produced, or 27 per cent.[37] The total number divided into racial groups at around the turn of the century is given in Table 1.3 which also shows the growing predominance of the Indians who now completely control this crucial part of the Trinidad sugar industry.[38]

Table 1.3 East Indian and Creole cane farmers in Trinidad, 1898–1908[39]

Year	*East Indian*	*Creole*
1898	2326	3824
1899	2826	3870
1900	2826	3591
1901	3819	4737
1902	4506	4850
1903	4443	4440
1904	4646	4685
1905	5424	5462
1906	6127	5446
1907	6557	5777
1908	5922	5619

Cocoa farming offered another opportunity for settlement and subsistence independent of the estates. At the turn of the century, cocoa was the most important export from Trinidad – much of it, again, grown on smallholdings of a few acres. Where independent peasant holdings were possible these appear to have lessened racial tension by effectively reducing direct competition. In Trinidad the Indians were soon occupying new lands in direct proportion to their overall strength in the population. Thus although between 1885 and 1890 they were taking only 24 per cent by area of the total land distributed while they constituted 35.10 per cent (70 218) of the population in 1891, the average for the period 1891–95 had risen to 34 per cent.[40] They were by no means as fortunate in Guiana, either in the volume or proportion of the land which they were able to acquire.

Wage levels and economic conditions

The overall economic development of each colony and, in particular, the way this impinged upon the lives of the various constituent groups is another related cause of heightened inter-group tension. In general, shortage of labour stimulated competition between employers and tended to improve the lot of the worker, while shortage of work had the effect of stimulating conflict between labourers. Even before the advent of the oil industry, Trinidad was more prosperous than Guiana, with competition between sugar and cocoa cultivators producing a more buoyant market for labour, although this had only marginal effects upon wages – possibly preventing them falling as much as they would have done during depressions. In Guiana the continued flood of Indians, and the lack of alternative avenues of employment, stimulated the demand for work while at the same time providing little pressure for the improvement of conditions on the estates themselves.

Perhaps one of the most important insights into the condition of the Indians in Guiana during the nineteenth century may be drawn from the report of the commission set up to enquire into allegations made by George William Des Voeux, who had been a stipendiary magistrate during the 1860s. His letter, sent from his new posting in St Lucia to the Secretary of State, Earl Granville, on Christmas Day, 1869, following riots in Demerara, was described by *The Times* as the severest criticism of public officers 'since Hastings was impeached for tyranny over the Lord of the Holy City of Benares and over the Ladies of the Princely House of Oude'.[41]

To Des Voeux himself it was intended as no such thing but rather a plea for a change in the system which allowed human beings to live in such conditions of degradation and exploitation. For example, on the punitive application of the labour laws concerning absconding, he reflected,

> while the law compelled me to punish for desertion, and the fear of causing a wholesale abandonment of the estates rendered it

> necessary to make this substantial, the half starved appearance of most of those convicted could not but raise unpleasant doubts as to the conditions of life on the plantations which caused them to prefer to it the precarious existence of a fugitive.[42]

The most fundamental criticism that he had to make was aimed not at the public officers directly but at the inordinate misuse of uncontrolled power by the planters. He charged that the conditions of health and welfare of the indentured immigrants would never improve while the doctors were employed by the estates and even the magistrates enforcing the labour ordinances invariably deferred to the planter interest.[43]

It was Des Voeux's conclusion on continued immigration that the arrival of the Indians may initially have had a salutary effect upon the Creoles but that the competition which they now offered had dispossessed this group to the point where immigration could not now be condoned. As he expressed it:

> The Negro labourers ... required competition as an incitement to industry, and the lesson which has been taught them has been doubtless wholesome and just, though a very severe one. But I would most respectfully urge that its severity is now becoming disproportionate to its justice, and every year more so.[44]

The report itself is remarkable for the fact that it denies the majority of Des Voeux's accusations while at the same time collecting information, and even adducing arguments, which show that his charges were *under-* rather than overstated.[45] On the specific charges that Des Voeux makes, the commissioners concluded that in default of surer knowledge and wider information he was personally not entitled to bring them.[46] Not only did they dismiss most of the points contained in the letter; they were of the opinion that its existence justified the attempts made by the planters to hide the very things that Des Voeux had unearthed.

Thus they vindicate the apparent reticence of the planters to reveal details of the indenture system by saying,

> if we have sometimes had cause to complain that witnesses from whom we have expected much have given us the minimum of information possible, we cannot but recognise that it was a difficult thing for members of the community to seem, by frank disclosures of the weak places in the system to make common cause with the common accuser.[47]

Despite this, Des Voeux himself was later to write that he obtained satisfaction – not so much from the Commission itself or from the unsympathetic official reaction (with the notable exception of James Crosby) as from the sudden expenditure on improving the conditions of the Indian workers which the planters felt necessary before defending their position.

One way the planters circumvented the minimum wage specified in the indenture contract was to make arbitrary distinctions between 'effective' and 'non-effective' labour. Even so, the Commission discovered a large number of remarkable discrepancies. For example, on Plantation Schoon Ord the manager claimed that his 263 'effective' male labourers were paid 48 cents per day and that they worked on average four days per week. This, the Commissioners concluded, must mean that his annual wage bill merely for the 'effective' male workers was 200 × 263 × 0.48 or $25 248. In fact the books for the estate showed that the total wage bill for *all* workers was only $10 471, 'that is to say, two fifths of the sum that, at 48 cents per working day, ought to have been earned by the effective indentured males only'.[48]

The exploitation of racial divisions

Apart from the ill-effects of the intense competition which the Indians brought to the labour market in Guiana, the report arising from Des Voeux's accusations also remarks on the inter-racial conflict induced by the tradition of having Creole drivers for task gangs on the estates – another notable difference from the situation in Trinidad. Coming as they did from Creole villages where many felt alienated from land which they felt to be rightfully theirs, the Creoles remaining on the estates are said to have used any positions of power they retained to make life as difficult as possible for the 'coolies':

> the African blood has asserted its superiority over the Asiatic, in the fact that a negro gang has always a negro for a driver, with here and there an exception in favour of a Portugese; but, upon the whole, it is most common for the Chinese to have a Chinese for a driver, and the Coolies a negro.[49]

While in these positions of power, the claim was that 'the negroes are apt to be violent and brutal, more from contempt than dislike, with Asiatics'.[50]

The Commissioners perceived the value of this mutual animosity for the stability of the planting interest for, with united opposition to the system being out of the question, the Africans would always take exception to agitation by the Indians. In an approving remark on this policy of 'divide and rule' they say:

> The Coolie despises the negro, because he considers him a being not so highly civilized as himself; while the negro, in turn, de-

> spises the Coolie, because he is so immensely inferior to him in physical strength. *There never will be much danger of seditious disturbances among East Indian immigrants on estates as long as large numbers of negroes continue to be employed with them.*[51] (emphasis added)

This would hardly have been the conclusion in Trinidad where, despite animosity between the racial groups, there was much more chance, even at this time when the slump in sugar was making itself felt, of united action on what could loosely be called a 'class' front. Certainly there is evidence of the Creoles combining in some protests with the Indians. For example, incensed at restrictive regulations governing Carnival in 1882, blacks joined with Indians in their defiance over similar repressions at Muharram.[52] On 30 October 1884 the police fired on a gang of 2000 people attempting to take their *tadjah* into San Fernando and thence to the sea, killing 16 and wounding 80. The presence of Creoles on this occasion in Trinidad certainly did not prevent trouble but seems to have fomented opposition to officialdom. One observer of the riots – a magistrate – commented that 'their number is estimated at two-thousand and they were accompanied by Creoles, dressed as Coolies'.[53] The leading role taken by the Creoles in what was essentially an Indian problem was again pointed out by an army officer:

> They came steadily on towards us, preceded by a great many creoles, also armed with sticks, who came up and stood all around us.[54]

In addition, one Creole, George Andrew, was given a six-month sentence for inciting Indians to violence.

Possibly the greatest source of conflict was over wage rates. In both colonies the Indians were blamed for reducing wage levels. It is not particularly significant to point out that wage rates may have fallen anyway as a consequence of the general depression after 1890 for, particularly in Guiana, the Indians were *perceived* as the main reason for the worsening plight of the Creoles. Part of the general opposition to continued immigration was often voiced in terms of the inequity of continuing a system whereby all members of the society paid for part of the cost of immigration by levies, duties and taxes, and not merely the planters who stood to gain directly. It was bad enough to see one's chances of work reduced, but to be forced to contribute was seen as positively suicidal. Perhaps the best statements of this feeling and the way that it incensed the Creoles of Guiana while only irritating them in Trinidad is contained in the papers laid before the Sanderson Committee of 1910.[55]

The Committee, in common with all previous and most subsequent enquiries of a similar kind, tended to come to conclusions consonant with planter interest and, in particular, the planters' views on the desirability of further immigration. On the latter question they were in no doubt:

> the continuation and extension of the system of immigration into British Guiana, British Honduras and the British West Indies of agricultural labourers from India is in the highest degree desirable....[56]

This was a view to which the Planters' Association in British Guiana readily subscribed. However, opposition to any such continuance and objection to what had gone before was forcefully expressed by the People's Association which, in part, claimed its representative legitimacy from the fact that seven of the 14 elected members in the Combined Court were drawn from its ranks.

As its general secretary, H. Aaron Britton, explained in his memorandum to the Committee, the Association was formed 'in the conviction that a strenuous and organized effort is necessary to secure for the people an adequate measure of recognition in the Colony's political and economic affairs'.[57] The Association was, in fact, a Creole pressure group set up to try and bring about a fairer deal for the Creoles in their losing struggle with the Indians – and, of course, with the planters themselves. They were in no doubt that the crisis was of such major proportions that their whole existence was in jeopardy. To them 'a crisis fraught with the gravest outlook for the future of the African race had arisen...'.

> At this moment the problem is not merely the material welfare and progress of the African population; it concerns whether adequate measures can be adopted to prevent the race from being eventually extinguished. The issue involved is the life or death of the people whose claims to the soil are paramount and who under wiser administrations should have formed by now a settled and prosperous peasantry.[58]

That they saw themselves as a race in decline and as a 'landless and disheartened populace' is not in itself surprising for, apart from the difficulties of obtaining land, poor health conditions and economic privation had led to enormous mortality and suffering. And the Creoles, on the whole, were without the safeguard, albeit minimal, of the estates' welfare and educational provisions. The Population Census for 1911 contained the statement that 'had there been no East Indian immigration the population would have shown a decrease of 9.8 per cent on the population of 1891'.[59] For the Creoles a large part of this situation was derived from appalling infant mortality rates, although they were by no means the only ones to suffer from high death rates overall.[60] The difference was, of course, that the Indians were constantly replenished by new arrivals. In addition, with the paternalistic care of the estates, the Indians suffered lower infant mortality although this was offset by very high death rates among male field workers.[61] While the Census denied the 'generally accepted and often expressed belief' that the Creoles were declining in numbers, it is hardly surprising that this belief should have been held in a society where, with continued large-scale immigration, the population had only risen by 17 713 to 296 041 in the intercensal period from 1891 and where for the decade after 1891 the mean death rate (31.65) had comfortably exceeded the mean birth rate (29.7).[62]

The fact that Creoles were generally landless was seen by the People's Association as the result of a deliberate policy by the planters. They noted that the Land Code of 1839 had not only set a high price for Crown Lands but, much more damaging, it had specified that a minimum of 100 acres was the smallest lot that could be acquired. It was only after the first change in 1890 and the subsequent one of 1898, when the sugar industry was in decline and the battle to retain labour became, for a brief period, of lesser consequence, that the planters acquiesced to the possibility of a landed peasantry.

The improved position of the freedman following emancipation was therefore destroyed by the planters when they 'persuaded the local legislature to deny to the African the right of settling on the soil as an agriculturalist'.[63] The process of alienation and the construction of an inherently antagonistic situation proceeded since 'having succeeded in demoralizing the local labour market by their own unenlightened tactics the planters clamoured for Asiatic immigration'.[64]

The People's Association were unequivocal in their judgement on the result of this policy and in their condemnation of the racist myths upon which it was based:

> With the advent of the indentured labourer a new period of repression began for the black race. The negro, it was asserted, 'required competition as an incitement to industry', and a class of immigrants was introduced who, because of his fewer needs, his ability to subsist on a smaller wage, and the legal restraints under which he carries out his indenture, has succeeded in almost completely displacing the African employed on the sugar estates.[65]

The Association were convinced that wages had fallen with the introduction of the immigrants and there seems little doubt that this was indeed so. But there were two other points which aggravated them still further when they compared their position with the Indian labourer. In the first place, they were paid the same rates for the same work as the Indians under indenture, whereas in Trinidad, which they cited with approval, the free labourers, whether Indian or Creole, were paid more to compensate them for the advantages of schools, hospitals, and housing which were provided by the estates. Second, it was their contention that Indians could live on lower wages than Creoles since the latter had been brought up to live in a 'British' fashion. After all,

> The negro has been Christianized and educated in accordance with British ideas and conceptions; his tastes in food and clothing approximate to those of the British, and he has been taught to think and to act in harmony with the particular civilisation of which he is a product.[66]

This was not, of course, true of the Asiatics but, contrary to the express dictates of the 1891 Ordinance, it 'is the East Indian under indenture who fixes the rate of wages rather than the free labourer'. And, as if all this was not bad enough, an added source of constant frustration was that not only had

> The system ... ended by virtually displacing the native labourer in the cane fields, except in respect to certain forms of work, such as cane cutting, which the East Indian, because of his feeble physique, is ill-fitted to undertake[67]

but also,

> the race to whose detriment the coolies were being introduced were made to contribute to the cost of a scheme of immigration designed either to supplant the negro or to coerce him into service with the planters at a wage inadequate for his proper maintenance.[68]

This particular complaint arose from the fact that in both colonies large proportions of immigration costs were derived from public revenues, in particular customs duties. The People's Association charged that only recently had the proportion contributed from public funds fallen as low as one-third and that the total cost of medical services, the immigration department and the recruiting office in Calcutta were publicly financed. What exacerbated this frustration was the fact that the estates not only received this benefit but they were also exempt from many of the other taxes which the small man had to meet. For example, much of their machinery and other imports were allowed in tax-free and the planters were also exempt from licences for mules and carts, whereas the peasant had to pay four and five dollars a year respectively for these essentials.

In the light of this well-argued and often eloquent plea from the Creoles it is interesting to note the response of the Committee and, indeed, of the Governor himself. Both dismissed this memorial in subjective and often emotive terms. In doing so they perpetuated the myths of the lazy, indolent African and added even further fuel to the fire of discontent that the Creoles felt both in relation to the planters and to the Indians. In forwarding an earlier memorial from the People's Association to Chamberlain on 14 July 1903, Governor Swettenham had begun by dismissing any claims that the Creoles may have felt to express an opinion on the grounds of their 'indigenous' occupation of Guiana. He then subscribed to the stereotype of irresponsibility and unfavourably compared the performance of the blacks with the white settlers of Canada, New Zealand and Australia! On their claim for greater representation and for the necessity of curtailing further Indian immigration he said,

> I have not been able to detect such a capacity for managing the affairs of the Colony as would warrant their being made responsible for that management, or would warrant the government in excluding others from the Colony for their sake.[69]

The Governor felt it was quite just for the labourers to be taxed, rather than the estates, and suggested that the country should receive ten times the 150 000 Indians who had already arrived. Rather predictably, Chamberlain concurred with the Governor's assessment of the situation and reaffirmed that these 'underdeveloped estates' should not fall into the incapable hands of the Creoles. This fact, together with the vast potential which Guiana was seen to offer,

> make it impossible for me to approve a policy which would make these extensive properties a close preserve for those who have not yet shown that they are both able or desire to make use of them.[70]

In a similar fashion, the Sanderson Committee itself was able to base its arguments for dismissing the claims of the disaffected Creoles on a contrast between the admirable qualities of the Indians and the lamentable shortcomings of those they had displaced. The report cites with approval and concurrence a section of the *Annual Report* for the Colony in 1902–3.

> It is to be feared that the ordinary Creole villager has not the same qualities of industry and tenacity of purpose as are possessed by the East Indian coolie who has served his time of indenture and elected to remain in the colony as a permanent settler. The emigrant from India understands what a struggle for existence means. The black man of the present class in Guiana does not; more than this, he is in many cases of a dreadfully wasteful and thriftless disposition.[71]

It is this view of the black Guianese which characterises the attitude of the planters and administrators alike during this period. For the most part they would dismiss the cries of the Creoles on economic grounds; that is, by suggesting that they had gained and not lost from immigration. For example, when the end of indentured immigration seemed near and the planters were desperately trying to mobilize support for continuing the system, one white owner, Fred Bascom, remarked,

> To those who believed that paying for the immigrants that the colony needs out of general revenue means taxing the labourers already in the colony to bring in others to take the bread out of their mouths, I would recommend a study of the history of their country. Such study would teach them that the coming of the coolie took the bread out of no man's mouth; on the contrary it produced an economic development that made it easier for everyone, from the highest to the lowest in the land, to make a better living.[72]

Even when it was recognized that the Creoles really might have suffered by immigration, to the planters it was the Creoles' own fault. James Rodway, President of the Royal Agricultural and Commercial Society and noted local historian, felt that the Creole had not 'competed fairly' but that if he did he

> could more than hold his own because he is stronger than the East Indian. But there is no such competition for these immigrants who work five days a week have no rivals. They stand alone in the colony as the only people who will keep the cane mills in working order. We may safely state that others may cut canes by the job, (but) there could be none to feed the mills if there were no East Indians.[73]

It was especially the case in Guiana that underlying these arguments there lay a deep-seated animosity towards the Afro-Guianese which was rabidly racist. Even that famous commentator on the races and ethnography of Guiana, E. F. Im Thurm, could not avoid this judgement when addressing the Royal Colonial Institute in London when he argued that 'it is all very well to say that a man is a man whether his skin is white or black; but it is certain that the vast majority of West Indian blacks – all but the very few really educated members of the class – are not men but children, great, strong, generally good tempered children, but almost always fickle, and essentially, though from mere thoughtlessness, cruel'.[74]

The alienation and disaffection that the Creoles of Guiana felt was projected very strongly in their evidence to the Committee of 1910 but it would not be fair to conclude that no similar representations were made from Trinidad. The Trinidad Workingmen's Association, under its president Alfred Richards, and honorary secretary Adrien Hilarion, also argued that the coming of the Indians had lowered wages and that it was quite wrong to continue a system whereby finance for continued immigration came from a tax on agricultural exports when, in the case of sugar, 40 per cent was grown without the aid of indentured labourers, and for cocoa this proportion rose to two-thirds. But what is so striking is that despite the truth of many of their claims, there was no suggestion of the racial persecution which characterized the Guianese representations.[75] Indeed, they even subscribe to the view that at least until 1870 the advent of the Indians was a good thing for 'it rendered a service by helping in various ways the descendants of the emancipated negroes to adopt habits of steady industry'.[76] After that date they contended that wages fell; on cocoa estates, for example, they fell from 60 cents per day to 35 cents.

If there is a contrast in the type and tenor of the objections raised by the Creoles to continued immigration into Trinidad and Guyana, there is one sphere where the response to such objections was consistent; the reply of the Governor. The Acting Governor dismissed the claims of the TWA in the following words:

> The members of the Trinidad Working Men's Association belong to the most part to the artizan class. They are apparently under the influence of men who have but little, if any, stake in the Colony, and who, even though convinced of their honesty of purpose, I should hardly consider to be capable of forming an impartial and reliable opinion on such a question as this.[77]

It could be argued, however, that while the effect of the replies to the claims of the popular representatives of the working class was the same for both colonies, there is an important difference between them. This was that the Acting Governor of Trinidad should have dismissed the TWA on *class* lines – that is, because they had 'little stake in the Colony', while in Guyana the inherent inadequacies of the *race* were the justification.

Conclusion

In this chapter I have tried to argue that while the migration of one ethnic group into a social system of one or more other ethnic or racial groups may define the parameters of future conflicts, it is not in itself sufficient explanation of those conflicts. Colonialism as it was manifest in both Trinidad and British Guiana certainly provided, as a system based in the last resort upon overt coercion, an inherently 'conflictive arena' but this has not been my main focus of interest. In both colonies the arrival of the Indians was a threat, but in one the lack of adequate land, the economic condition of the colony, and the policies and prejudices of planters and administrators alike, albeit constrained by these fundamental economic facts, were such as to turn this threat into a confrontation. Thus a situation was born where stereotypes emerged with greater virulence on all sides and served as they always do to divide further by justifying with an aura of rationality a basically false situation.

The fact that the greatest labour leader British Guiana ever had, Hubert Critchlow, could come to London in 1925 and describe the Indians as 'a menace to the other workers of the country' was the result of this emerging situation which was to provide one crucial component of later social and political developments.[78] In Trinidad, on the other hand, inter-ethnic divisions also emerged, but – to use Donald Wood's phrase – 'a *modus vivendi* has always been possible'.[79]

Notes

1 For British Guiana, see Dwarka Nath, *A History of Indians in British Guiana* (London: Thomas Nelson, 1950) and Peter Ruhomon, *Centenary History of the East Indians in British Guiana 1838–1938* (Georgetown: Daily Chronicle, 1947). For Trinidad, see M. J. Kirpalani *et al*, *Indian Centenary Review, 1845–1945* (Port of Spain: Guardian Commercial Printery, 1945).

2 See J. Graham Cruikshank, 'The beginnings of our Villages', *Timehri*, Vol. 8, August 1921, pp. 65–76.

3 At high tide, almost all the coastal lands of Guyana are beneath sea-level and are only prevented from inundation by an eleborate, and expensive, system of empoldering and drainage canals which were laid down originally by the Dutch colonists.

4 For further discussion of this point, see Rawle Fawley, 'The rise of the village settlements of British Guiana', *Caribbean Quarterly*, Vol. 3, no. 2 (1953), pp. 101–9. Also Eric Williams, 'The historical background of British Guiana's problems', *Timehri*, Vol. 26 (November 1944), pp. 18–34.

5 Rev. William Garland Barrett, *Immigration to the British West Indies: Is it the slave trade revived or not?* (London: A. W. Bennett, 1859, p. 6, emphasis in original).

6 In British Guiana a technique commonly used by the planters was to flood or overdrain the land and thereby destroy the crop of the smallholder.

7 See Dwarka Nath, *History of Indians*, Chapter II.

8 Adapted from G. W. Roberts and J. Byrne, 'Summary statistics on indenture and associated migration affecting the West Indies, 1834–1918', *Population Studies*, Vol. 20, no. 1 (1966), p. 129.

9 *Minutes of the Legislative Council of Trinidad and Tobago*, 21 May 1930. Cf. *Annual Report of the Protector of Immigrants, 1929.*

10 *Annual Report of the Protector of Immigrants for 1931*, Legislative Council Paper No. 43 of 1932.

11 *West India Royal Commission* Cd. 8655 (London: HMSO, 1897), Appendix C, Part II, pp. 126–7.

12 Roberts and Byrne, 'Summary Statistics', p. 127.

13 Those that did come from Madras were reputed to be better workers.

14 R. T. Smith, 'Some social characteristics of Indian immigrants to British Guiana', *Population Studies* Vol. 13 (1959), pp. 35–6. Smith found that immigrants came mainly from Basti, Azarnghar, Ghazipur, Gonda, Fyzabad, Allahabad, Gorakpur, Jaunpur, Shahabad and Lucknow. Cf. Judith Ann Weller, *The East Indian Indenture in Trinidad* (Puerto Rico: Institute of Caribbean Studies, 1968), espec. Appendix I, and pp. 123–6. Also Arthur H. Hill, 'Emigration from India', *Timehri*, Vol. 6 (September 1919), pp. 43–52.

15 See *Immigration Ordinances of Trinidad and British Guiana*, Cd. 1989 (London: HMSO, 1904).
16 Edward Jenkins, *The Coolie: His Rights and Wrongs* (London: Straham and Co., 1871), p. 95.
17 Barrett, *Immigration*, p. 3.
18 Rev. H. V. P. Bronkhurst, *Among the Hindus and Creoles of British Guiana* (London: T. Woolmer, 1882), p. 22.
19 Ibid., p. 26.
20 Surgeon-Major D. W. D. Comins, *Notes on Emigration from India to British Guiana* (Calcutta: Bengal Secretariat Press, 1893), p. 95.
21 Ibid., p. 4.
22 Comins, *Notes*, p. 16.
23 Ibid., p. 16.
24 Immigration Ordinance, 1891. Combined Court Paper No. 18 of 1891.
25 Comins, *Notes*, p. 50.
26 Immigration Ordinance, 1899, Legislative Council Paper No. 19 of 1899 and Immigration Ordinance, 1902, Legislative Council Paper No. 33 of 1902. All these ordinances are reprinted in Cd. 1989 (see note 15).
27 Comins, *Notes*, p. 50.
28 See Nath, *A History*, pp. 94–106.
29 Donald Wood, *Trinidad in Transition: The Years After Slavery* (London: Oxford University Press for the IRR, 1968), p. 270.
30 Ibid., p. 275.
31 William Des Voeux, *My Colonial Service* (London: John Murray, 1903), Vol. I, p. 131.
32 A. H. Alexander (Immigration Agent-General) *Statistics and Other Information prepared for Dr Comins, Protector of Immigrants, Calcutta in regard to Immigration from India* (Georgetown, Demerara: The Argosy Press, 1891). Large parts of this report were incorporated verbatim but unreferenced in Comins, *Notes*.
33 Comins, *Notes*, p. 2.
34 Ibid., p. 7.
35 See H. A. Will, 'Colonial Policy and Economic Development in the British West Indies, 1895–1903'. *Economic History Review*, Vol. 23, no. 1 (1970), p. 141.
36 The wage rates were normally about double. Indian weeders could expect 25–45 cents per day while Creole cane-cutters would be paid within the range of 60–85 cents.
37 Wood, *Trinidad in Transition*, p. 296.
38 At present approximately 40 per cent of sugar in Trinidad is grown by cane farmers.
39 *Report of the Committee on Emigration from India to the Crown Colonies and Protectorates* (Chairman: Lord Sanderson), Cd. 5194, BPP XXVII, 1910. Part III: Papers Laid, p. 115.
40 *Report of the West India Royal Commission* C. 8655, 1897. Appendix C, Part IV (Trinidad), Appendix H, p. 309. For the period from 1885 to 1908–9 the grants of Crown Lands sold to Indian immigrants amounted to 69 087 acres out of a total of 227 508 acres sold. See Sanderson Committee, Report, Cd. 5192, p. 69.
41 Des Voeux, *Colonial Service*, pp. 130–1.
42 Ibid., pp. 120–1.
43 Des Voux points out, for example, that in rural areas the magistrates would accept accommodation and hospitality from the manager or owner of a plantation and that it was customary for the latter to seat himself beside the magistrate during proceedings.
44 *Report of the Commissioners Appointed to enquire into the Treatment of Immigrants in British Guiana*, C. 393 (London: HMSO, June 1871), p. 11.
45 The Commissioners were William E. Frere, Sir George Young and Charles Mitchell.

46 Ibid., p. 29.
47 Ibid., p. 30.
48 Ibid., p. 32.
49 Ibid., p. 87.
50 Ibid., p. 87.
51 Ibid., p. 91.
52 The Muhurram Festival, though strictly speaking confined to Shi'ite Muslims, was generally supported by all Indians. In Trinidad it is termed after its leading deity as Hosein or Hose.
53 Letter from Arthur Child to Colonial Secretary, 31 October 1884. Reprinted in *Report and Corresondence on the Recent Coolie Disturbances in Trinidad* (Chairman: Sir H. W. Norman), C.4366 (London: Eyre and Spottiswoode, 1885), p. 11.
54 Major Bowles to Colonial Secretary, 3 November 1884. Ibid., p. 11.
55 Sanderson Committee, Cd. 5192: Report; Cd. 5193: Minutes of Evidence; Cd. 5194: Papers Laid.
56 Cd. 5192, p. 14.
57 Cd. 5194, p. 15.
58 Ibid., p. 15.
59 *British Guiana – Census Report for 1911*, p. V.
60 For the period 1891–1911, 71 542 Creoles died, of whom 16 573 were infants under one year of age.
61 Between 1891 and 1911, 72 696 Indians died, of whom 45 295 were male and 35 364 between the ages of 20 and 50.
62 Census, p. XXV.
63 Cd. 5194, p. 15.
64 Ibid., p. 16.
65 Ibid., p. 16.
66 Ibid., p. 19.
67 Ibid., p. 18.
68 Ibid., p. 19.
69 Reprinted in Cd. 5194, p. 31.
70 Chamberlain to Swettenham, 10 September 1903. Reprinted in Cd. 5194, p. 36.
71 Cd. 5192, p. 60.
72 Fred C. S. Bascom, 'The Labour Question', *Timehri* December 1912. Reprinted in *Indentured Immigration: Its ethnics and raison d'être* (Georgetown: The Argosy Co., 1913), p. 11.
73 James Rodway, 'Labour and Colonization', *Timehri*, Vol. VI (September 1919), p. 36.
74 E. F. Im Thurm, 'Notes on British Guiana', paper read at the Royal Colonial Institute, London, 13 December 1892, pp. 7–8.
75 The Commission of 1897 had sent round a questionnaire to sugar estates in Trinidad which revealed, on their own admission, that 14 out of the 20 who reported had lowered their wages in the previous few years – although all contended that this was due to the depression. See *Report*, C. 8655, Appendix C, Part IV (Trinidad), Appendix D, p. 307.
76 Cd. 5194, p. 114.
77 Knaggs to Secretary of State, 8 March 1909. Reprinted in Cd. 5194, p. 115.
78 Hubert Critchlow, in *Report of the First British Commonwealth Labour Conference* held at the House of Commons, 27 July–1 August 1925 (London: TUC and Labour Party, 1925), p. 83.
79 Wood, *Trinidad in Transition*, p. 304.

CHAPTER 2 Race and ethnic relations in Burnhamite Guyana

Ralph Premdas

Introduction

In Guyana, race relations between persons of African and Indian descent (hereafter referred to as Creoles and Indians) are marked by covert contempt and deceptive distrust. Inter-racial suspicion runs silently deep, each side engaged in a contrived drama of studied hypocrisy about inter-communal amity. To the casual observer, Creole–Indian relations may appear cordial. Many Creoles and Indians may live in mixed neighbourhoods in town or village, their children attending the same schools under a racially integrated staff and may participate in the same school-sponsored games, even saying the same morning prayers in school. Overt inter-racial interaction is plentiful, easy to be interpreted as evidence of unity and harmony. But these same people, in the privacy of their homes and racial communities, enact a script of racist antipathy to their cross-communal compatriot that shows how perilous every day is to open racial conflagration. Each side has contrived a set of secret intra-community symbols, idioms, and nuanced expressions that communicate group solidarity built on an understanding of collective contempt for the other side. Forced to live together by the dictates of the colonial past, inter-racial accommodation is in fact a 'cordial' state of conflict in which Indian submission to Creole political dominance changes place, and interweaves with Creole under-performance in relation to Indian economic dominance. Everywhere race enters into everything in a perennial struggle. In the end, the psyche and soul are scarred; each side equally dehumanized. This is race relations in a divided society.

To understand how this sad state of affairs came about, it is necessary to return to the colonial past when Guiana's plural society was first forged into existence from a diverse immigrant population settled to produce sugar and profits for imperial Europe. Early settlement pointing to racially-determined occupational structures and residential patterns as well as the values of racial dominance that attended colonial social organization planted the seeds of inter-racial conflict from the very beginning. A colony was created for profit built on the graves of the practically exterminated Amerindians and sustained by the agony of slave and indenture labour, for the benefit of European gain and dominance. A racially multi-layered plantation society would bequeath a legacy of communal fear and misunderstanding, built on virtual residential separation, which would harden into a society of fractured institutions set against itself. In the first part of this chapter, the colonial heritage will be traced to show how the seeds of racial strife were laid in plantation society. In the second part, the emergence of nationalist politics will be discussed to show how local leaders would fall victim to the inbuilt sectional structures of their society, exploiting its biases for personal ambition, and lighting the fire of open racial struggle between Creoles and Indians. In the third part, the seizure of power by one racial group over the other will be described, showing how colonially derived inequities were retained. Finally, a section is provided to offer an explanation of the conflict-ridden struggle of Creole–Indian race relations in Guyana.

Before proceeding, we shall take a brief look at some theoretical issues. The theoretical framework utilized in this chapter hypothesizes that ethnic conflict in culturally plural societies tends to be triggered in the first instance by competition for scarce resources. This method in the study of race and ethnic relations may be called 'the political economy approach'. Its bias is that the highly psycho-social collective phenomenon of communal strife can be reduced to economic and materialist factors. In the real world, few collective ethnic conflicts are definable solely or mainly in economic terms. Ethnic strife is multi-faceted, immensely complex, and often mysterious. For this reason, we need to look at other factors that feature in ethnic conflict. In the case of Guyana, while it will be argued that economic factors laid the first foundations of racial suspicion and division, thereafter the separation was sustained by cultural, residential and occupational patterns. Cultural differences assumed an abnormally larger role in sustaining separation and inter-group anxieties, and in particular, racial stereotypes institutionalized distorted perceptions of cross-communal compatriots.

Hence, in the evolution of Guyanese society, a matrix of early features was interwoven from differences in culture, residential areas and occupational patterns creating a deeply divided society. The struggle and competition for economic positions and privileges played a pivotal part in defining inter-group relations. But, in the end, it was not the economic, cultural and residential features that threw Guyanese race relations into a virtual state of civil war, but the introduction of nationalist politics. I do not believe that socio-cultural and economic cleavages themselves ignite ethnic strife. It was with the coming of universal adult suffrage and modern party politics that ethnic differences were exploited for communalistic and personal political ends. The truly flammable factors consist of open political competition in a zero-sum struggle for values conducted in an environment of rapid communications and high expectations. In this chapter, the various underlying factors will be discussed for their contribution to the structure of race relations in Guiana, but in particular, the political and economic factors will be chosen for their special explanatory roles.

The formation and foundation of an ethnically divided society

Guiana is often referred to as a 'Land of Many Peoples'. The country, populated mainly by descendants of immigrants, is constituted of six ethnic groups – Creoles of African descent, East Indians, Amerindians, Portuguese, Chinese and Europeans. A significant 'mixed' category also exists, consisting of persons who have any combination or mixture of the above groups. Table 2.1 gives the ethnic breakdown of the population. Africans and Indians constitute over 80 per cent of the total, imparting a bifurcated ethnic structure to the population. Nearly all of Guyana's people are concentrated on a five-to-ten mile belt along the country's Atlantic coast. The ethnically mixed population is loosely integrated by a Creole culture which has evolved during the last 250 years of Guyanese history. Nonetheless, strong social integrative institutions are few; they are rivalled by equally strong sub-cultural patterns which threaten periodically to burst the society asunder at its ethnic seams.

Table 2.1 The ethnic constitution of Guyanese society

	1960	%	*1970*	%
Black	183 950	32.8	227 091	30.7
East Indian	267 797	47.8	377 256	51.0
White	3 217	0.6	4 056	0.5
Portugese	8 346	1.5	9 668	1.3
Mixed	67 191	12.0	84 077	11.4
Chinese	4 074	0.7	4 678	0.4
Amerindian	25 453	4.5	32 794	4.4
Other	69	–	576	0.1
Not stated	233	–	–	–
Total	560 330		740 196	

The origins of Guyana's multi-ethnic structure go back to the first efforts at New World colonization attempted by Europeans. The area stretching from the Orinoco River to the Amazon, which includes the Guianas, came at one time or the other under the purview of French, Dutch and British explorers. In the early seventeenth century, the British started a settlement in Surinam, the French established two settlements in French Guiana and the Dutch planted settlements at various points in what is now Guyana. The Dutch began plantation production in the seventeenth century; when they were evicted from the colony by the British in 1803, the dominant economic organization of the colony was the plantation. Importation of Africans, East Indians, Portuguese, Chinese, and 'poor whites' in Guiana resulted from the nature of the plantation system which, to be viable, required massive amounts of cheap labour.[1] By 1829, 230 sugar plantations and 174 coffee and cotton estates existed in Guiana. Under British colonialism, cotton and coffee did not enjoy preferential prices. So they quickly succumbed to North American competition. Sugar production then became the dominant economic activity. Indeed, Guiana became little more than a huge sugar plantation.

The establishment of plantations was accomplished by the massive recruitment of African slaves. Resort to African sources of forced labour became necessary after the indigenous inhabitants, the Amerindians, had 'succumbed to excessive labour demanded of them'[2] while the 'poor whites' who were indentured from Europe failed to meet the rigours of plantation life.[3] In 1807, the British slave trade with Africa was halted. Slavery in the British Caribbean, however, was not abolished until 1833.[4] Labour shortages that followed emancipation explain the addition of Chinese, Portuguese and East Indians (from the Indian sub-continent) to the already existing ethnic groups in Guiana. Between 1835 and 1840 small batches of German, Portuguese, Irish, English, Indian and Maltese labourers were recruited. During 1853 even Chinese were tried. In the end, Asian Indians proved most adaptable, economical and available, although Chinese and Portuguese immigrants trickled in for over half a century. Between 1838 and 1917, approximately 238 960 indentured East Indian labourers arrived to work on the plantations.[5] At the expiration of their indentures, nearly two-thirds opted to remain as free, permanent residents.[6]

The pattern of the life of the ethnic groups in Guiana separated the communities in virtual cultural, residential and occupational compartments, allowing for interaction mainly in economic and trade areas. The Europeans lived mainly in exclusive, guarded residential enclaves on sugar estates and urban areas. They were predominantly planters and settlers and controlled most of the colony's economic wealth and official political positions. Partly because of their economic and political power, a colour–class stratification system evolved whereby things English and 'white' were valued highly while things African (Creole) and black were valued lowly. The ability to speak properly, to dress 'properly', and to be able to read and write were all marks of prestige defined with reference to 'English' culture. What gave the system its distinctive character was the element of colour. In effect, in this first phase of history, European ethnic superiority was established and European preeminence in monopolizing the preferred values of society was being institutionalized. Thus would emerge the basic outlines of a loose control system. The year 1838 witnessed a Creole exodus from the plantations.[7] At the end of the 'Free Village Movement' which lasted for a decade (1838–48), over 100 villages were established.[8] By the end of the nineteenth century, more than half of the African villagers would gravitate to urban centres where government jobs were available.[9] By the end of the first phase of European dominance, Creoles held the position of advantage over other non-European groups. They became educated and acquired industrial skills and training. By 1950, the Creoles dominated every department of the civil service,[10] while their portion of the plantation population was reduced to 6.8 per cent by 1960.[11]

Indians who remained in Guiana continued their close relationship with the plantations. Many were allotted land contiguous to the sugar estates in exchange for giving up their contractual right to return to India. A series of Indian villages sprang up within a radius of 15 miles of the plantations. Indians tended to work at first both on their private plots and on the plantations, but progressively many moved into full-time rice-farming on private plots. By 1946, the Indian outflow from the sugar estates left only a third as plantation residents; their urban presence was barely 10 per cent.[12] In the 1960s, 25.5 per cent of the Indian population were on sugar estates, 13.4 per cent in urban centres, with the remaining 61.1 per cent in villages.[13] Guiana's Indians then became predominantly rural dwellers serving either as sugar workers or farmers. They displayed distinctive patterns of cultural life, initially reflecting residues of their Indian cultural heritage. After the Second World War, however, the Indian quest for civil service jobs required them to acculturate to English ways. This became a significant force in the 1950s and 1960s when their cultural adaptation brought them into competition with their Creole compatriots for scarce job opportunities.

The other ethnic elements in the population were small, but they too established their own residential and occupational niches. Amerindians were assigned to 'reservations' mainly in the country's sparsely populated interior areas, while the Chinese and Portuguese gravitated to urban areas, where the former engaged in service industries such as restaurants and the latter in the professions and business.

Thus would a plural society be formed. Slavery and indenture were the twin bases on which successful colonization of the climatically harsh tropical coasts occurred. A work force of culturally divergent immigrants was recruited to labour on plantations in the New World. The different patterns of residence, occupation, and cultural orientations by the imported groups reinforced the original ethnic differences, laying, from the inception of settlement, the foundations of Guiana's politics. By the beginning of the twentieth century, certain features were clearly embedded in the social system. A communally orientated, multi-ethnic society was being fashioned. The system was dominated by Europeans, and an accompanying system of colonial laws and practices institutionalized racial inequality along a colour–class continuum. The wealth produced from the sugar plantations was repatriated to the metropolitan centre, leaving very little for the plantation workers. Creole–Indian rivalry developed over the remnants of the colonial pie. Inter-communal struggle, however, was restrained by the preponderantly rural–urban and occupational dichotomy that prevailed between the two major ethnic groups during the early colonial period.

Two patterns of behaviour emerged early to deepen the separation between Indians and Creoles: their voluntary association,[14] and the stereotypes they held of each other.[15] As the immigrants took roots in Guiana, they gradually developed voluntary associations to serve their specific interests. Prior to 1910, new voluntary associations existed; as the freed slaves and indentured immigrants stabilized around specific occupations and residential areas, they started to build community organizations to institutionalize their separate ways of life. By the 1920s, cultural organizations such as the League of Coloured People, the East Indian Association, the Chinese Association and the Portuguese Club sprung up to cater to social, cultural and religious needs of the several ethnic communities. This uni-ethnic pattern in the composition of voluntary associations has persisted to the present, extending to practically all kinds of clubs and groupings. The large economic organizations such as trade unions also became uni-ethnic, like the cultural and religious organisations, so that they were individually identified by the public as belonging to the 'Blackman', the 'Coolie', or the 'Potagee'. It is our contention here, that while it was almost inevitable that voluntary associations historically emerged as predominantly uni-ethnic bodies, this very fact in turn reinforced racial exclusivism and exacerbated ethnic divisions and fears. As mass political parties emerged after the Second World War, especially after 1955, when separated *de facto* Indian and Creole mass parties were launched, the voluntary associations supported and developed interlocking relationships with their own *de facto* ethnically-based parties. Mainly because of this interlocking ethnic relationship between party and voluntary associations, race relations were intensified and the bifurcation of the polity deepened.

In addition to voluntary associations, the evolution of stereotypes accentuated inter-ethnic divisions between Indians and Creoles. Typically, an Indian conceives of a Creole as: (1) physically strong and powerful. (Most Indians are relatively small in stature as compared with most Creoles.) While this appears to be a positive stereotype with regard to the Creole's physical endowment, most Indians view the physical power of the Creole as a threat to their security. (2) The Indian sees the Creole as economically undisciplined. Indians view the high consumptive habits of the Creole as irresponsible behaviour. Instead of saving some of the high earnings which come from good civil service and teaching jobs, as well as from cane-cutting on the sugar estates, the Creole, as seen by the Indian, spends all his money on liquor, dances, and good clothes. For the Indian, the 'economic extravagance' of the Creole accounts for the shabby houses in which Creoles live, and the paucity of Creole businesses. In holding this economic stereotype of the Creoles, Indians have failed to consider the numerous cases in their own villages and towns which attest to the economically conservative behaviour of many Creoles. For Indians, the 'economic irresponsibility' stereotype is not peculiar to a segment of the Creole population, but is true of all Creoles generally. (3) Indians view Creoles as culturally inferior. Most Indians regard the wholesale adoption of 'British' ways by Creoles as a mark of the Creole's inferiority. Although partly as bastardized as Creoles by British norms, Indians consider the Creole inferior for not retaining any traits of his cultural heritage. (Some cultural traits, which obviously have been retained are either not recognized by Indians or are condemned as 'juju' culture.)

On the other hand, typically, Creoles conceive of Indians as (1) physically weak and inferior. Creole disrespect of Indians substantially stems from the rather frail physical features of the Indian. Indians are 'dhall and rice coolies', a slur phrase which points to the dietary habits of Indians, who generally eat split peas, rice, vegetables and fish, but little meat. (Most Hindu Indians do not consume beef, and Muslim Indians similarly do not consume pork; the Creole eats both.) (2) The Creole considers the Indian economically miserly. Creoles view the Indian as a miserly person who sacrifices his dietary well-being and clothing habits for saving a few cents from every pay package. While this appears as a positive stereotype, most Creoles view this (exaggerated) behaviour trait as a threat in the long run to the superior status of the Creole in the colonial social hierarchy which has accorded the lowest rung to the Indian. (3) The Creole holds the Indian culturally inferior quite as much as the Indian holds the Creole culturally inferior. Most Creoles pride themselves on having acquired the English language and English norms (which in colonial British Guiana were the criteria for status and jobs), and regard the 'retarded' acquisition of English ways by Indians as a mark of the Indian's inferiority. Hence, Indians are frequently called derogatorily 'coolie babu', and Indian ways are called 'coolie culture'.

Thus a deeply divided society was formed. The foundations of inter-ethnic rivalry were forged on the anvil of the colonial policy of immigration and divide-and-rule. There is no evidence of any sort of inherent antipathy among the imported immigrants. It was, however, the manner in which colonial society was organized, stratified, and exploited that triggered and sustained inter-communal fears and rivalries. How each of the groups would fare and finally occupy a niche in the structure of colonial society will be traced in the next section.

Nationalist politics and communalism and the allocation of resources

Persistent struggle over a half a century (1891–1953) eventually yielded success in evicting the old plantocracy from their positions of privilege. In the early colonial phase, after pressure from the colony's emergent non-white middle class, the British colonial office liberalized the franchise requirements to enlarge political participation. In the 1850s eligibility to vote required property worth at least $7500 (BWI). The electorate then consisted of only about 900 persons, all Europeans, in a total population of about 130 000. In 1891, the franchise restrictions were lowered to about $480 (BWI) and were even further liberalized about a decade later so that by 1915 the voting list showed that the non-white population had made impressive gains.

These figures show that a remarkable event of potentially revolutionary proportions had occurred by 1915 – the Creole borgeoisie had grown into the majority group in the electorate and had, in fact, come to control the financial affairs of the colony.[16]

Professor Enloe commented on the impact that this control had on the allocation of public service jobs:

> As early as 1925, of the persons employed in the colonial bureaucracy, 84.7 per cent were listed as Negroes, while a mere 4 per cent were listed as East Indians. This despite the fact that already the East Indians, brought to the colony by the ship load as indentured labourers to work the sugar plantations after slavery was abolished, amounted to 41.97 per cent of the population, while Negroes represented only 39.36 per cent. Europeans, Portuguese, and light-skinned persons of mixed parentage continued to dominate the upper reaches of the civil service, right up to the mid-1960's.[17]

Initially, after emancipation, it was the Creole communal section among the non-white society that took advantage of European education. In 1835,

Christian denominational schools received a subsidy from the colonial government to provide limited public elementary education. Secular schools did not exist.[18] Most Indians saw the church-run schools as a cultural threat to their religious identity and therefore withheld their children. Further, Indians, most of whom engaged in full or part-time farming, utilized their children in the fields. The upshot was that 'by the end of the century, the Africans had come to dominate the public services at the national as well as the local level'.[19]

Although a compulsory universal education ordinance was passed in 1876, it was not until the 1930s that Indians were compelled to send their children to Christian denominational schools.[20] Then, slowly but inexorably, Indians converged on the schools, regarding them as the elixir to a new life free from the toil of agrarian drudgery. The repercussions reverberated mainly in the 1950s and onwards. Black Creoles, Mixed Races, and others found in Indians a new if not fierce competitor for the limited job opportunities. Creoles, in particular, faced the full brunt of this competitive assault and in turn this unleashed an intense round of rivalry for the resources of the state. The European segment, already small, was, with the passage of time, eased out as a major force in the struggle for jobs. Creoles and Indians confronted each other in ethnic competition that spilled over into party politics.[21] But Africans already had a clear advantage of nearly a century headstart and this consequently placed them on the defensive. Indians were seen as the new challengers in the same way that the Mixed Races and black Creoles were to the Europeans at the turn of the twentieth century.

In 1928, the Colonial Office acting under the pretence of the indebtedness of the Combined Court, suspended the 1891 constitution, which placed financial powers in the hands of the Black and Mixed Race middle class. A regressive Crown Colony system of government was imposed, returning decision-making control to the colonial administration.[22] One positive feature of the constitutional change was the enfranchisement of women, but the old property and income qualifications for the vote remained very restrictive. The leadership for change after 1928 would pass from the middle-class black bourgeoisie to a multi-racial and modernizing radical group which rejected piecemeal reform for a more fundamental rearrangement of the colonial order.[23] Trade unions emerged as the main mobilizer of popular sentiment.[24] A new era of politics was upon the colony. After the Second World War, the political framework would alter and with it the nature of the politics of resource distribution.

The denial of adequate reforms in the colonial order after the Second World War invited the emergence of a radical response. In 1946, a Political Affairs Committee (PAC) was formed by Dr Cheddi Jagan, a Marxist who had just returned from university training in the United States.[25] The PAC aimed at 'establishing a strong, disciplined and enlightened party equipped with the theory of scientific socialism'.[26] The PAC's ideology analyzed the colony's living conditions in class terms, appealing mainly to workers and farmers of all ethnic groups.

While the PAC was multi-racial in composition, its leader, Dr Jagan, was an East Indian. This fact would compel the movement, after its losses in the 1947 general elections, to recruit an African leader of equivalent standing.[27] The search led to the selection of Forbes Burnham, an outstanding lawyer who returned from London to Guiana in 1949. In January 1950, the PAC converted itself to the People's Progressive Party (PPP) and reaffirmed its commitment to a socialist society.[28] New general elections were scheduled for April 1953 under a constitutional arrangement that conceded universal adult suffrage and a limited cabinet ministerial system. Full participation in collective decision-making was finally at hand. The PPP was victorious, winning 18 out of 24 seats in the unicameral Legislature. The only explanation for such an overwhelming victory was the extensive collaboration of African and Indian constituents inspired by the joint bi-racial leadership of Jagan and Burnham.[29] The period 1950–53 was the Golden Age of racial harmony in Guiana. The control system had virtually collapsed while leaders assumed power.

Within five months after assuming office, the PPP suffered a major setback. During its 133-day rule, it openly threatened to nationalize the key foreign companies and radically rearrange the colour–class system.[30] Under the prodding of the plantocracy, the British government suspended the constitution, evicting the PPP from office. In turn, this triggered a major crisis within the PPP as explanations were sought for the ouster. Two main factions surfaced, one supporting Jagan and the other Burnham. New elections were slated for 1957 and in it a more radical socialist Jaganite faction faced a moderate Burnhamite faction. Their ideological stance apart, the Jagan and Burnham groupings obtained support mainly from Indian and Creole constituents respectively. In the elections, at the grassroots, racial appeals were widely used and the cross-communal goodwill between Creoles and Indians was shattered. Jagan won the elections, but as Premier of Guiana, he was now presiding over a state whose communal fabric was inflamed by electoral politics that pitted one ethnic segment against the other.[31]

Between 1957 and 1963, unprecedented racial turmoil racked Guiana, resulting in the removal of Jagan from power and the acquisition of leadership by Burnham. Burnham's complaints against Jagan's party were that it conducted a pro-Indian government and that it was discriminatory to Afro-Guianese.[32] Burnham's party, the People's National Congress (PNC) collaborated with a third splinter party, the United Force (UF), headed by a Portuguese businessman, Peter d'Aguiar who appealed mainly to Europeans, Portuguese Chinese, Mixed Races, Amerindians, and a small group of middle-class black Creoles and Indians.

In the 1961 general elections, Jagan's PPP defeated both Burnham's PNC and d'Aguiar's UF under the old first-past-the-post simple plurality electoral system. Jagan had obtained a disproportionately higher number of seats measured against his percentage of the popular votes. This fact served as the excuse that prompted the Opposition into a sustained set of severe attacks, strikes, demonstrations, and disruptions which would destabilize the Jagan government and enable the British Colonial Office to alter the electoral system to one of proportional representation.[33] With Jagan's group holding slightly less than 50 per cent of the adult votes, Burnham and d'Aguiar barely defeated Jagan's PPP in the 1964 elections. Ethnic strife grew to fearsome proportions. At one point virtual civil war ensued and mixed Indian–Creole villages became places of terror, requiring British troops to maintain communal peace.[34]

The role of ethnic competition is worth a brief analysis since it entailed the use of the public bureaucracy as a major instrument in the removal of a government. The joint bi-racial leadership of the independence movement by Jagan and Burnham concealed the fact that the government bureaucracy had come to be dominated by Creoles. The public and teaching services had emerged as the largest employer in the country and, more importantly, they were staffed by the best-educated and organized persons in the non-white population. If any regime wished to govern peacefully, it would not incur the wrath of the public bureaucracy. In Guiana's communal context, this basic fact of power became imbued with racial motivations. When Jagan and Burnham were together, the public service cooperated. Competition for state job opportunities was substantially based on merit. But after the eviction of the unified independence movement from office and the rise of racially-based parties, the bureaucracy assumed an active interventionist role in partisan politics.

> After the split in the national government, it was the Negro section of the population that was more advantageously placed in control of the machinery of government. This was seen in the fact that, although the Jaganite faction of the PPP defeated the Burnhamite faction at the elections held in 1957 and participated in the government as the majority party, it was not by any means in a position of strength. Quite apart from operating in a colonial situation in which the British government possessed wide powers of control over the governmental machinery, after a time the Jaganite regime became keenly aware of its lack of support from some of the crucial institutions and groups in the public bureaucracy. The People's National Congress (the Burnhamite faction),

> though not in government, was nevertheless in a position to embarrass and frustrate it.[35]

Jagan was in a quandary. Although he professed to be a socialist and recruited a racially mixed cabinet, he still had to meet some of the demands for jobs, services and projects in Indian political constituencies. The Jagan regime, coming to power in 1957, therefore embarked on a set of policies which sought to eliminate Christian control of schools and to orient economic planning in favour of rural industries.[36] Burnham's party protested vigorously against the 'agricultural bent' of the PPP's policies, charging the Jaganites with running an Indian 'Coolie government' and 'a Rice Government'.[37] The Jagan government also sought to rectify the ethnic imbalance in recruitment of the public service. In particular, Jagan feared the fact that the stability of his government depended heavily on a Creole-dominated police force.

In 1961 the Jagan government persuaded the British to accept that the victor in the 1961 elections would lead the country into independence. This was a most crucial fact, for the party in power after independence could redefine the rules of the game and remain in power indefinitely. For the highly politicized and insecure Indian and Creole segments, the 1961 elections could mean the indefinite domination of one group by the other.[38] It was on this vital issue that the Creole-dominated public service would be appealed to, politicized, and mobilized against the Jagan government. Two major unions, the Civil Service Association (CSA) and the Federation of Unions of Government Employees (FUGE), both Creole-controlled, represented public servants. Demonstrations and strikes in 1962 and 1964 against the Jagan regime witnessed the conversion of a neutral civil service into a politicized instrument of power in ethnically motivated partisan politics.

> The events between 1962 and 1964 which all but brought down the Jagan government were dramatic illustration of this. The PNC opposition was effectively using institutions over which it had control or influence in an attempt to embarrass and ultimately defeat the government – a fact of which it made no secret – and the Civil Service Association (C.S.A.) was one such institution. The political nature of the C.S.A.'s involvement could also be seen in part from the fact that although many of the issues remained unresolved after the change of government in 1964, no similar action has so far been taken by the C.S.A. against the PNC government.[39]

The Burnham government that succeeded Jagan in 1964 would itself suffer from similar boycotts and crippling strikes, but this time the mobilizer would be the Jagan forces who in opposition deployed the sugar-industry unions, which were overwhelmingly Indian-dominated. The fact that Africans resided mainly in the urban areas, especially in Georgetown, the capital, and Indians in the rural areas, partly restrained the inter-racial conflict. However, few racially interlocking endeavours existed to provide meaningful moderation in the conflict. The communal strife consequently became polarized, a special variant of intransigence locked in an uncompromising zero-sum struggle.[40]

It would be difficult to tell exactly what alterations in the state bureacracy and in the allocation of resources would have occurred under the racially unified PPP government of 1953. One could legitimately expect that allocation in government expenditures would have been diverted away from serving the interests of the plantocracy to serving the interests of the non-white working class. In its brief 133-day interregnum, the PPP had already signalled its intention to dismantle the monopolistic powers of the sugar planters. But apart from seeking to reorientate broad governmental programmes away from the European minority interests, it had hardly undertaken the task of redefining the role of the bureacracy to reconcile the communal structure of the society with the regime's egalitarian values.

Hence, no formula for inter-ethnic sharing of the benefits of government administration and programmes was enunciated. This essentially meant that a modified meritocracy practised around European values persisted. In practical terms those who acquired English ways and schooling obtained a head-start over those who lagged. When Jagan and Burnham parted company and formed their own parties, the communal conflict spilled over into the government administrative machinery. Upon capturing power in 1957 the Jaganite faction sought to rectify the racial imbalance in the Public Service. The Geneva-based International Commission of Jurists (ICJ Commission) was invited to do a survey of the problem. Table 2.2 shows the results.

Clearly Indians, who constituted about 51 per cent of the population, obtained only about 33 per cent of the jobs, while black Creoles and Mixed Races, who formed about 40 per cent of the population, obtained about 53 per cent. Europeans still controlled about five times as many jobs relative to their ratio in the population and those were among the most senior positions.

In part, the political contest among the racially divided population was not only over jobs and government allocations, but more significantly over averting ethnic domination. Consequently, in a tense situation of all-out communal confrontation, the ethnic composition of the police and coercive forces came to play a pivotal role. More so than in any government institution, the ICJ Commission found the gravest imbalance here. Table 2.3 demonstrates this.

Table 2.2 *Racial composition of staff employed in all Ministries and Departments in British Guiana*

	Negro	*Indian*	*European*	*Portuguese*	*Mixed*	*Chinese*	*Amerindians*
1. Senior staff, i.e. senior clerk level up	335	227	37	20	255	68	1
2. Clerical service below senior clerk level	697	543	1	17	222	23	5
3. Others below senior clerk level	6327	3830	2	69	843	68	282
Total	7359	4600	40	106	1320	159	288
Percentage of total	53.05	33.16	0.29	0.76	9.52	1.15	2.08

Source: Report of the British Guiana Commission of Inquiry, International Commission of Jurists, 1965, p. 84.

Table 2.3 Distribution of security forces by rank and race in British Guiana, 1965 (percentages)

	Negro	*Indian*	*European*	*Portuguese*	*Mixed*	*Others*
Police force						
Officers	80.3	9.1	1.2	1.0	7.9	0.5
Constables	72.8	21.9	–	0.1	4.3	0.9
Volunteer force						
Officers	83.9	5.8	4.4	1.5	2.9	1.5
Lance Corporals & Privates	89.5	9.8	–	0.5	0.2	–
Special service unit						
Officers	50.0	50.0	–	–	–	–
Constables	51.3	47.0	–	–	1.7	–
Special constabulary						
Officers	55.2	13.8	–	13.8	17.2	–
Constables	74.2	21.9	0.2	0.2	3.4	–
Prisons						
Officers	81.8	–	–	–	18.8	–
Prison officers	83.9	16.1	–	–	–	–
Fire Brigade						
Officers	85.2	3.7	–	1.8	9.2	–
Firemen	61.1	21.4	–	1.6	15.9	–
Total						
Officers	79.4	9.4	1.6	1.6	7.5	0.6
Others	75.1	20.6	–	0.2	3.5	0.5

Source: Report of the British Guiana Commission of Inquiry (International Commission of Jurists, 1965), p. 172.

These tables show that in the security forces Indians constituted 20 per cent and black Creoles and Mixed Races about 78 per cent. Professor Enloe offered an historical explanation for the imbalance: 'Police were recruited overwhelmingly from Africans, presumably because they were numerous in the towns and because they met the physical requirements such as height and chest measurement which smaller Indian frames could not.'[41] Overall, in the public service, including the police and security divisions, no principle of sharing or proportionality operated. Progressively as Europeans left the country, the contest for jobs was in the open competitive market among the non-white communal segments. At an early part of Guiana's history, Indo-African conflict was contained by the fact that these communal segments lived apart physically, with Creoles moving to urban areas and Indians remaining on sugar estates and in villages. But towards the turn of the century, Indians were coming to towns to compete for jobs and scarce urban-based opportunities. The conflict between these two groups, then, at least in part, has an objective basis in resource allocation. Table 2.4 illustrates the demographic settlement, showing that by 1960 Indians had become nearly one-quarter of the urban population. There they would seek out skills and training, further intensifying the conditions of inter-ethnic conflict.

The Burnham regime and ethnic domination

When the new government led by Forbes Burnham acceded to power in 1964, the first item on the agenda was to restore domestic tranquillity in the wake of the virtual ethnic civil war that erupted in Guiana during the previous three years. But this inevitably meant that Jagan's Indian-based party, the PPP, bore the brunt of the government's attack. Under a new National Security Act and a state of emergency, Jagan's party activists were ruthlessly suppressed, many arrested and held in detention for long periods of time without trial. The communal factor inevitably pervaded the entire law-enforcement exercise, casting a dark shadow of suspicion about the government's motives. It was during this period in 1965 when the Guiana Defence Force (GDF) was formed to add to the ruling regime's coercive capabilities. Like the Police Force, the GDF was recruited mainly from the Creole communal section.[42]

In the end this recruitment pattern would provide a powerful base for the maintenance of a Creole-led government in power.

To reconstruct Guiana from the ravages of the previous years' ethnic confrontation, the Burnham regime realized that the task must be multi-racial if only because the vital agricultural sector of the economy was under Indian control. Burnham pleaded for cooperation and appointed a few Indians to his Cabinet. But, like Jagan, who had made similar calls for multi-racial cooperation, Burnham learned that appeals to race during election campaigns, even though covert and subtle, were not easily forgotten. Further, the party in power was captive to its communalist base. Followers demanded patronage at the expense of a vanquished ethnic enemy. To deny them would risk losing political support; to cater to them would result in the further alienation of the opposition communal group.

Burnham was not happy with d'Aguiar, his coalition partner, who controlled the Ministry of Finance and restrained the PNC in literally

Table 2.4 Demographic settlement 1891–1960

Year of Census	*Negro*	*Indian*	*White*	*Portuguese*	*Mixed*	*Chinese*	*Other*
Sugar estates							
1891	14.44	79.36	0.93	1.12	2.42	1.59	0.14
1921	13.96	81.77	0.72	0.39	2.29	0.76	0.12
1960	14.74	80.45	0.58	0.18	3.35	0.38	0.31
Villages							
1891	61.20	26.70	0.33	4.31	6.11	1.03	0.32
1921	49.86	41.16	0.22	2.15	5.48	0.77	0.36
Urban centres							
1891	47.19	8.44	5.02	10.23	27.03	1.50	0.59
1921	50.59	11.34	3.45	8.54	24.08	1.60	0.40
1946	54.43	15.68	1.68	6.04	19.57	2.20	0.39
1960	49.00	22.13	1.22	3.78	21.72	1.81	0.34

Source: *Report of the British Guiana Commission of Inquiry* (International Commission of Jurists, 1965), p. 164.

rewarding its communal supporters. About six months before the 1968 general elections, the PNC induced a number of parliamentary defections from the PPP, gaining a majority in the National Assembly and sole control of the government. it then reconstituted the electoral commission with d'Aguiar's own partisan sympathizers and tampered with the electoral machinery. In what would be established incontrovertibly as rigged elections involving tens of thousands of fictitious votes, the PNC won an absolute majority of seats in the 1968 elections.[43] The electoral fraud was perpetrated under the supervision of a politicized and communally-lopsided police and military force.

The 'seizure of power' in 1968 was a watershed in ethnic relations in Guiana. In a racially plural society, the PNC, representing a minority African group (32 per cent), grabbed the government. To avert internal disruption, the PNC government embarked on purging the critical pillars of its power – the coercive forces and the civil service – of most of its non-African elements. Where communal malcontents did not strike and demonstrate, many migrated to Europe or North America. This was especially the case with the Europeans, Chinese and Portuguese. The massive migration of this group from Guyana left a society predominantly polarized between Creoles and Indians.

When Burnham seized power in 1968, he realized that the economy was essentially controlled by his communal opponents. He needed to rectify this problem in his favour, preferably to reverse the roles. Gradually he abandoned the capitalist structure of the economy, which favoured businessmen, big property owners, and land cultivators.[44] Towards the end of 1969, then, the PNC regime adopted a socialist framework for Guyana's reconstruction and in 1970 declared Guyana a 'Cooperative Republic'.[45] From private enterprise, the economy was to be founded on cooperatives as the main instrument of production, distribution and consumption. The regime thereafter floundered from crisis to crisis, lost US support, and suffered from persistent boycotts by the non-Creole population, particularly Indian sugar and rice farmers. It ran a gauntlet besieged by high unemployment (20–30 per cent), double-digit inflation, prohibitive fuel costs, demonstrations, boycotts and strikes. A vicious cycle of poverty was created by a pattern of polarized and unstable ethnic politics inter-mixed with socialist ideological and programmatic justifications.

Between 1971 and 1976, the government nationalized nearly all foreign firms, bringing 80 per cent of the economy under state control. This unwieldy public sector provided the job opportunities necessary to quell the increasing demands of PNC supporters for patronage. When the Burnham regime nationalized 80 per cent of the economy, this grossly enlarged the state bureaucratic apparatus. But the bulging public bureaucracy was not transformed into socialist organizations.

There is no question, however, that the country's economy had been radically altered. Professor Mandle pointed out that the rulers were not socialist but racialist in composition:

> The older colonial ruling class and its business firms have been banished and decision-making power now rests with a local elite of state and cooperative-based managers. In the Guyanese context, this assumes the form of the emergence of an urban Afro-Guyanese leadership under the auspices of the People's National Congress.[46]

The police, security and armed forces, in particular, were expanded to protect the besieged PNC government. In 1964, the police and auxiliary armed forces numbered about 3770; by 1977, it was estimated to be 21 751.[47] In 1964, there was one military person to 284 civilians; in 1976, it was one for every 37 citizens.[48] The budgetary allocation for the military rose from 0.21 per cent in 1965 to 8 per cent in 1973 to 14.2 per cent in 1976. That is, the increase has been over 4000 per cent. More than any other public service department, the police and coercive forces were overwhelmed by Afro-Guyanese. Burnham named himself Chairman of the Defence Board, where he took personal control over promotions and appointments. The main assignment of the armed forces was to supplement the police constabulary in maintaining law and order.

For a regime to maintain and extend Guyana's economic development, it would require programmes that encouraged agricultural production. Guyana lacks even a minor industrial capacity and its mining sector is small. It is upon agricultural production that the country's capability to feed itself depends. Sugar production is the backbone of the economic system as a whole and sugar workers are mainly Indians. In the mid-1970s the sugar companies, all foreign-owned, were nationalized. The next most significant agricultural industry was rice and this was almost wholly under Indian peasant production. When Jagan was in power, he provided several programmes such as credits, subsidies, marketing, technical assistance and drainage and irrigation to the rice industry. Hence, the PNC labelled the Jagan regime as a 'Rice Government' partisan to Indian communal interests. When the PNC acceded to power, the rice-growers were victimized, with most state subsidies eliminated. Rice production plummeted to half its original size. The government's Rice Marketing Board, which had a monopoly in purchasing the farmer's rice, was reorganized and staffed with PNC personnel. Rice farmers, under Jagan's instruction, boycotted rice production, creating grave shortages in the country.

Like the sugar industry, rice became a political and ethnic football. The PNC government wanted to eliminate its dependency on Indian agriculturalists for much of the country's food. In 1970, then, under its announced policy of 'Cooperative Socialism', the PNC attempted to locate landless Afro-Guyanese on state lands previously leased to Indian farmers. The Indian stranglehold on peasant agriculture provided Jagan's PPP with a powerful base of support. The strategy of Creole agriculture, involving redistribution of land and subsidies failed, for rice cultivation required years of experience for success. Despite victimizing them, Burnham's party continued to appeal to Indian farmers to produce. But cooperation was not forthcoming. As Mandle explained:

> Fundamentally at issue here is the nature of the PNC government. Briefly put, it is a regime which is manager-dominated, urban and predominantly Afro-Guyanese. The peasant and agricultural section of the population – largely of Indo-Guyanese descent – is inadequately represented within the government ranks. As a result, the ruling party and the government is poorly equipped either to mobilize the rural labour force or to call upon its goodwill in attempting to transform agriculture.[49]

The overall policy output of the PNC regime, even if it were to be interpreted foremost in socialist terms, pointed indisputably to ethnic favouritism and preference. The polarization of the races was probably attributable as much to ethnic chauvinism among PNC activists as to PPP boycotts and strikes against the government. The economic situation had deteriorated so badly that towards the end of the 1970s, the impact reverberated adversely on everyone alike, regardless of ethnic membership. Strikes and demonstrations and other challenges to Burnham's power increasingly came from all ethnic segments, including Creoles. The arsenal of coercive powers previously used against Indians was now used against Creole dissidents also.

The judiciary also came under the PNC regime's direct influence. The appointment of judges and magistrates was routinely based on party loyalty.[50] Thus, the use of the courts to challenge the legality and constitutionality of decisions of the regime was futile. In 1978, the government altered the constitution of the country so that the appointment of judges and magistrates fell under the purview of President Burnham. The new constitutional system inaugurated an executive presidency which was given to Burnham. The judicial system, then, became integrated into the regime's coercive and control arsenal to be used against political dissidents.

The fascistization of the state

Repression tends to breed the conditions of its creation; original factors become compounded as the opposition resists, impelling the state to increase the measures of repression. Soon, repression and counter-violence reduce the state to one marked by anarchy, dictation, suffering and almost hopeless poverty and misery. The Guyana case captured the dynamic of this reinforcing system of self-fulfilling prophecies. Not only have the screws of repression multiplied and tightened in Guyana in response to the need for more and more security, but as the screws were applied, the victims became more numerous and included erstwhile innocent, undecided and uninvolved persons who now became embroiled and alienated in the quagmire of government terror.

Clive Thomas uses the term 'fascistisation of the state' to describe events in Guiana:

> In this stage political assassination, direct repression of all popular manifestations, and a rapid growth of the security apparatuses of the state take place. These developments are propagandandised with the familiar claims of 'law and order', 'the necessities of development of a poor country', and 'we cannot afford the luxuries of democracy.' The fascistisation of the state is now very much on the way and from here on, the government through state-manipulation, propaganda, and force, make it unmistakably clear that it cannot be changed by legal or constitutional means.[51]

The use of formal and informal state-sponsored thuggery, harassment, inhuman treatment, assassination, terror and violence had become part of the repertoire of repression liberally applied to maintain the power of the PNC. Once the elections were rigged and parliament brought under control, all else followed, including the purging of the public service of communal and ideological enemies; purification of the armed forces and police of potentially disloyal personnel; politicization of the courts; the breakdown of the legal system as a constraint on arbitrary state action; public corruption and rape of the public treasury; the rise of PNC paramountcy and the personalistic powers of President Burnham; the breakdown of the economy and the impoverishment of the society with malnutrition and hunger widespread; and finally, the mass migration of a third of the population overseas.

In the 1970s, the PNC would be faced with a paradox of power: as it consolidated its control of the parliament, the courts, the coercive forces, the public service, and the mass media, it would become more insecure and become vulnerable to opposition attack. In the mid-1970s, a new organization called the Working People's Alliance (WPA), headed by historian Walter Rodney, appeared on the political scene. The WPA would organize and mobilize the entire spectrum of opposition forces, including Jagan's PPP, and unleash a fierce assault on the government. The WPA was a cross-communal organization, unlike the PPP which, although its leader Cheddi Jagan was socialist, was based on communal support of Guyana's Indians.

In confronting Burnham's PNC, the PPP merely achieved a standoff. To be sure, Jagan did succeed in periodically bringing the PNC government to a standstill through strikes and boycotts. The WPA was a different body, however; it was multi-racial and, above all, it was led, like the PNC, by an Afro-Guyanese.

If Burnham was able to maintain the loyalty of his communal segment and to cope with Cheddi Jagan by invoking the fear of Indian domination, he had no answer for Walter Rodney. Apart from being an African like Burnham, Rodney was also a socialist with a growing reputation among Third World intellectuals for his anti-capitalist radicalism. To add to these points, Rodney was a dedicated activist. He was successful in organizing anti-government strikes and demonstrations in government strongholds such as Linden, throwing the ruling regime into panic.[52]

To harass and intimidate the opposition, the government employed the 'muscular' sections of the PNC as well as the police, militia, state security, and army personnel, especially where the WPA and its supporters held meetings. This would be complemented by The House of Israel, a new organization headed by Rabbi Washington, an Afro-American refugee from US justice. The House of Israel gained the reputation as the thuggery-and-assassination arm of the government, for its open activities of intimidation and violence had never been questioned by the police.

> Father Bernard Drake, a Jesuit priest who was the photographer of the *Catholic Standard* was stabbed to death by members of the House of Israel on the streets outside the courts. His death was the most serious event in a pattern of violence which the government directed mainly against members of the WPA. Two activists were shot dead and many others imprisoned on spurious charges, while many of the sympathizers including senior management figures lost their jobs in the state sector on the grounds that they constituted security risks.[53]

In using state violence against its opponents, the government appropriated the term 'terrorist' to describe the opposition. The Inter-church Committee on Latin America gave a few recent examples:

> Twenty-two members of the PPP are currently charged with 'public terror' following the break-up of a PPP political meeting held prior to the 1980 elections. Nine members of the WPA were charged with causing 'public terror' after they had distributed leaflets from house to house on the eve of the December 1980 elections.[54]

Father Mike James, writing in *The Catholic Standard*, noted how arbitrary arrest and intimidation had become a norm: 'In recent years, security forces have felt free to arrest persons without explanation because they happened to sympathize with an opposition party, criticize the regime or merely attend an opposition public meeting.' The *Bar Association Review* of Guiana had called for an investigation of the brutality and terror that persons who were arrested experienced in custody.[55]

Walter Rodney was assassinated in 1980 but, prior to and after his death, 'Guyana had become a land of horrors. Democracy was no longer on trial here. The question was whether it would survive this [Rodney's] official crucifixion.'[56] State terror had become entrenched and pervasive as a mode of maintaining the PNC power. In the urban areas, especially Georgetown, the repression would become cross-communal, but in the rural areas where Indians predominate, it would assume a decidedly racist form. Rape, burglary and arbitrary arrests by the security forces had become so prevalent that Indian villages became places of terror. The police were viewed not as a solution but as the source of the problem. Indian homes in particular became a target of official search-and-seizure exercises, because as the economy deteriorated and inflation reduced the real salaries of the police and security forces, the need for public plunder as a source of revenue became compelling. Indian homes, then, became the main target of booty, and the police knew that theft and torture committed against the Indian community were likely to go uninvestigated or ignored by the courts. In effect, while it could be argued that the persistent pattern of theft and terror committed against the regime's communal enemies, and this meant mainly Indians since nearly all of the Portuguese and Europeans had migrated from Guyana, was committed on the initiative of police and security personnel, without formal approval of the PNC leadership, the fact remained that everyone knew what was happening and nothing was done to stop the plunder and terror. It could even be argued that once started for a specific purpose against only clearly identified political opponents, state terror lost control of its personnel, who privately perpetrated criminal acts against the Indian community. There is much plausibility to this argument, but it does not alter the source of ultimate responsibility, namely the ruling party, for setting a violent tone to Guyanese politics generally.

Finally, because of the diverting of scarce resources to pay for an inordinately expanded coercive apparatus, and because of persistent boycotts and strikes, the country became increasingly impoverished. Malnutrition, lack of elementary medical care, disrepair of public roads, schools, and other facilities, and the frequent interruption of water and electricity supplies cast the tenor of society as one in deep crisis. The Inter-church Committee on Human Rights in Latin America reported that

> the economic situation deteriorated rapidly, causing great hardship to the poorer members of the society and the right to life

> itself. Malnutrition is now widespread and is causing an increasing number of deaths in children according to doctors at the Georgetown Public Hospital. There has been a rapid deterioration in social and public services; health and education in particular have been severely affected.... The principal responsibility for this situation is (placed) on government policies rather than the state of the world economy.[57]

Conclusion

The dynamic of race and politics in Guyana has run a long gauntlet from white domination in a colonial system superseded by domination over another non-white group in the post-colonial period. The social and institutional context in which the politics of race relations has been played out has been the plantation, the rice field and the colonial town, all oriented toward producing a mono crop, sugar, for export. Competition over scarce resources in part structured the first expression of racial conflict. But thereafter a variety of factors – uni-ethnic patterns of occupation, residence, and voluntary organizations – exacerbated inter-ethnic divisions. When colonial politics yielded to nationalist politics, the role of personal ambition and mass parties soon distorted inter-communal cooperation.

In the end every party and leader exploited particularistic ethnic sentiments for narrow selfish ends, throwing the country in a tailspin of tragic racial bitterness. The Guyana model of race and politics is a clear, unequivocal illustration of what not to do in the sphere of race and ethnic relations.

Notes

1 Eric Williams, *Capitalism and Slavery* (London: André Deutsch, 1964).
2 Ibid., p. 7.
3 James Rodway, *Guiana: British, Dutch, and French* (London: T. Fisher and Unwin, 1912), p. 224.
4 Alan Young, *The Approaches to Local Self-Government in British Guiana* (London: Longmans, Green, 1958), p. 7.
5 Dwarka Nath, *A History of Indians in British Guiana* (London: Thomas Nelson and Sons, 1950), pp. 179–80.
6 Chandra Jayawardena, *Conflict and Solidarity on a Guiana Plantation* (London: Athlone Press, 1963), p. 14.
7 Rawle Farley, 'The Rise of the Peasantry in British Guiana', *Social and Economic Studies* (1954), p. 95.
8 Young, 'Approaches', p. 23.
9 Ibid.
10 *Report of the British Guiana Commission of Inquiry on Racial Problems in the Public Service* (Geneva: International Commission of Jurists, 1965), p. 164. (Hereafter referred to as the ICJ Report.)

11 Ibid.
12 G. W. Roberts, 'Some Observations on the Population of British Guiana', *Population Studies*, II (September, 1948), pp. 186–187.
13 ICJ Report, p. 165.
14 See Ralph R. Premdas, *Voluntary Associations and Political Parties in a Racially Fragmented Strategy. The Case of Guyana* (Georgetown: University of Guyana, 1972). Occasional Paper No. 2, published by the Department of Political Science.
15 See Ralph R. Premdas, 'Elections and Political Campaigns in a Racially Bifurcated State: The Case of Guyana', *The Journal of Inter-American Studies and World Affairs*, Vol. 14, no. 3, August 1972.
16 Cecil Clementi, *A Constitutional History of British Guiana* (London, 1937), p. 369.
17 C. Enloe, 'Civilian Control of the Military: Implications in the Plural Societies of Guyana and Malaysia.' Paper presented at the Interdisciplinary Seminar on Armed Force and Society, SUNY-Buffalo, Oct. 18–19, 1974 (mimeo), 5, p. 27.
18 For the historical background to educational development in Guyana, see M. K. Bacchus, *Education and Socio-Cultural Integration in a Plural Society* (Montreal: McGill University Press, 1970).
19 Raj K. Vasil, *Politics in Bi-Racial Societies* (New Delhi: Vikas, 1984), p. 69.
20 Bacchus, *Education.*
21 See Ralph R. Premdas, *Racial Politics in Guyana* (Denver, 1973); J. E. Greene, *Race vs Politics in Guyana* (Mona, Jamaica, 1974); Peter Newman, *British Guiana: Problems of Cohesion in an Immigrant Society* (London: Oxford University Press, 1964).
22 Paul Singh, *Guyana: Socialism in a Plural Society* (London: Fabian Society, 1972).
23 See Ralph R. Premdas, 'The Rise of the First Mass-Based Multi-Racial Party in Guyana', *Caribbean Quarterly*, 20 (Sept.–Dec. 1974).
24 Ashton Chase, *A History of Trade Unionism in Guyana* (Georgetown: New Guiana Co., 1964).
25 Cheddi Jagan, *Forbidden Freedom: The Story of British Guiana* (London: Lawrence and Wishart, 1954).
26 'The Aims of the Political Affairs Committee', *The PAC Bulletin*, 6 Nov, 1964, p. 1.
27 Premdas, 'The Rise of the First Multi-Racial Party in Guyana', pp. 10–13.
28 'Aims and Programme of the People's Progressive Party', *Thunder*, Vol. 1, no. 4 (April 1950), pp. 6–7.
29 Premdas, 'The Rise of the First Multi-Racial Party in Guyana', pp. 10–15.
30 Ashton Chase, *133 Days Towards Freedom in Guyana* (Georgetown: New Guiana Co., 1953).
31 See Ralph R. Premdas, 'Election and Political Campaigns in a Racially Bifurcated State', *Journal of Inter-American Studies and World Affairs* 12 (August 1972).
32 See 'Money Being Spent on Majority Party's Stronghold', *New Nation*, 24 Jan. 1959; 'We Want Nationalism Not Sectionalism', *New Nation*, 1 February 1958.
33 See Arthur Schlesinger, Jr, *A Thousand Days* (New York: Houghton Mifflin, 1965), p. 779.
34 Ralph Premdas, 'Guyana: Violence and Democracy in a Communal State', *Plural Societies*, Vol. 12, nos 3–4, Autumn–Winter 1981; Peter Simms, *Trouble in Guyana* (London: Allen and Unwin, 1966).
35 H. Lutchman, 'Race and Bureaucracy in Guyana', *Journal of Comparative Administration*, Vol. 4, no. 2, August 1972, p. 242.
36 See R. Hope and W. C. David, 'Planning for Development in Guyana: The Experience from 1945 to 1973', *Inter American Economic Affairs*, Spring, 1974.
37 See Ralph R. Premdas, 'Competitive Party Organisations and Political Integration in a Racially Fragmented State: The case of Guyana', *Caribbean Studies*, Jan. 1973, Vol. 12, no. 4, especially footnotes 30 and 32.

38 Ralph R. Premdas, 'Guyana: Communal Conflict, Socialism, and Political Reconciliation', *Inter American Affairs* 30 (Spring, 1977), Vol. 30, no. 8.
39 Lutchman, 'Race and Bureaucracy', p. 242. See also, *Report of the Commission of Inquiry into the Disturbances in British Guiana in February 1962* (London: HMSO, 2849, 1965); Ralph R. Premdas, 'Guyana: Destabilisation in the Western Hemisphere', *Caribbean Quarterly*, Vol. 25, no. 3, March 1980.
40 See R. S. Milne, *Politics in Ethnically Bi-Polar States* (Vancouver: University of British Colombia Press, 1981).
41 Enloe, Civilian Control of the Military', p. 27.
42 Enloe, 'Civilian Control of the Military'; see also her *Ethnic Soldiers* (Harmondsworth: Penguin, 1979).
43 Adrian Mitchell, 'Jagan and Burnham: It's Polling Day Tomorrow. Have Guyanese Elections Already Been Decided in Britain?', *The Sunday Times* (London), 15 Dec. 1968.
44 Jay Mandle, 'Continuity and Change in Guyanese Undevelopment', *Monthly Review*, Vol. 21, no. 2, September 1976.
45 See Forbes Burnham, *A Destiny to Mould* (London: Longman Caribbean, 1970); F. Burnham, *Towards a Cooperative Republic* (Georgetown: Chronicle Publishers, 1969).
46 Mandle, 'Continuity and Change', p. 11.
47 See George K. Danns, 'Militarisation and Development: An Experiment in Nation-Building in Guyana', *Transition* (Guyana), Vol. 1, no. 1, 1975, Jan.
48 Ibid.
49 Jay Mandle, 'The Post-Colonial Mode of Production in Guyana' (mimeo), p. 19. Department of Economics, Temple University, 1979.
50 See David DeCaries, 'Intense Political Pressures on Guyana's Judicial System', *Caribbean Contact*, June 1979.
51 C. Thomas, 'State Capitalism in Guyana: An Assessment of Burnham's Cooperative Republic', in *Crisis in the Caribbean*, ed. F. Ambursley and R. Cohen (New York: Monthly Review Press, 1983), p. 40.
52 Ralph R. Premdas, 'Communal Politics: Rodney's Guyana Revisited', *Revista Americana*, Spring 1985.
53 *Inter-Church*, Georgetown, 1976, p. 50.
54 *Catholic Standard*, 24 Oct. 1982, p. 1.
55 'Lawyers call for an Investigation into Police Brutality', *Guyana Update* (London), Sept.–Oct. 1984, p. 3.
56 *Guyana: Fraudulent Revolution* (London, 1983), p. 80.
57 *Inter-Chuch*, p. 72.

CHAPTER 3

Control, resistance, accommodation and race relations: Aspects of the indentureship experience of East Indian immigrants in Jamaica, 1845–1921

Verene A. Shepherd

In 1840, just two years after the termination of the Apprenticeship System in Jamaica, Stephen Harmer, overseer of Hope Pen in Manchester, in a letter to his brother in England, complained that

> I regret to say that this once fine country is Goeing [sic] fast to destruction through the want of continuous labour.... One half of the Negroes have scarely done anything since they were made free and them that do work demand very high wages from 4/- to 5/- per day and then they will not do even half a day's work for that.[1]

Harmer's 'lament' typified the reaction of Jamaican proprietors to the loss of their traditional command over labour in the years following the complete abolition of slavery. Jamaican ex-slaves, however, refused to work under the unfavourable conditions offered by these proprietors and evinced a preference for non-estate occupations wherever these could be secured. This situation had been anticipated by Lord Glenelg in 1836 when he posited that, 'During slavery, labour could be compelled to go wherever it promised most profit to the employer; under the new system it will find its way wherever it promises most profit to the labourer.'[2]

To solve what was then popularly termed the 'labour problem' in Jamaica, several immigration schemes, mostly under the bounty system, had been tried since 1834.[3] The failure of these schemes to provide the proprietors with cheap, reliable and controllable workers led them to agitate for state-regulated immigration. By 1842 the more influential proprietors had managed to convince the British Government that immigration was the antidote to emancipation. Consequently, a Select Committee of the House of Commons recommended in 1842 that

> One obvious and most desirable mode of endeavouring to compensate for this diminished supply of labour is to promote the immigration of a fresh labouring population....[4]

This 'fresh labouring population' would supply the wage workers – essential ingredients for the continued advancement of the cause of capitalism in the metropole; for, according to the quintessential pro-immigrationist, Edward Gibbon Wakefield,

> Property in money, means of subsistence, machines and other means of production, does not as yet stamp a man as a capitalist if there be wanting the correlative – the wage worker, the other man who is compelled to sell himself of his own free will.[5]

In Jamaica, as in Trinidad and Guyana, it was East Indian immigration which seemed to offer most hope for the planters and other proprietors. About 25 000 Indians had migrated to Mauritius between 1834 and 1839 and British Guiana had experimented briefly with Indians under the ill-fated Gladstone Experiment in 1838.[6] Those early experiments had been riddled with problems, causing the Indian Government to impose prohibition. With the establishment of a new system of controls, Indian emigration had again been allowed to Mauritius in 1842. India seemed to offer boundless resources of cheap unskilled labour and presented fewer political obstacles to emigration than, say China – another proposed source of labour. These considerations combined with the increasing frustration with Creole and other forms of bonded labour migration being tried, led the Colonial Office to approach the Government of India at the end of 1843 proposing the establishment of labour migration between India, Trinidad, British Guiana and Jamaica. The first batch of 261 Indians arrived in Jamaica on the *Blundell* in May 1845.[7] Between 1845 and 1921, when indentureship was abolished, the island imported approximately 37 000 Indian labourers.[8]

Jamaican planters were optimistic about the benefits to be derived from use of bonded Indian labourers. A primary hope was that Indian immigrants would provide them with a 'controllable' labour force. It was also expected that regular importation of immigrants would create a surplus pool of labourers and cause a reduction in prevailing wage rates. The moral rectitude of such a scheme and the implications for Indian–Creole relations of the stated economic effects, were not issues with which Jamaican proprietors were particularly preoccupied. Missionary bodies such as the Baptist Union, however, constantly warned that poor race relations in the island between Indians and Creoles would result.[9] The intention of this chapter is to examine, from the early history of East Indian immigration into Jamaica, the extent to which the Indians provided the planters with the hoped-for 'controllable' workers, and how far the missionaries' prediction of poor Indian–black relations during the operation of the system of indentureship, 1845–1921, became a reality.

I

Jamaican proprietors employed a variety of measures in an effort to render East Indian immigrants a 'controllable' labour force. The first strategy was to secure Indian labourers under a contract system. The rationale for contracts was that where labour was not sufficiently cheap and servile, the free play of market forces must be interrupted and an element of extra-economic compulsion in the form of long contracts be introduced. Despite planter agitation for long contracts, the British Government at first refused to allow Indians to be indentured for more than one year. By 1850, they had relented sufficiently to allow three-year contracts and, by 1862, five-year contracts were general. A further advantage for proprietors was that Indian labourers were resident on the properties on which they were contracted. They were required to work for nine hours a day, six days a week in gangs under Indian or Afro-Jamaican headmen. To further secure labour, planters successfully agitated for the imposition of a compulsory ten years of continuous residence in the island before the Indians became entitled to return passages to India.[10] Above all, Indian immigrants were controlled by a set of restrictive laws, with penal clauses attached, which sought to restrict their mobility.[11] According to Haraksingh, in analysing planter attitudes to East Indians in Trinidad,

> throughout the indenture period the assumptions and premises of slavery continued to inform management attitudes. The need to keep the workers under the strictest control was never questioned. In this context there was established an elaborate system of coercion which included laws curtailing freedom of movement outside the estate.[12]

In order to lodge a complaint against his employer, for example, the immigrant first had to obtain permission from that same employer to leave the estate and go to the Protector of Immigrants' office. It is apparent from this that, as under slavery, Indian workers were confined within the estates. Indeed, none was allowed to venture beyond the estate boundary without a pass. The rationale for such restriction was that, like the slaves before them, Indians were prone to marronage and had to be restrained from such vagabond instincts. This attitude was not confined to Jamaica. Tinker has shown that even after the expiration of his contract the Indian worker in

Mauritius had to carry a *livret* or pass with his photograph.[13] A number of punitive devices were also imposed upon indentured workers for what were deemed 'offences against the labour law'. Such 'offences' included unlawful absence from work, downright refusal to work, wilful indolence, and so on. Punishment for such offences ranged from such extra-legal methods as floggings on some estates, to heavy fines and imprisonment. Furthermore, time spent in prison served to lengthen the immigrants' indentures, for periods spent in jail were not discounted.[14]

These various control strategies were partially successful. Not all Jamaican proprietors utilized Indian indentured servants, but for those who did, such labourers restored to them a degree of control over labour which they could not exercise over Afro-Jamaicans. Indians, after all, represented a resident, contracted labour force subject to the total authority of the proprietors for at least five years. But were Indians entirely controllable? That is, did they accept planter control uncomplainingly? Contemporary official reports, indeed, tried to convey the image of the 'docile coolie'; but the evidence conflicted with the stereotype. There is ample documented evidence to indicate that Indians from time to time employed a variety of means to register their disaffection with certain repressive aspects of the system of indentureship. These included late payment of wages, inadequate wages and rations (for the newly arrived) and harsh punishment for actions deemed offences against the labour law. The Indians' reaction to these conditions were varied and ranged from resistance to accommodation.

II

The failure of Indian indentured servants in the Caribbean to uncomplainingly accept the conditions of their servitude has led to the introduction of another dimension to resistance studies in the region. While still dominated by slave resistance studies, the historiography reflects the increasing attention being paid to protest among indentured labourers. In his recent bibliographical review of the historical writing on migration into the Commonwealth Caribbean, however, Alvin Thompson expressed the view that even this increasing interest in protest among the Indians was not adequate. According to him,

> the aspect of the plantation system that has received least attention is that regarding [Indian] resistance and revolt. There is still need for a comprehensive work on the subject since Indian resistance and revolt clearly had a major impact on plantation life.[15]

While acknowledging the need for more work on this subject, Thompson's review clearly indicates that the greatest gap in the literature exists in the case of Jamaica, as some pioneer work has already been undertaken by historians in Trinidad and Guyana.[16] In doing this micro-analysis involving Indians in Jamaica, the definitions formulated by Frederickson and Lasch to delimit the somewhat indistinct boundary between resistance and accommodation will be utilized. Their model will also be followed in deciding whether or not all forms of non-cooperation on the part of the indentured immigrants constituted resistance.[17] In order to place the discussion which follows in the context of the Frederickson–Lasch formulation, it is first necessary to explain their use of the term 'resistance'. According to them,

> resistance is a political concept. Political activity in the strictest sense is organized collective action which aims at affecting the distribution of power in a community.... More broadly, [resistance] might be said to consist of any activity either of individuals or of groups, which is designed to create a consciousness of collective interest, such consciousness of collective interest being the pre-requisite for effective action in the realm of power.[18]

Although organized resistance is not the only form of political action, it is the form generally used by people for whom the possibilities of conventional politics are largely absent. Those who did not band together in violent confrontations employed various personal strategies of accommodation. The most common have been categorized by Frederickson and Lasch as 'intransigence'. The latter they distinguish from resistance. It does not imply any sense of solidarity or underground organization of workers, but is, rather, a personal strategy of survival. It can help to sustain a high morale but, on the other hand, can just as easily lead to futile and even self-destructive acts of defiance.[19]

Based on these definitions and explanations, it is possible to state definitively that Indian immigrants in Jamaica, as in Trinidad, Surinam and Guiana, employed both accommodationist techniques and political resistance to survive in or escape from, a form of total institution analogous to slavery.[20]

III

Indian immigrants in Jamaica employed a variety of intransigent actions to register their dissatisfaction with their status as indentured servants and with the failure of employers to honour all the terms of their contract. These included day-to-day protest such as malingering, 'wilful' indolence, outright refusal to work, constant requests for leave of absence, desertion, and unlawful (short-term) absence from work. All these forms of protest represented breaches of the immigration law and were punishable by fines and imprisonment.

Of the forms of protest mentioned above, only desertion was aimed at securing for the indentured labourer who attempted it his complete freedom from indentureship, and this will be treated first.

Desertion was a feature of the system of Indian indentured servitude from its very inception. Some of the early immigrants imported in the 1840s wandered off the estates and the Inspector of Immigrants, Garsia, reported various cases throughout the 1860s in his personal letterbook.[21] Surgeon Major D. Comins's report of 1891, however, indicated that the rate of desertion up to 1891 was not considered alarming.[22] Nevertheless, like other forms of protest, desertion was considered a breach of the Immigration Law which governed not only the conditions of employment of the immigrant but also his conduct. The law defined a deserter as

> any Immigrant who at any time except Sundays or on holidays or festivals is found during the ordinary hours of work at a distance of more than two miles from the estate on which he is indentured and fails to produce a certificate of exemption, or a written ticket of leave signed by his employer....[23]

Such an immigrant could be arrested without warrant by any police constable, once it was determined that he was a *bona fide* deserter, and either taken back to his estate or to an Inspector, or Justice. The latter step had to be taken in cases where the accosted immigrant refused to disclose the name of the estate from which he had absconded.[24] Employers usually reported cases of desertion to the nearest police station within 24 hours of their detection.[25] As periods of desertion were reckoned against an immigrant (which he would have to serve at the end of his five years),[26] employers were advised to keep a register of all cases of desertion.[27] Other employers were also prohibited from employing immigrants who had succeeded in deserting from a particular estate and who were not caught and returned to the estate from which they had deserted.[28] Some Indians, on being accosted, tried to escape the charge of desertion by pretending to be on their way to the Protector of Immigrants or the Resident Magistrate to lodge a complaint or seek advice.[29] In such an event, the case was decided on the basis of whether or not they had reasonable ground for making such a complaint or seeking such advice.[30] Some deserters also produced false documents, thus fraudulently pretending to be free. When cases of fraud were detected, a fine of £2 was imposed.[31]

Convicted deserters either paid a fine of £5[32] or served 30 days in prison.[33] Perhaps because of the risks involved, only a small proportion of the total number of indentured immigrants deserted each year. In addition, as Table 3.1 indicates, the majority were usually caught and returned. The percentage caught and returned each year gives an even more accurate picture of the general failure of desertion to provide escape for indentured servants. In fact, of the years for which figures are available, only in 1914–15 and 1920–21 were the majority of deserters successful in their escape.

Table 3.1 *Cases of desertion, 1910–21*

Year	*No. of Indians under indenture*	*Number of cases of desertion*	*% of indentured population*	*Number caught and returned to estate*	*% caught and returned each year*
1910–11	2892	33	1.14	26	78.78
1911–12	2841	28	0.98	No figures available	–
1912–13	4152	52	1.25	No figures available	–
1913–14	4000	35	0.87	No figures available	–
1914–15	3911	36	0.92	16	44.44
1915–16	2913	69	2.37	58	84.05
1916–17	2884	17	0.58	14	82.35
1917–18	2736	61	2.22	44	72.13
1918–19	872	15	0.11	11	73.33
1919–20	560	19	3.39	11	58.00
1920–21	562	15	2.66	6	40.00
Total		380		186	

Source: Annual Reports of the Protector of Immigrants, 1910–21.

The myth of the docile Indian, in Jamaica, was shattered by the frequency of malingering, 'wilful indolence', unlawful absence from work and downright refusal to work. According to Law 23 of 1879 [Section 95 (15)], these offences were regarded as serious breaches of contract and fetched penalities not exceeding £3 upon conviction. The fact that such offences formed a large percentage of the cases brought before the Resident Magistrate and the Protector of Immigrants in each year, attests to the fact that the threat of fines did not deter the Indians. In 1914–15 alone, a total of 256 cases of wilful indolence were brought before the Resident Magistrates and the Protector. (See Tables 3.2 and 3.3.) Many employers described the Indians as incorrigible idlers who would never reform even though they were always punished.[34] The Protector of Immigrants, Charles Doorly, admitted that very often punishment was only applied 'by way of setting an example to others on the property who perhaps are not too zealously inclined'.[35]

Refusal to work and unlawful absence also accounted for a number of the cases before the Protector and the Magistrate. In 1914–15, 123 cases of downright refusal to work were recorded and 70 cases of unlawful absence. Careful records of unlawful absence were kept. Table 3.4 shows figures for the whole island of this offence. When compared to the total number of indentured workers, however, these percentages became less significant. In fact, between 1911 and 1916, only 1.55 days on average were lost per year on account of absence from work.

Nevertheless, penalties for these two offences were severe. For refusal to work, the offender could either pay a fine of £3 or serve two months in prison. Prison terms were also given for unlawful absence.[36] Very often immigrants were imprisoned for these labour offences since many were unable to pay the fines levied. Of the 15 East Indians in prison in 1902, for example, seven were serving sentences for labour offences.[37] Tables 3.2 and 3.3 clearly show that in the majority of cases, Indians brought before the Protector of Magistrate for labour offences were convicted.

IV

More violent signs of discontent, classified as true political resistance, were organized strikes, riots and protest marches to the Protector of Immigrants or to the police station.

Strikes, riots and protest marches occurred throughout the indentureship period, though they were more marked in the twentieth century. These were usually spontaneous and localized and never reached the proportion of planned islandwide revolts. The usual causes for strikes, riots and protest marches were non-payment of wages or the failure of employers to pay wages on time, disputes over task work, dissatisfaction with the headmen, dispute over rations and ill-treatment of indentured workers by employers. In some cases, violence accompanied strikes. In all cases, the aim was to better working conditions for all indentured servants and force employers to conform to the term of the contracts.

The first recorded strike of Indian indentured servants actually occurred in the early years of Indian immigration – in 1847 – just two years after the start of Indian immigration into Jamaica. In that year, all the indentured Indians from an estate in Hanover downed their tools and marched to Lucea to lodge a complaint against their employer. Their principal complaints were ill-treatment, and failure to receive food rations in conformity with the agreement made with them previous to leaving India.[38] This is how a contemporary writer calling himself 'Publicola' described the scene in 1847:

Table 3.2 *Proceedings against immigrants for breaches of the Immigration Law before the Protector of Immigrants, 1901–21*

Year	*Number of indentured immigrants*	*Number of complaints*	*Number of convictions*	*Number dismissed*	*% of convictions to population*
1901–2	1175	95	91	4	7.74
1902–3	1819	119	117	2	6.30
1903–4	1245	114	107	7	8.50
1904–5	N O F I G U R E S A V A I L A B L E				
1905–6	1427	117	104	13	7.20
1906–7	2200	174	173	1	7.86
1907–8	2832	107	105	2	3.77
1908–9	2605	122	119	3	4.56
1909–10	3749	119	112	7	3.00
1910–11	2892	296	291	5	10.00
1911–12	2841	327	320	7	11.26
1912–13	4152	296	296	None	7.12
1913–14	4000	398	398	None	9.95
1914–15	3911	337	324	13	8.28
1915–16	2913	249	242	7	8.31
1916–17	284	194	191	3	6.66
1917–18	2736	108	108	None	3.94
1918–19	872	74	74	None	8.49
1919–20	560	29	29	None	5.18
1920–21	562	29	29	None	5.16

Source: Annual Reports of the Protector of Immigrants, 1901–21.

Table 3.3 Proceedings against immigrants before the resident magistrate, 1901–20

Year	*Number of indentured immigrants*	*Number of complaints*	*Number of convictions*	*Number of cases dismissed*	*% of convictions to indentured population*
1901–2	1175	29	25	4	2.12
1902–3	1819	68	67	1	3.68
1903–4	1245	83	82	1	6.50
1904–5	NO FIGURES AVAILABLE				
1905–6	1427	70	70	None	4.90
1906–7	2200	157	157	None	7.13
1907–8	2832	132	132	None	4.66
1908–9	2605	150	150	None	5.75
1909–10	3749	88	87	1	2.32
1910–11	2892	98	96	2	3.31
1911–12	2041	171	170	1	6.00
1912–13	4152	202	202	None	4.86
1913–14	4000	241	241	None	6.02
1914–15	3911	348	343	5	8.77
1915–16	2913	202	202	None	6.92
1916–17	2864	55	55	None	1.92
1917–18	2736	14	14	None	0.51
1918–19	872	1	1	None	0.11
1919–20	560	4	4	None	0.71

Source: Annual Reports of the Protector of Immigrants, 1901–20.

> Rambling some evening last week about dusk towards the suburbs of the town of Lucea, my eyes caught the light of several fires, and my ears were greeted with the sound of human voices in wild harmony, mingled with the notes of tambourine and bamboo flute. Such revelry being unusual in this retired spot I hastened on to gratify my curiosity. On reaching the place from whence the sounds proceeded, a novel scene presented itself to my view; about forty coolies, in groups of four or five were squatted on the ground around murky fires; some looking after their pots of rice, which were under the culinary process, while others were singing; some were clapping their hands by way of accompaniment, but all seemed engaged to their satisfaction for the time being. The glow of light from the fires cast a faint shadow on their strongly marked countenances: their gaunt figures half clad in flowing drapery, and strange jargon, all conspired in exciting my imagination to a belief that I had fallen on an encampment of a tribe of Gypsies, but I came to the conclusion that they had met there to celebrate one of their religious festivals....[39]

In fact, the Indians had stopped to make their supper after a long march. Clearly, they were well-prepared for their journey to Lucea. This early pattern of resistance continued into the twentieth century. They were not very frequent, however. Indeed, there were only 18 recorded strikes in the period up to 1921. One of the more serious strikes. which was accompanied by violent rioting, took place on Moreland Estate in St James in July 1907.[40] All the indentured workers on this estate stopped working and made a general attack on the manager and his assistants, using sticks, stones and whatever else they could find. On receipt of the news, the Protector immediately visited the scene. On investigation, he found out that the riot was due to the fact that debts owed by the immigrants to a provision shop kept on the estate by the owners had been illegally deducted from their wages without their consent. To settle the dispute, the Protector, F. L. Pearce, ordered the overseer to refund the amounts deducted.[41] Other strikes accompanied by violence took place in 1910, 1913 and 1918.[42] In 1916–17, there were several cases of unrest among the Madrasis in St Mary on account of poor wages and conditions of work.[43]

A unique protest march occurred in 1913–14. In that year, the indentured Indians on Orange Hill Estate in St Mary marched to the immigration office with a chain measuring 37 feet instead of 33 feet. They complained that they were being made to do more work on account of this 'long' chain. On investigation, however, it was found that it was the immigrants themselves who had lengthened the chain in an effort to get rid of an unpopular headman. They were subsequently punished.[44] A similar case occurred in 1919, only this time it was the headman himself who was guilty and was summarily dismissed.[45]

The Indian leaders of these riots, strikes or protest marches were usually seasoned immigrants. Walter Rodney reported that fresh arrivals were more malleable and consequently, planters specially favoured the continual influx of new Indian immigrants.[46]

Political resistance was resorted to particularly where other methods had failed; for in an attempt to seek redress for grievances, immigrants at times tried the legal method – that is, taking their employers to court for breaches of the beneficent clauses of the immigration law. In theory, the magistrates were also obliged to move against planters who did not conform to the industrial law. However, immigrants regularly went before the courts as victims of a legal system which brought the force of the law directly on the side of the planters.[47] Indeed, in Jamaica, only in isolated cases were employers convicted and fined, as for example, in 1913, when the overseer of an estate in Portland was prosecuted for assaulting an Indian worker. He was fined £3, costs awarded to the complainant, amounting to £1.9s.[48] No other employer conviction was noted for the period 1903–10.[49]

Employer convictions were also rare in other East Indians importing countries. Emmer recorded that in the period 1873–1916, representing the entire period of Indian immigration in Surinam, only 10 per cent of employers charged with offences under the labour law were convicted, compared to 71.4 per cent of indentured workers so charged.[50] Similarly, Tinker notes for Mauritius that, in 1893, only 78 of the charges made against employers resulted in convictions, in contrast to 7476 indentured workers convicted before the courts for offences committed.[51]

V

The Indians' protest over aspects of their servitude received some external attention. The practice of imprisoning indentured workers for breaches of contract, for example, came under severe attack in the twentieth century. Colonies were urged, particularly after the submission of a report on Indian immigration, by Chimman Lal and James McNeil, two Government of India officials, in 1913, to abolish imprisonment for purely labour offences. Governor Manning of Jamaica did not agree with those who felt that the power given to employers to proceed against indentured immigrants for breach of contract ought to be removed. He felt that this would be detrimental to the immigration system since there would be no other effective means of enforcing the performance of the contract.[52] After all, physical punishment, though infrequently resorted to, was illegal,[53] and in cases where fines could be paid in lieu of imprisonment, this was often done. This was the cause of complaint among some planters in 1902. It was felt that, especially in cases where there was concerted action on the part of workers, they all subscribed to pay the fine. The Protector in 1902 felt that this made the prison sentence nugatory and so proposed that power should be given to him to convict and send refractory indentured immigrants to prison without the option of a fine.[54] Though this was not conceded, immigrants nonetheless ended up in prison as not all were able to afford the fine, despite the impression created by the Protector.

The frequent imprisonment of immigrants for labour offences was a bone of contention in other East Indian importing countries. In Fiji, for example, the penal labour laws were applied with severity. In 1892, there were 4423 Indians under indenture in Fiji. Of these, 1625 received convictions, the main offence being that of 'unlawful absence'.[55] Despite protests over these servile conditions, however, the system of indentureship continued with only minor changes in the conditions of immigrants until 1921.

VI

The second concern of this chapter is to examine the view held by missionaries in Jamaica that the immigration of East Indians would affect race relations between Indians and Creoles. This is because one of the hopes of the planters and other proprietors in Jamaica was that the presence of indentured immigrants would create competition for estate jobs, thereby depressing wage rates and forcing Creole workers back on to the estates in more reliable numbers. This situation, it was feared, would lead to animosity between the two groups of labourers and even result in violent confrontations. Indeed, according to van den Berghe's typology of competitive race relations, economic competition often determines race relations in capitalist societies where equal subordinates compete for scarce resources. Such competition usually manifested itself in racial prejudice, expressed in such ways as aggression and avoidance behaviour.[56]

However, fears that the importation of Indian indentured labourers would create competition for jobs and that the overstocked labour market which would develop would serve to depress existing wage rates failed to materialize in the nineteenth century. As a result, this century was not characterized by widespread open conflict between Indians and Creoles over economic issues. Indeed, only one case of violent confrontation between Indians and Creoles in Jamaica in the nineteenth century has, so far, come to light, and stemmed from a petty quarrel among Indian and Creole labourers on Danks Sugar Estate in Clarendon. According to the report of the incident carried in the *Falmouth Post* of 20 May 1845, an Indian

Table 3.4 Percentage of working days lost by East Indian labourers on estates in the parish of St Mary on account of lawful/unlawful absence from work, 1911–12

Name of plantation	Name of employer	Mean no. of labourers employed		Unlawful absence		Absence with leave	
		M	F	M	F	M	F
Green Castle	Hon. Sir J. Pringle	39 1/4	15 1/2	.05	–	6.82	10.90
Coleraine	Hon. Sir J. Pringle	59 1/2	24	.05	–	12.78	26.95
Chovey	Hon. Sir J. Pringle	68	25 3/4	.28	–	9.06	14.53
Agualta Vale	Hon. Sir J. Pringle	16 1/4	6	–	–	8.06	21.84
Cape Clear	Hon. Sir J. Pringle	21 3/4	8 1/2	–	–	7.00	6.92
Koningsberg	Hon. Sir J. Pringle	23	8 3/4	–	–	8.56	10.36
Hopewell	Hon. Sir J. Pringle	35	12	.07	.20	7.19	12.13
Tramolesworth	Hon. Sir J. Pringle	48	20	–	–	11.10	13.51
Brimmer Hall	Hon. Sir J. Pringle	32 1/4	12 3/4	.06	–	9.31	24.22
Trinity	Hon. Sir J. Pringle	45 1/2	13	.05	.03	7.89	11.59
Nutfield	Hon. Sir J. Pringle	27 1/2	17 3/4	.08	.17	11.09	15.60
Nonsuch	Hon. Sir J. Pringle	44 1/2	20	–	–	7.29	10.79
Newry	Hon. Sir J. Pringle	44 3/4	19 1/4	.10	.07	8.37	11.98
Orange Hill	Hon. Sir J. Pringle	49 3/4	21 1/4	1.20	.56	6.76	10.12
Upper Ft Stewart	Hon. Sir J. Pringle	35	11 1/2	.22	–	6.96	12.31
Lower Ft Stewart	Hon. Sir J. Pringle	26	12	1.30	.32	9.26	10.94
Gibraltar	A. C. Westmoreland	33	15	1.04	.13	9.39	11.37
Esher	A. C. Westmoreland	19	6	.44	2.67	10.45	12.76

Table 3.4 (cont'd)

Name of plantation	Name of employer	Mean no. of labourers employed		Unlawful absence		Absence with leave	
		M	F	M	F	M	F
Water Valley	J. H. Scarlett	20	8	.45	.07	10.79	14.80
Rosend	E. E. Broughton	21 1/2	8	–	1.02	9.39	10.39
Osborne	R. L. Benbow	19 1/4	8	–	–	8.13	16.59
Charlottenburgh	W. H. Westmoreland	11 1/4	5 1/2	.34	.31	8.26	12.62
Grey's Inn	Grey's Inn Estate Ltd.	28	9 1/2	3.56	.23	12.78	19.87
Clermont	H. G. Constantine	8	3	–	–	8.72	9.79
Fontabelle	Hon. R. P. Simmonds	7	2	–	–	18.74	27.66
Quebec	Hon. R. P. Simmonds	6 1/4	4	–	–	18.37	17.39
Wentworth	United Fruit Co.	21	8 3/4	–	–	10.00	22.38
Platfield	T. M. Grey et al	19 3/4	7 1/2	.18	.09	9.45	19.27
Halcot Farm	H. D. Graham	21 1/4	9	.02	–	9.90	12.40
Montrose	J. M. Fletcher	10	4	.24	–	7.84	9.81
Frontier	Admin. General	18	5	.03	.12	8.71	6.75
Itar Boreale	E. E. C. Hosack	43 3/4	17 3/4	.09	.14	8.49	21.02
Lady Hole	E. E. C. Hosack	24 1/4	9 1/4	–	–	6.91	12.89

Source: Protector of Immigrants Report, 1911–12.

Table 3.5 Percentage of days lost by unlawful absence, 1911–20 (Jamaica)

Year	Percentage of days lost Male	Female
1911–12	1.54	.75
1912–13	1.55	.53
1913–14	1.75	.76
1914–15	1.12	.98
1915–16	1.77	1.13
1916–17	No figures available	
1917–18	No figures available	
1918–19	3.78	1.40
1919–20	5.33	3.79

Source: Annual Reports of the Protector of Immigrants, 1911–20.

labourer on Danks accused a Creole labourer working in the millyard of deliberately allowing a horse to step on his foot. The Indian, offended by the incident, retaliated by hitting the Creole. A fracas developed as a result as other Indian and Creole workers immediately joined in the fight on the sides of their respective countrymen. Several workers were wounded in the ensuing fight. The headman, who came to investigate the source of the fracas, found his path blocked by Creoles who also tried to hide the Creole labourer involved at the start of the fight. The indentured Indian labourers consequently surrounded this hiding place, calling for justice to be done. The case was at first referred to the Court of Assizes for settlement, but later the parties involved 'made up' out of court. It is possible that similar local, petty incidents occurred where Indians and Creoles worked together on the same estates; but this does not seem to have been the norm.

One possible reason for the low level of open conflict between Indians and Creoles in this period over economic issues could be that the volume of Indian immigration was comparatively small and, further, was not as sustained as in Trinidad and Guiana. In Trinidad, for example, Indian immigration continued even when the sugar market was depressed.[57] In Jamaica, this was not the case. Furthermore, the great political opposition to Indian immigration being financed out of the public purse, and planter preference for Creole labourers, limited Indian immigration to times when Creole labourers could not be obtained in adequate numbers. In his evidence before the Sanderson Committee on Indian immigration in 1909, Governor Olivier expressed such planter preference. He stated that 'Jamaican planters exhibit a preference for Creole labourers. When they can be obtained, employers will not employ one more coolie labourer than is necessary.'[58] Consequently, Jamaica received only 7 per cent of the approximately 543 914 Indians imported into the Caribbean between 1838 and 1917.[59] Afro-Jamaicans were, therefore, not displaced from this 'favoured' position by the importation of Indians.

Far from fearing their importation in the nineteenth century, Creoles came to anticipate and welcome Indians. Several contemporary sources attest to this fact. After the arrival of the first batch of Indians in 1845, for example, the *Falmouth Post* reported that 'the few negroes who were present at the first landing of the East Indians seemed rather pleased than otherwise and mingled with them readily'.[60] A somewhat similar report was contained in the *Morning Journal* after the *Athenian* landed. In its editorial of 15 April 1847, it stated that

> Indians who arrived on the *Athenian* were cordially welcomed by their black brethren who generously offered them oranges, sugar-cane, and various description of fruit, as well as bread cakes [sic] and trifling articles of clothing for the children....[61]

The *Morning Journal* further reported that 'the immigrants have been well treated by the peasantry in the country, who have promised to do all in their power for the "strangers who have come to a strange land"'.[62]

Continuing on this note of amicability was the Indian official, Surgeon Major Comins's account of Indian-Creole relations in Jamaica in the nineteenth century. According to Comins, 'as a rule, Coolies and Negroes get on well together and live amicably on the estates'.[63] Sohal feels that Creoles welcomed Indians as potential consumers for their provision crops. Apparently, on one occasion when Creoles on an estate were told that 'lots of Coolies are coming', they jokingly replied, 'make them come now massa, they will buy our provisions fro' we'.[64] The blacks clearly perceived the economic benefits which would accrue to them, as an established peasantry, from the presence of labourers who did not have the advantage of provision plots from which they could meet their food needs.

Another explanation for the comparatively low level of Indian–Creole conflict in this period lies in the fact that Creoles did not view Indians as settlers. They saw them as transient 'slave coolies' who would return to India at the expiration of their ten-year compulsory residence in Jamaica. Indeed, repatriation commenced in 1853 as Indians, making use of the provisions in the immigration law for their repatriation, returned to India from Jamaica.[65] Furthermore, Indian–Creole contact during the period of indentureship was limited. Creoles generally lived off the estates in their free villages, while Indians lived on the estates in barracks spatially separated from those of the few Creoles who might still have resided on the estates. Even where they worked on the same estates Indians and Creoles were usually separated into different gangs under their respective headmen

– though in a few cases black headmen were placed in charge of Indian gangs. One is forced to agree with Gillion's conclusion in his analysis of a comparable social situation – Fijian–Indian relations in the period of indentureship – that such separation precluded conflict.[66]

The absence of open conflict was not an indication that Indians and Creoles necessarily liked each other. The Creoles may initially have tolerated Indians because they were 'strangers in a strange land' and were no threat to their immediate economic interests; but still derided them as 'slave coolies' as they had accepted contract labour – shunned by Creoles – on the estates, in conditions little removed from slavery.[67] Using the yardstick of European culture, Creoles also felt that Indians were culturally inferior to them.

The Indians, for their part, brought with them to the Caribbean the characteristic northern Indian contempt for darker-skinned people, coming as they did from a country with an entrenched caste system. According to 'Publicola', 'they, [the Indians] fancy they are a superior race, and openly avow their dislike of them, [the Creoles]'.[68] Brereton further suggests that, by the guidelines of caste, Indians decided that Creoles were 'hopelessly polluted', and so assumed a superior attitude to them.[69] A similar view was expressed by van den Berghe who, in his analysis of Indian–Creole relations in East Africa, observed that the Indians themselves were caught in the racist dynamics of colonial society, for they assumed cultural superiority over Africans. Their intense pride in their cultural heritage, according to him, 'led them to ... accept as axiomatic their ethnocentric belief in their cultural superiority over Africans'.[70] Phenotypical characteristics, such as hair texture, were also used by Indians to claim superiority over Creoles.[71] Such attitudes encouraged stereotyping and laid the foundations for mutual prejudice and antipathy between the two races. As in other colonies, the mutual contempt held by Creoles and Indians for each other, reinforced the existing network of prejudice surrounding race and colour in Jamaican society.[72]

These feelings on the part of Indians and Creoles caused them to avoid social interaction. For those working on the same estates, contact was not extended to after working hours. Such behaviour has been described by Blalock as one of the subtle manifestations of racial prejudice in situations involving potential intimacy.[73] An indication that limited social interaction took place among Indians and Creoles on the estates is Comins's report on sexual relations between them. According to him, Indian–Creole relations did 'not go so far as sexual intercourse'.[74] What seems certain is that Creole women in this period exhibited an aversion to sexual relations with Indian men. This is clearly demonstrated in a letter from the Governor of Jamaica to the Earl of Kimberley in 1871. Grant, basing his comments on the attitude of Creole women to Indian men on the report of the Agent General of Immigration, informed Kimberley that 'the indisposition of Creole women to form connections with [male] Indian immigrants appears to remain unchanged'.[75] This attitude on the part of Creole women in Jamaica seems to have been a reflection of the general attitude in other East Indian importing countries which had a Creole population. Henry Taylor of the Colonial Office had requested information on Indian–Creole relations from British Guiana, Trinidad, St Lucia, St Vincent, Grenada and Mauritius. From the replies he received he concluded that 'connections between creoles and Indians are not increasing or likely to increase'.[76]

The aversion to sexual relations was equally evident on the part of the Indians, according to Jamaica's Agent General of Immigration. In a letter to the Colonial Secretary he explained:

> This indisposition seems to me to be equally strong on the part of the Coolies, as they appear rarely to forget the family and race associations of their own country. I have found many who have been in this colony upwards of twenty years still only mixing with their own people....[77]

The male-dominated nature of Indian immigration (by itself) does not even seem to have forced Indian men to find sexual partners among Creole women. Indeed when, towards the end of the nineteenth century, limited sexual interaction took place between Indians and Creoles, they were more usual between Indian women and Creole men rather than between Indian men and Creole women. According to Comins, writing in 1893, 'in very rare cases cooly women cohabit with negroes, but I have never seen any case of a man being married or living in concubinage with a negro woman'.[78]

Rather than develop relationships with Creole women in this period, the Indian men competed for the favours of the few Indian women. This inevitably led to the development of polyandry in the colonies and also caused an increase in uxoricide as jealous Indian men took revenge on unfaithful wives and paramours.[79]

While both Indians and Creoles frowned on the development of sexual relations, however, other levels of interaction on the estate seem to have been tolerated. During the period of indentureship, for example, Creoles were active participants in the Muslim Hussay Festival.[80]

VII

In recognizing planter attempts to transfer the docility thesis from slaves to Indian indentured servants, Walter Rodney, opposing this view, observed that 'it takes a very jaundiced eye to read a people's history as a record of undiluted compliance and docility'.[81] Indeed, as this chapter has attempted to show, the evidence of protest conflicted with the myth of the 'docile coolie'. Indians were increasingly dissatisfied with the plantation and used various methods of protest either to escape from it or to force improved conditions of labour. Admittedly, as the quantitative data presented have shown, the proportion of Indians who actively resisted was small compared with the total number under indenture at any one time. The majority, in fact, seemed to have used accommodation as a means of survival under a plantation system in which power was monopolized by the proprietors. Nevertheless, the very existence of protest, no matter how limited, was an indication that residential, contracted labour did not necessarily imply totally 'controllable' labourers.

With respect to race relations involving Indians and Afro-Jamaicans, it has been demonstrated that these two subordinate groups did not violently confront each other over the economic impact of immigration. Despite the planters' hopes, East Indian indentured labour was not numerically significant enough to affect wage rates. At the same time, it failed to create competition for jobs and render Creole labourers more available. Indian labour might not have been socially disruptive and might have enabled some planters to continue production, but it did not 'save' the sugar industry in Jamaica as it did in Trinidad and Guyana.[82]

Notes

1 Stephen Harmer to Henry Harmer, 11 February 1840, MS 765, National Library of Jamaica.

2 Circular Despatch to the Governors of the Plantation Colonies, 30 June 1836, quoted in W. E. Riviere, 'Labour Shortage in the British West Indies after Emancipation', *Journal of Caribbean History* 4 (1972), p. 4.

3 For an elaboration of these early immigration schemes, see K. O. Laurence, 'Immigration into the West Indies in the Nineteenth Century', *Chapters in Caribbean History*, 3 (Barbados, 1971).

4 *Report from the Select Committee on West Indian Colonies, 1842*, (PP, 1842 (47a) XIII) Resolution II.

5 Marx attributed this quotation to Gibbon Wakefield. It was quoted in Alan H. Adamson, 'The Impact of Indentured Immigration on the Political Economy of British Guiana', in Kay Saunders (ed.), *Indentured Labour in the British Empire, 1834–1920* (London and Canberra, 1984), p. 42.

6 Laurence, 'Immigration into the West Indies', pp. 10–11, 21–4.

7 Central Government File (hereafter CGF) 1B/9/3, Papers of the *Blundell*, Jamaica Archives.

8 V. A. Shepherd, 'From Rural Plantations to Urban Slums', *Immigrants and Minorities* 5, 2 (1986), p. 130.

9 Public Record Office, CO 318/173, Anti-Slavery Correspondence, 1847. See also, V. A. Shepherd, 'Indians and Blacks in Jamaica in the Nineteenth and Early Twentieth Centuries: A Micro-Study of the Foundation of Race Antogonisms', in Howard Johnson, (ed.), *After the Crossing: Immigrants and Minorities in Caribbean Creole Society* (London, 1988), pp. 95–112.

10 See V. A. Shepherd, 'Transients to Citizens', *Jamaica Journal*, 18 (1985), 17–26.

11 CGF 1B/9/17, 'Laws Operating in 1903 for the Treatment of Coolies', Immigration Office, 6 March 1903, Protector of Immigrants Papers.

12 K. Haraksingh, 'Control and Resistance among Overseas Indian Workers: A Study of Labour on the Sugar Plantations of Trinidad, 1875–1917', *Journal of Caribbean History*, 14 (1980), p. 75.

13 H. Tinker, 'Into Servitude: Indian Labour in the Sugar Industry, 1833–70', in S. Marks and P. Richardson (eds), *International Labour Migration: Historical Perspectives* (London, 1984), pp. 90–111.

14 London, India Office Records V (30) 1991, No. 4, Surgeon Major Comins's Report on Jamaica, and CGF 1B/9/27, The Earl of Crewe to Charles Doorly, 2 November 1908.

15 A. Thompson, 'Historical Writing on Migration into the Commonwealth Caribbean: A Bibliographical Review of the Period c. 1838–c. 1938', *Immigrants and Minorities*, 5 (1986), p. 152.

16 Among these are D. Nath, *A History of Indians in British Guiana* (originally published 1950, 2nd edn London, 1970); B. Mangru, 'Imperial Trusteeship in British Guiana with Special Reference to the East Indian Indentureship Immigrants, 1838–82, Myth or Reality?', MA Diss., University of Guyana, 1976; T. Ramnarine, 'The Growth of the East Indian Community in British Guiana, 1880-1920', D. Phil. Diss., University of Sussex, 1977; G. Tikasingh, 'The Establishment of the Indians in Trinidad, 1870–1900', PhD Diss., University of the West Indies, St Augustine, 1973; Haraksingh, 'Control and Resistance among Overseas Indian Workers'; W. Rodney, *A History of the Guyanese Working People, 1881–1905* (London, 1981).

17 G. M. Frederickson and C. Lasch, 'Resistance to Slavery', *Civil War History*, 13 (1967), 315–29.

18 Ibid., p. 317.

19 Ibid., p. 326.

20 For a restatement of the existing views on resistance, accommodation and intransigence, see D. Geggus, *Slave Resistance Studies and the Saint Dominique Slave Revolt: Some Preliminary Considerations*, Occasional Papers Series No. 4 (1983), Florida International University, Latin American and Caribbean Centre.

21 Garsia's Letterbook on East Indian Immigrants, MS 35, National Library of Jamaica.

22 Comins's Report, Section 38.

23 Doorly's memo. on 'The Laws Relating to East Indian Immigrants', and the Sanderson Committee Report, p. 71.

24 Jamaica Law 23, 1879, Section 89.

25 Jamaica Law 23, 1879, Section 88.

26 Jamaica Law 23, 1879, Section 39 and Jamaica Law 20, 1891, Section 19.

27 Jamaica Law 23, 1879, Section 87.

28 Jamaica Law 23, 1879, Section 90.

29 Jamaica Law 23, 1879, Section 91.

30 Jamaica Law 20, 1891, Section 16.

31 Jamaica Law 23, 1879, Section 93 (7).

32 Jamaica Law 23, 1879, Section 93 (16).

33 Jamaica Law 23, 1879, Section 93 (16). For Surinam, Emmer says that few indentured workers ran away. In 1890, after 18 years of immigration, only 161 had taken to the bush, mostly to abscond to British Guiana. See P. Emmer, 'The Importation of British Indians into Suriname (Dutch Guiana), 1873–1916', in Marks and Richardson, *International Labour Migration*, p. 109.

34 CGF 1B/9/27, Manager of Golden Grove Estate to the Protector of Immigrants, 4 December 1909. Also Comins's Report, Section 13.

35 Protector of Immigrants' Report (hereafter PIR) Jamaica, 1910–11.

36 Jamaica Law 23, 1879, Sections 47 and 95 (15). See also letter from the Constabulary Office, Port Maria, St Mary, to the Protector of Immigrants, 19 November 1909.
37 PIR, 1901–2.
38 CO 142/7, *Morning Journal*, 14–15 April 1877, p. 3.
39 Ibid., 'Publicola' to the Editor.
40 PIR 1907–8.
41 PIR 1907–8.
42 PIR 1910–18.
43 PIR 1916–17. For Surinam, Emmer records that only a few uprisings occurred. Between 1873 and 1916, the whole period of immigration into Surinam, only five uprisings were recorded. See Emmer, 'The Importation of British Indians into Surinam', p. 109.
44 PIR 1913–14.
45 PIR 1919–20.
46 Rodney, *A History of the Guyanese Working People*, p. 155.
47 Rodney, *A History of the Guyanese Working People*, p. 152.
48 PIR 1913–14.
49 PIR 1903–10.
50 Emmer, 'The Importation of British Indians into Surinam', p. 107.
51 Tinker, 'Into Servitude', p. 81.
52 CO 571/3, Jamaica Despatch No. 92, Gov. Manning to Harcourt, 16 March 1915.
53 CGF 1B/9/17, Clerk of Courts, St Mary to the Protector of Immigrants, 22 January 1910.
54 Correspondence No. 20, Protector of Immigrants Papers, the Protector to the Colonial Secretary, 1902.
55 H. Tinker, *A New System of Slavery: The Export of Indian Labour Overseas, 1830–1920* (Oxford, 1974), p. 194.
56 P. van den Berghe, *Race and Ethnicity: Essays in Comparative Sociology* (New York, London, 1976), pp. 20–41.
57 B. Brereton, *Race Relations in Colonial Trinidad, 1870–1900* (Cambridge, 1979), p. 190.
58 Sanderson Committee Report. Evidence of Gov. Sydney Olivier, 1 July 1909. It should be noted that the importation of Indians was greater during the years of Creole immigration to Cuba and Central America.
59 G. W. Roberts and J. Byrne, 'Summary Statistics on Indenture and Associated Migration Affecting the West Indies, 1834–1918', *Population Studies* 20 (1966), p. 129.
60 *Falmouth Post*, 20 May 1845.
61 CO 142/7, *Morning Journal*, 15 April 1847, p. 3.
62 Ibid.
63 India Office Records (hereafter IOR) V; (30) 1991, No. 4, *Comins's Note on Emigration from India*, 1893, Sec. 49, p. 26.
64 H. S. Sohal, 'The East Indian Indentureship System in Jamaica, 1845–1917', PhD Diss., University of Waterloo, Canada, 1979, p. 38.
65 V. Shepherd, 'Transients to Citizens'.
66 K. L. Gillion, *The Fiji Indians: Challenge to European Dominance, 1920–1946* (Canberra, 1977), p. 14.
67 F. Henriques, *Family and Colour in Jamaica* (London, 1968), p. 48; and G. Knox, 'Race Relations in Jamaica', PhD Diss., University of Florida, 1962, p. 226.
68 CO 142/7, *Morning Journal*, 14–15 April 1847, 'Publicola' to the Editor, p. 3.
69 Brereton, *Race Relations*, pp. 188–9.
70 P. van den Berghe, *Race and Ethnicity*, p. 294.
71 A. S. Erlich, 'Race and Ethnic Identity in Rural Jamaica: The East Indian Case', *Caribbean Quarterly*, 22 (1976), p. 21.
72 Brereton, *Race Relations*, p. 89.

73 H. M. Blalock, Jr, *Towards a Theory of Minority Group Relations* (New York; London; Sydney, 1967), p. 51.
74 Comins's Report, p. 26.
75 CO 137/459, Gov. J. P. Grant to the Earl of Kimberley, 8 Nov. 1871, Despatch No. 161.
76 Ibid., Minute Paper by Henry Taylor.
77 CO 137/459, Enc. in Despatch No. 161, Alexander, Agent General of Immigration, to the Colonial Secretary, 19 Oct. 1871.
78 Comins's Report, p. 26. This numerical disparity was a matter of concern throughout the period of Indian immigration and led to the stipulation by law of a minimum ratio of 40 females to every 100 males. This ratio was not always maintained, however (CO 571/3, Immigration Correspondence).
79 For an elaboration of this point see V. A. Shepherd, 'The Emigration of East Indian Women to Jamaica and their Experiences in the Plantation Society, 1845–1945: A Working Paper', Social History Workshop, UWI, Mona, Jamaica, 8–9 Nov. 1985 and 'Emancipation through Servitude?, Caribbean Societies/Women, Colonialism and Commonwealth Seminar, Institute of Commonwealth Studies, London, 17 March 1988.
80 H. S. Sohal, 'The East Indian Indentureship System in Jamaica, 1845–1917', PhD Diss., University of Waterloo, Canada, 1979 and V. A. Shepherd, 'Separation vs. Integration: The Experiences of the Indian Group in the Creole Society of Jamaica, 1879–1945', M. Phil Diss., University of the West Indies, Jamaica, 1985.
81 Rodney, *A History of the Guyanese Working People*, p. 151.
82 For a comparative analysis of the differential economic effects of Indian immigration on Trinidad, Guiana and Jamaica, see W. Green, 'The West Indies and Indentured Labour Migration', in Kay Saunders (ed.), *Indentured Labour*, pp. 1–41.

Part II

Religious and cultural practices

CHAPTER 4 Hindu elements in the Shango/Orisha cult of Trinidad

Noorkumar Mahabir and Ashram Maharaj

I am always there, and any time you need me, call me
Call me for sickness – any time you want me, call me
I am coming to defend you.

Words of Ogun/St Michael when he manifests on a devotee.

O unconquerable Hanuman, where your name is ceaselessly chanted, there diseases vanish and pains and miseries come to an end.

Hanuman Chalesa (a panegyric to the monkey-warrior)

Introduction

Acculturation occurs when two or more ethnic groups come into intimate contact with each other over time. The contact provides an opportunity for each of the respective groups to adapt in varying degrees to an alien/new cultural form or orientation, particularly when there are common or transferable elements and when particular needs or situations arise.

Acculturation in the religious sphere (religious syncretism) has been one of the major focal points of research in the New World with pioneer work done by M. and F. Herskovits (1947).[1] They have documented the manner in which African slaves accommodated themselves to various aspects of the European culture they encountered in a Trinidad village. Later scholars[2] have found that a combination of such New World phenomena as the European–African superordination–subordination pattern, the long period of slavery which prevented the retention of full African culture, and certain similarities in form between Christian and West African religions, gave rise to Vodun in Haiti,[3] Revivalism in Jamaica, Santeria in Cuba,

Candomble in Brazil and Shango/Orisha in Trinidad. Little work however, has been done on the evolution of cultural reinterpretation between groups of Africans and East Indians. In 1961 Michael Horowitz and Morton Klass were the first to begin work in this new area, the result being a paper, 'The Martiniquan East Indian Cult of Maldevidan'.[4] Later, A. and L. Mansingh (1980) sought to explore the possible contributions of the Hindu presence to the Rastafarian movement in Jamaica through the smoking of ganja, wearing of dreadlocks, using the salutation 'Jah', isolating menstruating women, maintaining a vegetarian diet, etc.[5] And in Trinidad, which has been hailed as 'a rainbow country' because of its unique blend of races and cultures, the social reality of Hindus and Catholics has blossomed into the celebration of the Feast of La Divina Pastora, the former referring to a miracle saint as 'Siparee ke Mai' and the latter as 'La Divina'.[6]

This chapter seeks to document and account for the East Indian, particularly Hindu, presence in the Orisha Cult of Trinidad. We hope it will serve to illuminate areas of the Orisha belief system that the standard anthropological and film-documentary procedure has not concerned itself.

The Social and Cultural Matrix

Before attempting to document possible East Indian influences on Orisha faith, it is necessary to consider the acculturative structure which was set in place and which gave shape to this syncretic cult.

The social matrix of plantation life was the dominating factor in the acculturative process between East Indians and Creoles after Emancipation. Although Creoles generally expressed contempt for the Indians' religion, culture, style of dress and family life, while Indians tended to regard them as untouchables because of their colour and meat-eating habits, conflict between the races was rare, and when it did arise, conspicuous.[7] Indeed the two numerically major races enjoyed a higher degree of interaction in Trinidad when compared with the situation in Guiana. This peaceful relationship was remarked upon in 1861 by a colonial officer:

> I have made it the subject of a special inquiry and observation, and I believe that neither the Creole nor the coolie have even dreamed of a national hostility toward each other.[8]

As early as the 1850s Creoles were joining the East Indian Sh'ia Muslim Hussay processions where they sometimes took respectable positions as drummers and bearers of the *tazias* (imitation mausoleums).[9] The few free Creoles who stayed on the plantation shared similar experiences and conditions with the indentured Indians, though having specialized tasks. When not confined to the plantation environment, the two races sometimes lived close together in villages,[10] having the advantages of daily social intercourse with each other.

Though there may have been some reluctance to participate in and adapt/adopt other cultural forms due to racial and fundamentalist Christian prejudices encouraged by the planter-class, Creoles and Hindu polytheism accommodated unexpected transmutations and combinations of religious beliefs and practices. For the few Creoles who attended the large Indian ceremonies,[11] there was the opportunity for remembering and thus reinforcing/retaining some of their almost-forgotten traditional practices. That to assume a continuous process of mutual influence between the two cultures in some aspects of beliefs and behaviour is not unreasonable is further indicated by the following citation:

> A striking example of agreement on basic beliefs is the combining of African and East Indian traditions of magic practice. Hindu pandits perform a 'High Mass' for their Negro clientele who have not had their prayers answered in the Christian churches, Shouter temples, or Shango yards. In the same way, Indians employ Negro obeahmen for curing and for manufacture of 'trick' and 'guard' amulets.[12]

Indeed there were and are obvious similarities between the two religious systems of the Creoles and Indians. In fact some of the Yoruba slave immigrants to Trinidad had already accepted Islam in Africa.[13]

Contact with elements of another culture could be made not only physically but sometimes through the spirit-world. Shangoists believe that the personality-soul may wander about in sleep or during a trance in search of special knowledge.

> The type of possession known as 'soul projection' is found in Trinidadian cults when, during the 'mourning' rites conducted by the Shouter leaders for both Spiritual Baptist and Shangoists, a person's 'spirit' wanders to distant lands such as Egypt and India seeking spiritual knowledge and 'gifts' (spiritual talents).[14]

In the case of those of the Spiritual Baptist faith, the dreams and visions are more important than in Orisha and serve to influence major decisions in their lives.[15] Through a dream-experience one may feel compelled to incorporate certain congenial aspects of another culture into one's own.[16] This was and is particularly so of the Orisha worshippers.

One researcher, Frances Henry, found that since the 1970s a most interesting development in membership patterns emerged in this Trinidad cult.[17] It was the new role of East Indians in what had always been considered a Creole religion. She noted that despite the presence of East Indians in Trinidad society for over one hundred years, participation in a Creole religion was neither desired by the Indians or their Creole hosts.[18] A most intriguing development in the 1970s was the emergence of an East Indian Orisha leader who had a very large and active, primarily Creole membership.[19]

> Mr Smith is said to give the best and largest feast in the country today.... As long term observer in Trinidad, I was impressed with the range and breadth of his knowledge particularly in view of his non-African origins.... He did, however grow up in a racially mixed village and some of his neighbours who were in Shango influenced him as a child.... In so doing, he abjured his Indian ethnicity and became culturally Black. He has been disowned by his family but very well accepted by Black friends, neighbours and Shango followers.[20]

How Mr Smith 'abjured his Indian ethnicity' the author did not say;[21] for, as we shall see later, because of the similarities, it is easier to blend Indian beliefs, rituals and iconographies into Orisha worship than to separate them out. Mr Smith's leadership, however, has been instrumental in attracting other Indians to attend to and participate in this kind of practice, thereby changing the racial composition of Orisha followers.

Another, equally intriguing development is the hosting of an Orisha ceremony by a devout practising Hindu/Indian farmer at Longdenville, Central Trinidad, in which his entire family participated and which was presided over by a Creole leader (*amombah*). Whereas in 1965 the anthropologist, George Simpson, saw East Indian men as active participants,[22] in almost every cult-centre we visited at Tacarigua, Tunapuna, Curepe, D'Abadie, Longdenville, Enterprise and Moruga, we saw at least one Indian participant, who was invariably female and who had cohabited with an African cult-member.[23] The majority of Indians, though, merely visit the leaders for medicinal and psychological services.

East Indian participation in an essentially Creole cult indicated that there may be a 'loosening' or 'opening-up' of the formerly closed ethnic enclaves in Trinidad society as old racial prejudices are becoming worn with the passing of each successive generation. Though East Indians dominate certain geographical areas, they may also now be found sprinkled among the predominantly Creole villages. There is, therefore, on the basis of ethnic origins, no perceptibly segregated area in Trinidad.[24] According to the anthropologist J. D. Elder, through the Shango/Orisha cult, the Creoles of Yoruba ancestry in Trinidad 'have thus not only integrated religion but also the whole community – the outsiders, the non-African groups, the late-comers and the East Indians'.[25]

The evolution of Shango/Orisha

Some of the slaves, before leaving Africa, had interacted culturally with tribes of other kingdoms, each having its own language and religion.[26] The Yoruba tribe, many of them being Orisha worshippers, was well represented among the African slaves. The Yoruba cult developed during the nineteenth century in Trinidad mainly as an amalgam of remembered practices from African villages and of elements of Catholicism. Because of the blending of religious elements in Africa itself, and the nature of the slave trade to the New World, the cult apparently was not transported *in toto*.

Shango is really the God of Thunder of the Yoruba people of Nigeria, but his name is given by others to the complex of Creole worship in Trinidad. Elements from neighbouring faiths in the plural society of Trinidad were woven into the religious movement. In an isolated village in Trinidad, the Herskovitses (1947) found that the Shango/Orisha cult combined elements of the Yoruba traditional religion, Catholicism and the Baptist faith.[27] The extreme remoteness of this village and its entirely Creole population are important variables responsible for the absence of possible East Indian influences. Interestingly, a minister of a Spiritual Baptist Church in New York observed that the West Indian Baptist religion, as practised, evolved completely in the Caribbean:

> In some areas where there was exposure to Roman Catholic and Hindu religious practices, manifestations of African tribal and Hindu deities, as well as Roman Catholic saints form part of the Baptist experience.[28]

The Minister was obviously referring to Yoruba traditional components which the Baptists had adapted to their faith. The European-borrowed traits and reinterpreted European elements in Orisha are identified in the names of Catholic saints, Catholic hagiography, the Bible as a ritual object, the words and melodies of Catholic songs, books of magic, the cross and the crucifixes, candles, shepherd's crooks, keys, incense, rosaries, and divination by gazing into a crystal ball, a glass of water, or the flame of a candle.[29] There are no traces of Carib, Arawak or American Indian influences in this syncretic cult and very few whites take active part up to this day.[30]

The anthropologist Molly Ahyee has noted that syncretism of the Yoruba Orisha tradition in Trinidad was not only through the acculturation of Christian practices, but the accommodation of Hinduism, Islam and other branches of religious philosophy.[31] The integrated complex of drum, chant, dance, liturgy, shaped ritual, spirit possession and animal sacrifice which mark the worship of gods in the Orisha cult are akin to the Kali-Mai (Black Mother) cult of Hinduism in Trinidad.[32] Some items are common to both Kali worship and Orisha ('parallel tradition') from inception; others are absorbed through the process of transmutation. Suffice it to say at this point that both the East Indian Kali-Mai and African Orisha cults are lower-class forms of folk culture with its tradition of familial property-holding, apolitical participation and little formal organization. Forms of Orisha worship in Trinidad find their counterpart in the procession, broom dance, reverence to ancestors and use of certain ritual paraphernalia in the Indian Shia Muslim observance of Hussay.[33]

The Pantheon

The Yorubas admit the existence of many gods (spelt with a lowercase 'g') as intermediaries (Orishas) between man and the Supreme Being, the Creator of the Universe.[34] Simpson found that in Nigeria, Shango (god of thunder) is the only deity worshipped in the Shango cult. Other Yoruba gods have their own priests, societies and cult centres.[35] In Trinidad he found Shango to be only one of dozens of 'powers' (saints/spirits), many of which have been reinterpreted because of contact with European and Indian cultural traditions. This pliability shown by the Yoruba people is manifested in Africa itself, as we have seen, when the gods of the other tribes are taken over and incorporated into a system already an integrated whole but in separate centres.[36]

The polytheism of this essentially West African religion has been reinterpreted in Trinidad by equating certain Yoruba gods with mainly Catholic saints.[37] But

> New powers are constantly being adopted into the faith. In order for this to occur, the adopted power must be recognised by the sponsor of a given centre. Regional differences are important factors in such recognition, for example Mahabil (an East Indian power) has many devotees in the South and in Port-of-Spain but is not recognised in Tunapuna. Although many East Indians live in Tunapuna, sponsors in Tunapuna are exclusively black.[38]

That was in 1980, according to the researcher, Stephen Glazier. But in 1988 we visited three shrines at Tunapuna and found all of the officiants recognized at least one East Indian 'power'.[39] Protestantism offered no such imposing galaxy of venerable saints and thereby did not open the opportunity for syncretism as the Catholic Church did elsewhere.[40]

The one hundred or so active cult centres in Trinidad contain about sixteen major Orishas (gods/deities/spirits) recognized by the Yorubas. They include Shango (after whom the cult is named),[41] Elegba, Omile, Alafin, Obalufon, Eshu, Obatala, Erinle (Airelay), Oya, Oba, Ibejii and Maina Leterre. Some of these, for example Ifa (god of divination) are not known in Trinidad. The more popular powers who have been given Christian counterparts are Abtala (St Benedict), Elephon (Eternal Father), Osain (St Francis), Shakpana (St Francis), Shango (St John) and Ogun (St Michael). Among the major deities of this African-derived cult, Ogun and Osain should be of special interest to us because they are also looked upon by Shangoists as 'Indian powers'.

Ogun is the ancient god of war, the hunt and iron; and therefore all instruments made of iron are consecrated to him. Very rarely needed as a deity of war, Ogun is still important to hunters, surgeons, barbers, butchers, blacksmiths and, through an extension of his authority, motor drivers and mechanics. In fact, he is called Osinmale – the chief among the divinities.[42] Orisha worshippers in Trinidad also associate Ogun with Hanuman (Mahabir) of the Hindu pantheon, who is the celebrated monkey-chief of the *Ramayan* epic.[43] Hanuman, a mythical leader of a large troupe, was an ally to Rama, the hero of the religious text, in the war against Ravana, the demon king of Lanka. The Yorubas hold the belief that when one's path is not clear or when one encounters difficulties, appeal must be made to Ogun for help. Likewise, ceremonial worship is done to Hanuman (*rote*) mainly to remove difficulties and to dispel evil. To the Yorubas, Ogun is believed to be capable of providing prosperity to his devotees. A couplet from the panegyric to Hanuman reads: 'O Hanuman, you are the repository of all spiritual powers as well as all worldly and material wealth.'[44] Ogun is depicted with 'massive shoulders'[45] and Hanuman is conceived as 'repository of immeasurable strength'.[46] Conscious of the obvious similarities between the two saints, Yorubas have fused the two into one in the Orisha cult of Trinidad. Indeed Shangoists insist that 'God is one but people see him in different ways because of respective cultures' – also a Hindu concept.[47]

Asahin (Osanhin, Osayin) a Yoruba god of medicine, known as Osain in the Trinidad Orisha cult, is the equivalent of St Francis in the Christian Church, and is called upon in treating certain types of disease, especially illnesses caused by evil spirits. Crowley (1957) observed that the 'Yoruba god Osain is syncretized with the Muslim saint Hossein, grandson of Mohammed, and is described by his Negro devotees as a "wild coolie man".'[48] But Husain (Hossein) is considered more of a warrior than a doctor in the East Indian Sh'ia Muslim observance of Hussay in Trinidad. In the Hussay ritual-complex, women nevertheless pray to him for the blessing of children, the casting of a *jinn* (evil spirit), the recovery of an illness or some other wish.[49] In the spirit-world, Osain has several brothers just as Husain has a brother, Hassan.

Included in the Orisha pantheon are saints of lesser importance like Oshun/Osho[50] who is paired with the Hindu Ganga-Mai (Mother), both being the tutelary divinities of water and believed to be a healing and fertility goddess.[51] Some Hindu deities like Lakshmi (goddess of Wealth and Light), Durga (destroyer of evil), Shiva (patron of ascetics; dark-skinned with matted locks and serpent) and Ganesh (the elephant-headed god of wisdom) are not associated with any of the Yoruba gods but are given reverence by the fact that lithographs of them are displayed on the Orisha shrines. Other Orisha 'powers' like Sadhu and Baba seem to be a confused reinterpretation of deities distantly related to those in the Hindu pantheon.[52] Indeed adherents to the Orisha faith, and Creoles in general, are quite unclear about the distinction between the beliefs and practices of Hindu and Muslim Indians in Trinidad. Accordingly, the degree of Indian influence on the Orisha cult is determined mainly by the way Asian components are conceived to be culturally adaptable by the Creoles. It cannot be understood then why the Yorubas in Trinidad do not equate the Hindu Dee (Baba?)[53] with the Orisha Oko,[54] both being guardian spirits of the land to whom animal sacrifices are made by farmers.[55]

Ceremonial rituals and practices

Most of the elements common to both the Orisha and East Indian religions may be explained by the theory of a 'parallel tradition' rather than of open borrowing from the other. This is not to deny that there is and was some degree of cultural integration at work between the two religious systems.[56] Practices like cooking ritual food, feeding of devotees, drumming, singing and chanting characterize the Yoruba annual feast (also attended by people of other faiths)[57] but are also to be found in Hindu ceremonial worship (witnessed by a white European in the 1880s).[58]

The Orisha *chappelle* (church) contains inner and outer shrines. Invariably two of these shrines ('stools') in the yard are dedicated to Ogun/Hanuman and Osain/Husain because they are considered 'high' (major) powers to many priests/priestesses. On the shrine of Ogun is placed a cutlass, sword or piece of metal which has been identified as his symbol.[59] In Hindu iconography Hanuman, the monkey-warrior, is represented by a mace made of steel held in his hands and resting on his shoulder.[60]

On the outer shrine of Ogun, a red flag affixed to a bamboo pole 23 feet in height is erected. The Hindus also plant a red flag on a bamboo staff (*jhandi*) in honour of Hanuman. In Nigeria and India the erection of flagstaffs is not common and therefore seems to be a West Indian phenomenon.[61] For Osain/Husain a yellow (or yellow and brown) flag is erected, but the pole is shorter. In front of every Baptist house there are flags ('signals') on bamboo poles of varying lengths, each colour representing a different nation: navy-blue represents the Chinese, light-blue or red the African, yellow the Syrian and white and yellow the Indian.[62] All other flags are rectangular in shape except those of Ogun and Osain which are triangular. Orish participants say that the triangular shapes represent distinct 'Indian spirits'. Significantly, Hindu flags which are set up to mark the sanctity of a place are triangular. In some Yoruba cult-centres, the Orisha and Indian flagstaffs are kept apart in the yard. Both Shangoists and Hindus attach some significance to the fluttering of the flags. Shangoists believe that the flags are 'talking' in a 'spirit language'. Hindus consider the fluttering to be a constant reminder to the celebrant of the obligation he/she took when it was hoisted.

On the shrine of Ogun are placed a red goblet of water, half a bottle of puncheon rum, a red candle and sometimes a lithograph of Hanuman (Mahabir). On the shrine of Baba, Simpson found *diyas*, Hindu earthen lamps filled with coconut oil.[63] In fact we discovered that many Yorubas in Trinidad celebrate Divali – the Hindu festival of lights – but on a smaller scale. [64] The Hindu custom of lighting *diyas* at dusk near the *jhandi* (flagstaff) finds its parallel in the lighting of candles for Ogun and Osain only, 'the Indian spirits', at dusk at their respective shrines.[65]

Water is an important ritual element in both the Orisha and Hindu belief systems. Three drops are thrown in the ground of the Orisha ceremony to call, calm or dismiss a power. In the *puja* (Hindu ceremonial worship) water is necessary for sipping and sprinkling and for bathing the images. It not only suggests purification, but also the element pervading all life.[66] Unlike the Orisha practitioners, Hindus do not use olive oil for sanctification.

In Nigeria, wine, and not puncheon rum as in Trinidad, is given to Ogun and Osain. The Baptists make no use of rum during their ceremonies. In the 1880s, a visitor to Trinidad noted the following:

> One of the South India gods, named Madrivele, had the marvellous faculty of entering houses through the smallest crevice; he used to display an inordinate fondness for fowls and rum, and he would help himself freely to these at all times. Hence at the sacrificing to Madrivele, the eating of chickens and the drinking of copious libations of rum play an important part.[67]

Madrivele is one of the old deities particularly revered by adherents to the Kali-Mai cult. Propitiation to the Black Mother is still made by pouring puncheon rum in the cracked halves of coconut shells.[68] Offerings to Dee, the Hindu guardian spirit of the land, are also made in the form of lighted cigarettes and white rum.

There is a similarity in the ritual use of blood between the Orisha and Kali-Mai worshippers. Both give blood as food to the gods at the time of a ceremony and both groups touch blood to the foreheads to all present at their ceremonies. This act of putting *tikka*, as the Hindus would call it, is done by the priest or celebrant by dipping his finger in a brass plate of blood. Indeed the Hindu goddess Kali is associated with the ritual of slaying animals to appease her lust for blood.[69] But while Kali officiants may lick the blood, Orisha participants merely allow some of it to flow from the sacrificial animal on the shrines of particular saints. The sacrificial animal for Kali, like Ogun/Mahabir, must be a healthy goat or fowl.[70] Shangoists, like Kal-Mai devotees, must follow a strict, unsalted, meatless diet before the ceremony. Those Orisha members who wish to summon 'the Indian powers', Ogun and Osain, must eat rice and *dhal* (split-peas), a diet particularly associated with East Indians of Trinidad.[71]

Osain, the divinity controlling medicine, receives offerings of honey, a frizzled-feathered fowl and a land turtle. One Orisha leader said that the turtle is associated with this Indian spirit because of its likeness to the shape of the dome in a mosque.[72] The use of the turtle as a ritual object is not only absent in Hindu religious performance but is hardly known in the Yoruba culture of West Africa. Moreover, Osain is not a major deity in Nigeria and his symbol is not a turtle or broom but an iron staff with a zoomorphic head. [73] Hindus nevertheless believe that it was the tortoise that found the earth in the ocean and was thus a precursor of Lord Vishnu in his *kurma* incarnation.[74]

The 'implement' identified with Osain is the cocoyea/coconut broom (*shayshay*), a symbol of cleanliness. It is used by both Orisha and Hindu practitioners for the same purpose of healing (*jharay*) people who are afflicted with some form of evil.[75] By a process of stroking the patient several times over the body and reciting sacred formulae, the person is supposed to be 'cleansed'. In the Kali-Mai cult the priest would circle the patient three times and brush him/her with a neem branch tied to a bamboo stick.

In both West Africa and Trinidad, special stones are utilized as ritual objects. Every Orisha temple in Trinidad has a collection of sacred stones ('pierres') believed to have fallen from the sky. They are kept on white plates. They must be washed each year with a mixture of certain leaves and water and must be fed from time to time by pouring olive oil on them.[76] A European visitor in the early 1870s found that the Trinidad Hindu temples had 'a stone or small stump on which offerings are made of red dust and flowers'.[77] A popular stone 'found under miraculous circumstances' and 'believed to be a Shiva *lingam* (phallus)' was found in Penal.[78] The basic and most common Hindu object of worship in Trinidad is the *lingam* which denotes the male creative energy of Shiva.[79]

The snake generally appears both in Hindu and Yoruba symbolism and art.[80] The python is particularly honoured in West Africa while any small snake in Trinidad is believed to be the spirit of an ancestor. At an Orisha cult centre in D'Abadie, one was preserved in a bottle and was associated with one of the Osain brothers. At an Orisha ceremony we saw a member being possessed not by the python, but the cobra. His body and arms were arched as he danced with a candle, lit at both ends, in his mouth. He made a hissing sound, asked for gainda (marigold) flowers and milk, and his utterances were regarded as oracles. The motif of the snake may be seen in the design of ornaments, necklaces and anklets kept by both Shangoists and Hindus. Significantly, the snake invariably adored by the Hindus is the cobra (*naag*).[81] It is represented in the lithograph of Shiva (wrapped around his neck) and in the semi-circular grass-knife which is kept on the Orisha inner shrines.

At the Orisha ceremonies, celebrants possessed by Osain (the master of Fire) placed a lighted wick into their mouths and/or walked through fire or lighted coals without being burnt. This rite was perhaps reinforced by the Madras Indian religious feat of walking repeatedly through a pit of flames without being burnt.[82] The act was done mainly by the Kali-Mai devotees as a test of faith. The feat attracted African and other spectators as early as 1884 at Mucurapo.[83] In her writings, a Spiritual Baptist of Trinidad makes mention of the Indian Fire-Pass or Fire-Walking Ceremony which she had witnessed as a child in the 1920s at St James.[84] During the Hussay procession, men performed the fire-rod dance (*banaithi*) by twirling bamboo poles with balls of fire at each end.[85] The dance, which attracted large crowds in the 1880s, was symbolic of the lighting of the way for the great spirits, Hasan and Husain.

At the Orisha ceremonies, devotees invoke the 'powers' by playing their respective rhythms on the drums and singing their respective songs.[86] At the Hindu Kali-Mai ceremonies, the chants vary but the rhythm on the *tappu* remains the same. Ogun, the divinity of iron and war, is the first to be summoned by the Shangoists.[87] For both Kali-Mai and Orisha worshippers, the presence of the spirit is revealed by convulsive shiverings and shakings of the celebrant's body and by abnormal utterances. When an Orisha spirit manifests on a person he/she would ask for and dance with the implement associated with that power; for Ogun it is the sword and for Osain the broom.[88] In the Madras Indian sect, the person on whom Kali has manifested would push out his/her tongue.[89] When Osain 'mounts' a celebrant, he/she would dance with a yellow goblet on his/her head, dribble, and the left foot and hand would appear to be paralyzed. This is an indication that Osain was wounded at some time.[90] In the Hussay ceremony in Trinidad, the soldier, Husain, is depicted as killed rather than wounded in the battle of Kerbala in AD 680. The spirits of Husain and his brother are believed to visit, but do not possess, the faithful celebrants and abide with them for ten days during which time special services are observed.[91] In both Orisha and Kali worship, a power may manifest on any member, irrespective of race. Thus Simpson found that 'two East Indian men were active participants, and Shango manifested vigorously on one of them' and was told by one informant that 'what a person is afraid to do, he does when possessed.... I never like Indian people, but I went to "mourn" and Mahabil came.'[92] In the Kali temples in Trinidad there are a few African participants, one of whom we found to be a former Baptist, possessed by Mother Kali herself.

Both Yorubas and Hindus pay homage to ancestors by offering food and drink in the yard to the spirits of deceased relatives during an annual ceremony.[93] The Yorubas also believe that one of the ways whereby departed ancestors may return to the living is when the soul is reincarnated into one of the newborn.

Yorubas seek protection from many diseases from Ogun, in the same way as Hindus seek the services of Hanuman who had brought medicinal herbs for the wounded Rama in the mythical battlefield. While both Shangoists and Kali-Mai practitioners prepare medicines with herbs for certain illnesses, the former also use leaves for the ceremonial washing of sacred stones and sacrificial animals. The manner in which the Orisha officiants spread the mango leaves in the mouth of the *kalsa* (urn), shows obvious East Indian influence. Indeed the *kalsa* itself, like the *lota* (brass jug), *tharia* (brass plate) and the yellow *sari* (dress) and white *dhoti* (loin cloth) worn by Osain devotees,[94] is an essentially Hindu religious trapping. So too is the use/terminology of *lipay* (plaster) and *gobar* (cow dung) when applied to the outer shrines of Ogun and Osain, and the preparation of food: *roti*, *parata*, *dhalpuri*, *chaityne* and delicacies made mainly by Indian women during the Orisha ceremonies.

The Orisha practice of planting two banana trees in the *palais* (inner sanctuary)[95] seems to have disappeared, but is kept by the Hindus in the centre of the altar (*bedi*) as a symbol of fertility.[96] Incense, camphor, brass handbells, conch and the red ixora (for Ogun/Mahabir) and yellow/orange gainda (marigold) flowers are used in both Hindu and Orisha worship for the same purpose of inviting the saints to the ceremony. Though one Orisha leader mentioned that in a vision she 'was carried away in an Indian temple and the people were beating *tassa* (drums)...'[97] and though the Africans were playing *tassa* in the Hosay processions[98] as early as the 1880s, the Yorubas never made use of this Indian percussion instrument in their ceremonies. Instead, they use the varied rhythms of the Yoruba *igbin*, *dudun* and *oumeme* to induce possession by one of the powers/forces. And though all of our African informants claim to speak Hindustani or an Indian language when they wish to invoke, or function as an oracle for Ogun or Osain, we found only a few of them had a working knowledge of Hindi. In possession trance, nevertheless, it is very common to speak tongues other than those known to the person; though Simpson himself found 'no East Indian songs or prayers during Shango ceremonies'.[99]

Conclusion

In the interpretation of Creole and Indian civilizations in Trinidad, the eclecticism of Shango and Hinduism provides unlimited opportunities for syncretism. Among the reinterpretations of African elements in Orisha worship that Simpson found are: the names and some of the characteristics of the spirits, the multiple soul concept, utilization of the spirits of the dead, divination by throwing kola-nuts, ritual acts in initiation ceremonies, ritual objects (ceremonial broom, thunder stones, clay pots, double-bladed wooden axes, rattles, drums) perfumes or 'oils', the use of blood, use of leaves, and use of stones.[100] Indeed some Shango leaders maintain that Creoles and Indians are of one family, as could be seen in their similarities of beliefs and rites, and that Creoles are really dark-skinned Hindus.[101] One leader, who had heard about the Hindu religious epic, *The Ramayan*, argued that the main difference between Hinduism and Orisha is the language, but that the Shangoists 'go more in-depth'. Many Baptists and Shangoists perform *puja* (Hindu ceremonial worship) which they refer to as 'sitting down prayers' in which a *pandit* (Hindu priest) officiates.[102] Both Hindus and Orisha participants believe that every age has its own prophet and that people pray to the same god in different forms. By incorporating African, Indian and other elements, the cult members contribute to the perpetuation of a 'multi-cultural heritage' in Trinidad.

In recent years the fundamental Christian Churches – the Pentecostal, Jehovah's Witnesses, Open Bible, and others – have been making open and pointed attacks on Creole and Indian traditional religions. Their agents have made an almost thorough penetration into the lives of these people by the use of propaganda media and other modern techniques. Through the American satellite beamed on local television sets, they have thus become the very symbol of Western culture and civilization. Their churches have mushroomed everywhere, even in the most rural areas, and membership has been found even among the elderly folks. Though Orisha and Hindu followers apprehend more than one deity simultaneously and have accommodated Christ into their respective systems, the fundamentalists are intolerant because they believe that their god is a jealous and exclusive one. These forms of folk culture have been quite helpless in resisting the incursions of this new wave of conversion. The result is that large sections of the Creole and Indian communities have broken the images of their forefathers and uprooted the flagstaffs that had been replanted on new soil on this side of the Atlantic.

Notes

1 Herskovits, M. and F., *Trinidad Village* (New York: Alfred A. Knopf, 1947).

2 See, for example, Gates, Brian, *Afro-Caribbean Religions* (London: Ward Lock International, 1980).

3 See, for example, Courlander, H. and Bastien, R., *Religion and Politics in Haiti* (Washington: Institute for Cross-Cultural Research, 1966).

4 Horowitz, M. and Klass, M., 'The Martiniquan East Indian Cult of Maldevidan', in *Social & Economic Studies*, Vol. 10, no. 1, UWI, Jamaica, 1961, pp. 93–100.

5 Nettleford, Rex (ed.), *Rastafari* (Jamaica, Caribbean Quarterly Monograph, 198?). See especially Mansingh, A. and L., 'Hindu Influences on Rastafarianism', pp. 96–115.

6 See 'La Divina Pastora', in *Tribune*, Trinidad, 10 April 1988, p. 6. There is also the lesser-known thesis, 'The Influence of the tassa on the making of the steelband' by Mahabir, Noorkumar (Trinidad: unpublished paper, 1983). The attempts to syncretise Indian musical rhythms with calypso have gained much popularity in Trinidad.

7 Brereton, Bridget, *Race Relations in Colonial Trinidad, 1870–1900* (Cambridge: Cambridge University Press, 1979), pp. 189.

8 Sewell, William G., *The Ordeal of Free Labour in the British West Indies* (London: Frank Cass & Co., 1968, first published 1861), p. 132.

9 Wood, Donald, *Trinidad in Transition: The Years after Slavery* (London: Oxford University Press, 1968), pp. 152–3.

10 Brereton, Bridget, op. cit. In his autobiography, one reputable African healer, diviner and seer wrote that there was an Indian woman who kept a shop near her mother's house in Grenada and that his wife herself was 'an Indian, full Indian'. Smith, M. G., *Dark Puritan* (Jamaica: Extra-Mural Studies, 1963), p. 51.

11 See Mangru, B., *Indenture and Abolition* (Toronto: TSAR, 1993), pp. 43f.

12 Crowley, Daniel, 'Plural and Differential Acculturation in Trinidad', in *American Anthropologist*, Vol. 59, 1957, p. 822.

13 In the early nineteenth century, the Muslim Hausa under Uthman dan Fodio were engaged in a war against the largely polytheistic Yorubas. Warner, Maureen, 'Africans in 19th century Trinidad', in *African Studies Association of the West Indies. Bulletin* No. 5, publisher unknown, 1972, pp. 27–58.

14 Simpson, George E., *Religious Cults of the Caribbean: Trinidad, Jamaica and Haiti* (Puerto Rico: Institute of Caribbean Studies, 1970, first published 1965), p. 32.

15 While some East Indian spirits may assist Orisha/Shango worshippers, others may seek to do harm. The grandchild of a Yoruba elder tells of her ordeal: 'I was playing with other children in the schoolyard when I saw an old Indian man dressed in a white *dhoti* coming up to me. I shouted to the other children but they said they saw nobody. I felt afraid and my head began to swim and I fell down. The other children ran away. I do not remember anything until later when I found myself at my grandfather's home.' Elder, J. D., *The Yoruba Ancestor Cult in Gasparillo* (Trinidad: cyclostyled copy, 1969), p. 11.

16 The psychologist may interpret this as a deep urge to make contact with another ethnic group, but which is repressed in conscious life due to, among other things, the exclusiveness of the Hindus and the arrogance of the Yorubas.

17 Henry, Frances, 'Religion and Ideology in Trinidad: The Resurgence of the Shango Religion', in *Caribbean Quarterly*, Vol. 29, Nos 3 & 4, Jamaica, UWI, 1983, pp. 63–9.

18 More East Indians have joined the Spiritual Baptist faith which is also essentially Black in composition.

19 Henry, Frances, 'Religion and Ideology', p. 67. A leader who also appears to be Indian is Ralph Frank. 'The Who and the What of Orisha Worship: Part 2', in *The African Presence in Trinidad and Tobago* (Trinidad and Tobago Television Production, 1985. Script by Gould, Joy).

20 Henry, Frances, 'Religion and Ideology'.

21 Perhaps Mr Smith had to publicly declare that he had denounced his Indian cultural heritage – his name testifies to this – since he was instructed and confirmed by Papa Neeza, the undisputed Orisha King of Trinidad, who 'was intolerant of the entry into the Shango religion of people who were not Africans'. It is quite paradoxical that the same famous Yoruba leader said in an interview at his Lengua Compound in 1951 that 'Shango religion in Trinidad is very mixed up.' Elder, J. D., *African Survivals of Trinidad and Tobago* (U.K., Paria Press, 1988), p. 22.
22 Simpson, George E., *Religion Cults*, p. 17.
23 At an evening Shango/Orisha feast in 1978 Frances Henry counted six Indians and 175 Blacks. She estimated total membership in Trinidad to be at least 10 000 in the 100 active ceremonial establishments. Except for the feast at Longdenville, we witnessed an average of one Indian among 20 Africans.
24 Elder, J. D., 'The Yoruba Ancestor Cult in Gasparillo'.
25 Ibid., p. 20.
26 Fermor, Patrick L., *The Traveller's Tree: A Journey Through the Caribbean Islands* (London: John Murray, 1951, first published 1950), p. 283. See also Craton, Michael, 'Slaves, Culture, Resistance and the Achievement of Emancipation in the British West Indies, 1783–1838' in Walvin, James (ed.), *Slavery and British Society 1776–1846* (London: Macmillan, 1982), pp. 100–22.
27 The relations existing between the Spiritual/Shouter Baptist, a predominantly Christian religion and the Shango/Orisha are complex. The latter is identified with drumming and animal sacrifice while the former rites ostensibly focus exclusively on the Holy Trinity. Whenever the two faiths overlap in beliefs and practices, the fusion is termed 'Shango Baptist'. Accordingly, each faith may be viewed as one end of a continuum. See Glazier, Stephen D., 'African Cults and Christian Churches in Trinidad', paper presented at Twenty-Third Annual Meeting of the African Studies Association, Pennsylvania, 1980.
28 'West Indian Spiritual Baptists are keeping up in faith in Brooklyn' in *Express*, Trinidad, 13 September 1985, p. 35.
29 Simpson, George E., *Religious Cults.*
30 'We believe in the brotherhood of mankind.... The Orisha belief system recognises and respects all other religious traditions of mankind.' Abimola, Wande, 'The Orisha Tradition: A World View', in *The Religion of the Orisas* (Trinidad: Orisa Movement, 197?).
31 Ahyee, Molly, 'Orisha tradition and culture', in *Trinidad Guardian*, 30 October 1983, Trinidad, pp. 21 and 31. 'Caribbean supernaturalism... ethnically is a composite of European demonology, African ancestor worship and fetishism, Asian mysticism and several minor systems of metaphysical phenomena which have evolved as native forms within the larger body of supernaturalism in the Caribbean as a whole.' Elder, J. D., 'Folk Beliefs, Superstitions and Ancestor Cult Activities in Relation to Mental Health Problems', Trinidad, unpublished paper, 1970.
32 Mahabir, N. and Maharaj., A., 'Kali-Mai: The Cult of the Black Mother in Trinidad', Trinidad, unpublished paper, 1985.
33 Mahabir, N. and Maharaj, A. 'Hosay as Theatre', Trinidad, unpublished paper, 1984.
34 Johnson, Samuel, *The History of the Yorubas* (London: Routledge and Kegan Paul, 1969, first published, 1921), p. 26.
35 Simpson, George E., *Religious Cults.*
36 Herskovits, Melville J., *The Myth of the Negro Past* (Boston: Beacon Press, 1958).
37 Khayyam, Ahamad, 'Follow Shango and you may have to account', in *Blast*, Trinidad, 12 September 1986.
38 Glazier, Stephen D., 'African Cults'.
39 A Shangoist in Grenada admits: 'I like the Indian Powers very well, because they are powerful...' Smith, M. G., *Dark Puritan*, p. 127.

40 Pitt, E. A., 'Acculturative and synthetic aspects of religion and life in the islands of St. Vincent and other predominantly Protestant islands and areas of the West Indies', in *Actes du IV*, Vienne, 1952, pp. 385–90.
41 Shango is known as 'Chango' in the USA. He has double claim to popularity as god of thunder and one of the early legendary kings of Oyo.
42 Omosade, Awolalu J., *Yoruba Beliefs and Sacrificial Rites* (London: Longman, 1979).
43 Dowson, John, *A Classical Dictionary of Hindu Mythology and Religion, Geography, History and Literature* (London: Routledge & Kegan Paul, 1972), pp. 116–17.
44 Vidyarthi, D. N. (tr.), *Hanooman Chaleesa* (Trinidad: Hindu Foundation for Religious Advancement, 1983).
45 Gleason, Judith, *Orisha: Gods of Yoruba* (New York: Atheneum, 1971), p. 49.
46 Vidyarthi, D. N., *Hanooman Chaleesa.*
47 See Mahabir, N. and Maharaj, A., 'The Hindu View of Christ', in *Moksha* (Trinidad: Indian Review Publication, 1986).
48 Crowley, Daniel, 'Plural and Diffcrential', p. 823.
49 Mahabir, N. and Maharaj, A., 'Hosay as Theatre', p. 10.
50 She also corresponds with Saint Philomene.
51 Interview with Shango/Baptist leader, Mr Percy 'Sugar' Lemaitre, Tunapuna, b. 1913.
52 Interview with Orisha leader, Fitzie, Enterprise, b. 1957. See also Simpson, George E., 'Religious Cults', p. 3.
53 See Mahabir, Noorkumar, 'Hindu Festivals, Ceremonies and Rituals in Trinidad', Trinidad, unpublished paper, 1987.
54 Gates, Brian, *Afro-Caribbean Religions.*
55 It is perhaps that propitiation to Dee (where rum is also offered) is one of the more private Hindu practices.
56 It is the view of an African critic that few authors have been concerned with the process of syncretism. See 'Syncretism', in *Tarikh*, Vol. 2, no. 1, Nigeria, Historical Society, 1977, pp. 1–3.
57 Elder, J. D., *African Survivals of Trinidad and Tobago.*
58 Collens, J. H., 'The feasts, which are very common, are generally in honour of some god...', p. 191.
59 In Nigeria, the usual symbols of Ogun are a cotton tree, a stone and a piece of iron.
60 'At Curepe.... on the pediment of the (the temple) stood an effigy of Hanuman, the Monkey-God. A little club rested on his shoulder, and one knee was advanced in the first step of a grave religious saraband', Fermor, Patrick L., *The Traveller's Tree*, p. 166.
61 Interview with Orisha Leader, Peerly Lashly ('Mother Queen'), Moruga, b. 1948.
62 Felix, Lynette, 'A Comparison between the Shango Cult and the Spiritual Baptist Community in Port of Spain', Caribbean Studies Project, UWI, St Augustine, 1971.
63 Simpson, George E., *Religious Cults*, p. 33.
64 Interview with Orisha leaders Fitzie, Mother Cole Besson of Enterprise b. 1927 and mother Bessie Bannister of D'Abadie b. 1918.
65 Orisha informants say that the candle lights for a longer time when compared to the *diya*.
66 Mahabir, Noorkumar, 'Hindu Festivals, Ceremonies and Rituals of Trinidad', p. 8.
67 Collens, J. H., *Guide to Trinidad* (Trinidad, n.p., 1888), p. 191.
68 Mahabir, N. and Maharaj, A. 'Kali-Mai: The Cult of the Black Mother in Trinidad'.
69 In the height of religious fervour, wounds are self-inflicted by participants of the Hussay observance as an expression of grief and love for the slain martyr, Hussain.
70 Hanuman is not associated with animal sacrifices in any Hindu sect or cult.
71 Interview with Peerly Lashley.
72 Interview with Fitzie.
73 The current market value of a land turtle is $150. The tortoise is not mentioned in

Omosade, A. J., *Yoruba Beliefs*; Afolabi Ojo, G. J., *Yoruba Culture* (London: University of London Press, 1966); Ellis, A. B., *The Yoruba-Speaking Peoples of the Slave Coast of West Africa* (Lagos: Pilgrim Books, 2nd edition 1974) and Parrinder, Geoffrey, *West African Religion* (London: Epworth Press, 1961). It is mentioned, however, as a symbol of the feminine qualities of persuasion by the Ibo and Ijaw tribes of Nigeria in Talbot, Percy J., *Some Nigerian Fertility Cults* (London: Frank Cass, 1967, first published 1927).

74 Bhattacharji, Sukumari, *The Indian Theogony* (Cambridge: Cambridge University Press, 1970).

75 There is the rite of the broom-dance in the Hussay ceremony.

76 Simpson, George. E., *Religious Cults.*

77 Kingsley, Charles, *At last a Christmas in the West Indies* (London: Macmillan, 1896, first published 1871), p. 300.

78 Niehoff, A. and J., *East Indians in the West Indies* (USA, Milwaukee Public Museum, 1960), pp. 120–1.

79 Heinrich, Zimmer R., *Myths and Symbols in Indian Art and Civilization* (Princeton: Princeton University Press, 1974, first published 1972), p. 126.

80 Parrinder, Geoffrey, *West African Religion*, op. cit., p. 50. See also Ojo, G. J., *Yoruba Culture.*

81 Crooke, William, *Religion and Folklore of Northern India* (New Delhi: S. Chand & Co., 1925), pp. 383–99. In northern India, rice and milk are given to snakes as protection/appeasement against snake-bites. It is believed that snakes give cures to certain diseases.

82 Mahabir, Noorkumar, 'The Indian Fire-walking ceremony in Trinidad', in *Divali Nagar* (Trinidad: National Council of Indian Culture, 1987), pp. 32–3.

83 *The New Era*, Trinidad, 18 August 1884, p. 3.

84 Whittington, Viola-Gopaul, *History of the Spiritual Baptist and Writings*, Trinidad, private pub., 1983, p. 18.

85 Mahabir, N. and Maharaj, A., 'Hosay as Theatre'.

86 Yoruba song to Osain:

kay ree, kay ree, Osain eelay	Osain is now in our presence to dance and
kay ree, kay ree, Osain eelay	take part in our ceremony.
Oscain ce power	He promises to remain with his brother (ie Michael)
kay ree, kay ree, kay ree	Help him in everything which is done
Osain eeelay	in the ceremony.

87 'Francis Henry recalls her three months with "Pa Neezer", the Shango King', in *People*, Trinidad, Inprint, Vol. 7, no. 4, November 1981, pp. 61–5.

88 Simpson, George E., *Religious Cults.*

89 Mahabir, N. and Maharaj A., 'Kali-Mai: The Cult of the Black Mother in Trinidad'.

90 Interview with Mother Doreen Alvarez.

91 Grant, Kenneth J., *My Missionary Memories* (Halifax: Imperial Publishing Co, 1923), p. 69.

92 Simpson, George E., *Religious Cults*, pp. 33 and 12.

93 See Awolalu, J. D., *Yoruba Beliefs*, and Mahabir, N. and Maharaj, A., 'Pitri-Paksh: A Fortnight of Spirits', in *Divali.*

94 The Orisha leader, Isaac, of Oropouche, wore *dhotis* continuously for a year-and-a-half. Interview with his wife Peerly Lashley. Mother Doreen Alvarez of Curepe wears a yellow *sari* when she wants to summon 'the Indian spirit' Osain.

95 Brown, Wenzell, *Angry Men – Laughing Men: The Caribbean Caldron* (New York: Greenberg, 1947), pp. 265–71. The banana is an object sacred to Shango in West Africa. See Afolabi Ojo, G. J., *Yoruba Culture*, p. 172.

96 Lackan, Rabindranath, *Plants of Religious Significance to the Hindu population of Trinidad and Tobago* (Trinidad: California Hindu Temple 198?).

97 Interview with Mother Jessie Bannister.
98 Simpson, George E., *Religious Cults.*
99 See Rampersad, Felix A., 'The Hosein Celebration and its Significance', in *Trinidad, Gem of the Caribbean* (Trinidad, publisher unknown, 196?).
100 Simpson, George E., *Religious Cults.*
101 Interview with Baptist leader, Winston Cornliff of Tunapuna, b. 1933.
102 Interview with Baptist leader, Mother Bishop Eudora Thomas of Tunapuna, b. 1934 and Orisha leader, Peerly Lashley.

We are grateful to anthropologist Chris Waith of the University of Western Australia for his comments on the first draft of this chapter.

CHAPTER 5 'Official' and 'popular' Hinduism in the Caribbean: Historical and contemporary trends in Surinam, Trinidad and Guyana

Steven Vertovec

The religious traditions of Hindus in the Caribbean are the products of over one hundred and forty years of inadvertent permutation, deliberate alteration or innovation, and structurally necessary modification. Caribbean Hindu traditions are also currently in process of transformation, and will doubtless continue to undergo changes for a host of reasons or purposes. This should come as no surprise since, to paraphrase Burghart,[1] reformulating Hindu beliefs and practices in light of shifting contexts is as old as Hinduism itself (an issue examined also by van der Veer in Chapter 6). In fact mutability is one of the hallmark characteristics of many concepts, rites, social forms and other phenomena generally subsumed under the rubric of 'Hinduism'. In India, the range of such phenomena is so large, varied, and variable that many scholars have criticized the use of any single notion or category 'Hinduism'.[2] However, in the Caribbean, historical courses of change have been such that a generally unitary Hindu religion has indeed arisen. Still, though a standardized and institutionalized orthodoxy has come to dominate the religious life of Hindus in each of the major communities in the Caribbean, more variegated beliefs and practices nonetheless occur on local levels. These developments are perhaps described best in terms of 'official' and 'popular' forms of Hinduism.

Hinduism, descriptive categories, and the diaspora

Since the 1950s, anthropologists and others have found heuristic value in the notions of 'Little Tradition' and 'Great Tradition' for addressing the diversity within and relation between local and India-wide Hindu religious phenomena.[3] 'Little Tradition' has generally referred to highly parochial non-Brahmanic (usually low-caste) and non-Sanskritic beliefs and practices; these tend to invoke minor or potentially malevolent deities and supernaturals, often toward pragmatic ends. The 'Great Tradition' of

Hinduism, on the other hand, has been said to include mainly the beliefs and practices found in Sanskrit texts and maintained by Brahmans across the entire subcontinent; these invoke the highest or most widely-known pantheon of deities, and also promote transcendent or philosophical ideals.

Much of the literature describes dialectic relations between these two categories (sometimes doing so in terms of 'classical *vs* folk' or 'textual *vs* practical' religion).[4] Many scholars have come to agree that these kinds of categories can often obscure the continuity of types or 'levels' of religious phenomena by reifying an artificial polarity. Instead, perhaps, such terms should represent Weberian ideal types placed on the ends of a kind of descriptive continuum;[5] depending on what is being undertaken, the activities of Hindus in India could then be represented at one point or another on the continuum. In such a model, for example, Hindu belief and practice might be described as being towards the 'Little Tradition' or pragmatic end when a person employs a low-caste specialist to invoke a blood-demanding deity during an exorcism, and towards the 'Great Tradition' or transcendent end when the same person makes a pilgrimage to a major Vaishnavite site; subsequently, other concepts and activities (elements of domestic worship; acts or obeisance to holy men; participation in certain oblatory rites, and so on) may be placed in-between according to their means and ends as conceived by the worshipper. The most important thing to recognize is that such categories or models are merely abstractions pertaining to phenomena which are inextricably linked in believers' minds and in their social relations.[6]

With reference to the Hindus who now reside in a wide variety of contexts outside India, the categories of 'Little' and 'Great' Tradition are of even more limited value. For a host of reasons and in different ways, the range of religious phenomena so long associated with the Hindu 'Little Tradition' has been narrowed or displaced altogether among migrants and their descendants. Throughout the Hindu diaspora, there has occurred a general course of change which has 'led from village and caste beliefs and practices to wider, more universalistic definitions of Hinduism that cut across local and caste differences'.[7]

Anthropologists have described this trend in similar ways: regarding Hinduism in East Africa, one notes the occurrence of a 'complete fusion of "big" and "little" tradition elements';[8] regarding South Africa, it is suggested that migrants' beliefs and practices have evolved into a 'regional Hinduism' in their own right;[9] regarding Trinidad, Hindu phenomena characteristic of different analytical 'levels' and drawn from various regions of India have been described as historically 'homogenized' in the new context and, regarding Surinam, we read that 'Rituals and ceremonies peculiar to specific castes disappeared, as well as the division between a brahmanical religion of the higher castes and a folk religion of the lower castes.'[10]

Especially due to the relatively small size and socially isolated status of their communities, a single corpus of belief and practice has usually come to be pervasive among Hindus in each post-colonial context outside India.[11] Thus to continue to describe the variety of Hindu beliefs and practices among overseas Hindus in terms of 'Little' and 'Great' Traditions – even by way of an ideal-type continuum – would be for the most part an irrelevant exercise.

Instead, it is suggested here that the notions 'official' and 'popular' religion may be more useful in describing strands or 'levels' of Hinduism in places like the Caribbean. 'Official' religion can be taken to mean a set of tenets, rites, proscriptions and prescriptions which are promulgated through some institutionalized framework: this usually entails a formal network of priests (often hierarchically structured) and/or a lay organization which determines orthodoxy and orthopraxy, arranges and administers a variety of socio-religious activities, usually controls some sort of communication network (such as publications or pronouncements dispensed through subordinate bodies – especially temples), and is often directly involved in religious education through schools and other programmes. 'Popular' religion can be understood basically as beliefs and practices undertaken or maintained by lay believers: these include orthodox practices undertaken outside 'official' auspices (especially domestic worship, but also including local festivals which celebrate mainstream deities or saints), so-called superstitious (magic–religious) and/or charismatic phenomena (such as healing rites, spirit-possession and exorcism, pursuits of miraculous ends, or steps taken to ward off evil forces), and 'cult' phenomena (collective religious activity directed toward some specific but usually unorthodox focus, such as an extraordinary person, sacred place or item, or supernatural being propitiated by a relative minority).

'Official' and 'popular' features are found in every world religion today, although in Hinduism (in India or abroad) they have a rather unique newness. Largely because it is without a founding prophet, central sacred text, geographical focal point or institutionalized priesthood, the sizeable cluster of traditions which has come to be deemed 'Hinduism' has, until relatively recently in its long history, been without an 'official' dimension. The resultant heterogeneity of belief and practice is Hinduism's leading characteristic, and has been cause for the anthropologists' conundrum of 'Great/Little Tradition'.

However, especially since the British imposition on India and the subsequent 'Hindu renaissance' of the early nineteenth century, there has been an increasing rationalization and institutionalization of Hindu beliefs and practices.[12] Consequently, a variety of organizations have arisen in India to provide Hinduism with new 'syndicated', 'corporate', or other 'official' forms. These range, for example, from the Brahmo Samaj and Arya Samaj (both of which advocate largely doctrinal and social reforms) through the Sanatana Dharma Raksini Sabha and Bharata Dharma Mahamandala (which arose, it might be said, as counter-reformist bodies seeking to standardize 'Great Tradition' tenets) to the Hindu Mahasabha and Shiv Sena (which have advocated conservative Hindu political activism). Still, their impact on Hindu religious traditions across India has been variable and sporadic (especially regarding village-level phenomena), and their membership or activity has been undercut by caste and class considerations. Outside of India in places like the Caribbean, on the other hand, such organizations have come to play a dominant role.

In order to trace adequately the development of 'official' Hinduism in the Caribbean, it is first necessary to examine migrants' religious backgrounds and early social conditions in the colonies. This chapter concentrates on the largest Hindu communities, those in Surinam, Trinidad and Guyana, where estimates suggest that Hindus respectively comprised 25 per cent, 25 per cent and 34 per cent of each country's total population of around 491 000 in Surinam, 1 062 000 in Trinidad and Tobago and 884 000 in Guyana during the mid-1980s.[13]

The Hinduism that came

Throughout the period which witnessed the large-scale migration of Indians into the Caribbean under schemes of indentured labour, a total of 238 909 Indians arrived between 1838 and 1917 into what was then British Guiana, 143 939 into Trinidad during 1845–1917, and 34 304 into Surinam between 1873 and 1916; subsequent to the return of a number of migrants (32 per cent, 22 per cent and 34 per cent respectively) following the expiration of their five-year terms of indenture, this amounted to net immigration figures of 153 362 in British Guiana, 110 645 in Trinidad, and 22 745 in Surinam.[14] Hindus formed the overwhelming majority of these transplanted populations (around 85 per cent in each case).

Most migrants came as individuals, recruited piecemeal from vast areas of north-east and south-west India. Depending on their original region, district and village, migrants would have experienced substantial differences in culture (including language and dialect, dress, cuisine, caste composition and structure, architecture and village layout) and economy (including agricultural production and labour relations, taxation and patronage, land distribution, local and distant markets). Their religious backgrounds, too, were highly idiosyncratic, reflecting parochial traditions of worship, pilgrimage, and festival observance as well as incorporating locally recognised sacred landscapes, varying influences of Islam or particular Hindu sects, dominating roles of castes with particular religious patterns.

The first major, geographically derived differences in socio-religious heritage can be inferred between migrant groups from North India (passing through the port of Calcutta) and South India (passing through Madras). Table 5.1 provides figures for these migrations during relevant years of operation.[15]

Table 5.1 Migration from Calcutta and Madras to British Guiana (1845–62) and Trinidad (1845–60)

	Madras	*Calcutta*	*Total*
British Guiana	11 459 23.5%	37 270 76.5%	48 729 100%
Trinidad	4 992 22.0%	17 624 78.0%	22 616 100%

Source: Geoghegan, 1873: 79, 80

Thus in the early years of indentured immigration, there was a sizeable South Indian presence in the two main receiving colonies. Drawn from a number of Tamil districts (including Trichinopoly, Ramnad, Tanjore and Salem) and Telegu districts (as far apart as Nellore, Ganjam and Vizagapatam), the South Indian Hindu migrants would tend to exhibit general religious characteristics of Shaivism (involving ascetic practices and non-Brahmanic rites directed towards Shiva), and to a lesser extent, Shaktism (involving ecstatic behaviour associated with cosmic power and healing derived from various goddesses). Regional variations in belief and practice were doubtless present among the South Indians, as they were among the far more numerous North Indian migrants. Table 5.2 provides data on the areas of origin for the latter migrants who passed through the port of Calcutta.[16]

Of the main North Indian areas of origin, Bengal, Bihar and Orissa have long been dominated by Shaktism (though Vaishnavism, or devotion to Vishnu and his incarnations, has had some influence particularly from the Chaitanya sect in Bengal), while eastern and western Uttar Pradesh (in what used to be called the Northwest Provinces or United Provinces of Agra and Oudh) and the Punjab are mainly Vaishnavite. Regardless of the regional religious patterns, however, each area is dotted with important, age-old centres of pilgrimage devoted to particular deities, which hold great sway over the religious orientation of surrounding vicinities. These include

Table 5.2 Areas of origin (by per cent) and total numbers of Indian migrants to Surinam,[1] Trinidad, British Guiana, 1874–1917

	Surinam	*Trinidad*	*British Guiana*
Orissa	0.1	0.1	0.1
West Bengal[2]	0.9	0.9	1.0
Central Bengal	0.4	0.4	0.4
East Bengal	0.1	0.1	0.1
Bihar[3]	14.3	13.5	14.6
NW/United Provinces[4]	48.6	50.7	52.0
Oudh	28.1	24.4	24.6
Central Provinces	0.5	1.4	0.6
Central India	1.6	2.5	1.3
Ajmere	–	0.1	–
Punjab	1.6	1.9	1.5
Native States[5]	1.5	2.4	1.2
Nepal & Native States[6]	0.6	0.4	0.6
Bombay, Madras, etc.	0.9	0.7	1.4
TOTAL	99.2	99.5	99.4
Total number of migrants, 1874–1917	30 555	94 135	140 085

Source: Annual Reports, Protector of Emigrants, Calcutta

1 No migration to Surinam recorded in 1874–75, 1875–76, 1885, 1887, 1897, 1900, 1903, 1910, 1911, 1915 or 1917.
2 Includes Central Bengal after 1906.
3 Includes Orissa after 1912.
4 Called 'Northwest Provinces' (today's Uttar Pradesh) until 1902: thereafter called 'United Provinces of Agra and Oudh', though Oudh continued to be tabulated separately.
5 Between 1897 and 1917.
6 Migration from Nepal only recorded between 1874 and 1885; thereafter 'Nepal and Native States' recorded together between 1886 and 1896. Recruitment in Nepal discontinued after that final year.

Shaivite, Vaishnavite and Shakti or Goddess sites (listed respectively for each) in West Bengal (Bishnupur, Kenduli, and Amta), Bihar (Sonpur, Gaya), eastern UP (Varamasi Ayodhya), western UP (Garmukhtesar, Soron, Deoband) and Orissa (Bhubaneswar, Puri Jaipur). In addition to propitiating the 'higher' Sanskritic gods, other deities are regionally popular as well, such as Gaininath, Naika, and Dharha in Bihar[17] and Bhumiya, Sitala, Joginya and Panch Pir in Uttar Pradesh.[18]

Though the bulk of Hindu migrants were drawn from three provinces, they came from a great number of districts within each, among them Cawnpore, Ghazipur, Basti and Azimgarh in the 'Northwest Provinces', Shahabad, Patna, Durbhiga and Gaya in Bihar, and Lucknow, Fyzabad and Gonda in Oudh. Each district – and further, each village – recognized an array of supernatural beings and had various traditions associated with them. Such beings would locally include a protective village deity (*gramadevata*, often called a *dih*), saints or martyrs, ghosts, demons, witches as well as sacred or malevolent trees, river banks, wells, stones and animals.

A widely heterogeneous caste composition among Hindu immigrants also had religious consequences, since certain beliefs and practices were specific to these as well. Further, not only did certain castes have special deities and rites, but these varied from locale to locale. Thus one contemporary observer wrote that

> the manners and customs of the various castes vary from one end of the Province [UP] to the other.... A custom or mode of worship prevailing among a caste in Saharanpur or Ballia may or may not extend as far as Aligarh on the one side or Allahabad on the other.[19]

For instance, among some of the castes which came in large numbers from Uttar Pradesh to the Caribbean, Ahirs (cowherders) traditionally worshipped Bittiya and Vinchyabasini Devi in many places, but also Birnath in Mirsipur district and Bangaru Bai in south Bhandara: Kurmis (cultivators) generally worshipped Thakurji, but also Surdhir in Goruckpur and Babi Fir in Basti; and among Chamars (leatherworkers), a host of deities were worshipped from place to place, including Jagiswar, Nagarsen, Kuanwala, Sairi Devi and Parmeshwari. Finally, each lineage or clan within a caste had rites and other practices centring on a deity special to themselves (*kuldevata*).

Therefore, in sum, the Hinduism which came to the Caribbean was comprised of a profusion of religious traditions determined by the heterogeneity of the Hindu migrants themselves. Out of such a profusion, however, common forms were forged.

Early Hinduism in the Caribbean

Patterns of Hindu worship during the early years of Indian presence in the Caribbean seem to have been diffuse, by all available accounts. Goat sacrifice – reflecting presumably non-Brahmanic activity – was observed in Trinidad in 1849 and in 1855, when a goat 'wearing garlands of red flowers and surrounded by pans of washed rice and bottles of molasses and rum... was beheaded to the sound of drums...'.[20] In 1865, a Christian missionary in Trinidad visited

> a place where the Hindus sacrifice. There was a pole with a small flag flying, a small altar of mud, and near it two stakes... a sort of yoke into which the neck of the goat to be sacrificed is placed and its head severed at one blow. The blood is burned on the altar and the body made a feast of.[21]

The same missionary explained that at this time, Hindu rites were bound to occur anywhere, since 'They had no temples. Gatherings for worship were conducted at any selected spot by their Brahmans or priests': moreover, 'each priest had his own disciples'.[22]

Uncoordinated and perhaps random rites and practices at that time would be quite expectable, given the basic fact that early migrants on colonial estates were so linguistically disunited due to their diverse areas of origin. Bengali, Hindi, Maithili, Magahi, Punjabi, Telugu, Tamil, tribal languages and others were spoken by the immigrants, as were dialects such as Kanauji, Avadhi, Bhojpuri, Brajbhasa and Tondai Nadu. A missionary in British Guiana pointed out,

> nearly all these languages spoken in India are in free and constant use among them in the Colony, and only a very small portion among our immigrants can understand more than one language.[23]

He explained that

> The proprietors or managers of sugar estates purposely choose men speaking three or four separate and distinct languages not understood by each other, in order to prevent combination in cases of disturbances among them....

'When these people meet in Trinidad,' one contemporary Englishman wrote, 'it strikes one as somewhat strange that they may have to point to water and rice, and ask each other what they call it in their language'.[24] Gradually through the years, a common, creolized Indian tongue or 'plantation Hindustani'[25] developed in each Caribbean context (based largely on Bhojpuri and Avadhi, and blended with non-Indian languages especially in the case of Sarnami in Surinam).[26] Until that time, however, collective religious activity was doubtless hindered by lack of effective communication among the transplanted Hindus.

Religious activities among the indentured Indians were quite tolerated – even facilitated – by plantation managers, as long as these activities did not conflict with economic production. [27] Yet, given the breadth of religious traditions which characterized the migrants' backgrounds, consensus on devotional focus and procedure was probably hard to achieve at first. In British Guiana, for instance, Bronkhurst suggested that Vaishnavites and Shaivites were 'strenuously contending for the supremacy of the chief object of their worship, and the consequent inferiority of the other'.[28] (It is perhaps more plausible that Bronkhurst actually discerned some division between North Indians, mainly comprising followers of the former broad orientation, and South Indians, generally equated with the latter, because among North Indians alone such contention between Vaishnavites and Shaivites would be less likely since they have co-evolved for centuries in that part of the subcontinent.) There has been no major distinction between Vaishnavites and Shaivites in Surinam,[29] basically because the colony never received shipments of South Indians.

Some Hindus may have tried to continue propitiating traditions directed toward regional, village, caste or kin group gods, but the basic fact that they were an amalgam of Indians, thrust together on plantations far from India, militated against any such successful continuity. The absence of shrines, legend-filled landscapes, and co-believers would spell the rapid relinquishment of parochial traditions – psychologically distressing though this may have been to many migrants. Certain sects or orders were more successful in maintaining their ways, however, since these were roughly institutionalized prior to migration.

Towards the end of the nineteenth century, Comins[30] described the presence of Ramanandis, Kabir panthis, Aghor panthis, and Swaminarayanis in Trinidad, the traditions of which have remained in one form or another up to the present day.

Eventually, more durable, collective modes of Hindu worship were established in the colonies, evident particularly in the creation of temples. In many estates and nascent villages, small shrines (in the form of raised platforms with clay images) persisted through the nineteenth century. Yet very gradually, more elaborate structures were constructed, often with the help and encouragement of the estate management (who, Moore suggests,[31] saw this as a way to keep the Indian workers socio-culturally isolated and therefore more easily manipulated). Underhill[32] pointed to one of the earliest temples in Trinidad, while the novelist Charles Kingsley provided the first detailed description of such structures observed in 1871:

> Their mark is, generally, a long bamboo with a pennon atop, outside a low dark hut, with a broad flat veranda, or rather shed, outside the door. Under the latter, opposite each door... is a stone or small stump, on which offerings are made of red dust and flowers. From it the worshippers can see the images within.
>
> ... Sometimes these have been carved in the island. Sometimes the poor folk have taken the trouble to bring them all the way

> from India on board ship. Hung beside them on the walls are little pictures, often very well executed in the miniature-like Hindoo style by native artists in the island. Large brass pots, which have some sacred meaning, stand about, and with them a curious trident-shaped stand, about four feet high, on the horns of which garlands of flowers are hung as offerings. The visitor is told that the male figures are Mahadeva, and the female Kali....[33]

Bronkhurst likewise gave us a good account of Hindu temples in Guiana:

> A Hindu temple is not constructed like a Christian sanctuary.... It is not intended to accommodate a crowd of worshippers within its walls. Its worshippers stand outside in an area opposite the door which is the only entrance belonging to thc building. The priest, the representative of the people, is the only person who enters the temple through that door in order to perform the duties of his office in the presence of the idol, which stands at the lower end of the door, and so placed that the worshippers from outside might have a full view of, and fall down before it. There is no window to a Hindu temple to let in light or admit air. The room, including the small space which is called the residence of the idol (*Swami stalam*), before which burns a small oil lamp, and the space sufficiently spacious for the temple utensils, the offerings, and the officiating priest to stir or move about, is always dark and awe-inspiring.... These hut-temples are considered so sacred by the coolies, on account of the visible presence of the deity – the idol – they worship, that no unclean person can enter any of them without the preparatory ablutions being performed.... (Italics in original.)

These small *shivalas* and *kitis* (or *kutiyas*), also described in Trinidad by Froude,[34] appear to have closely resembled those normally found in villages of Bihar and Uttar Pradesh. In Guiana, only two small temples were observed by a Royal Commission in the 1860s; by the onset of the 1890s, at least 33 Hindu temples were to be found, funded through individual donation or group subscription. By the early twentieth century, such structures were commonplace in most estates and Indian villages.[35]

The celebration of Hindu festivals, too, grew in number and importance by the early part of this century. Lengthy and elaborate plays (Ram Lila, Krishna) depicting stories of the gods were performed in estates and villages in the nineteenth century, and Diwali and Phagwa (Holi) were the most popular annual events celebrated by Hindus in the colonies by the turn of the century. And whereas Comins, based on a visit of a mere ten days, believed there were few Indian festivals celebrated in Surinam, Emmer suggests that no less than 32 Hindu festivals were annually recognized on Surinamese colonial estates.

Some of the earliest Hindu activities became notorious, however, which led to their suppression. One was a practice in which a devotee would impale various points of his flesh with hooks and subsequently swing by them from a pole. Oddie notes that during the nineteenth century, this was widespread in both Bengal (where it was known as *chrak puja*, a penitential rite directed to Shiva) and in South India (called *soodaloo* or *chedul*, a self-sacrificial rite to a goddess).[36] This proved too 'barbaric' for white colonists, and hook-swinging was banned in British Guiana in 1853.[37] Another extraordinary Hindu activity was fire-walking, a *shakti*-oriented practice which – though carried out in Bihar and the tribal states as well as in South India – became wholly associated with the immigrant 'Madrassis'.[38] In Trinidad, Collens reported that 'it is not observed by Hindus of Northern India, but, on the contrary, is repudiated by them'.[39] Though publicly suppressed, fire-walking continued in 'Madrassi' circles in both Trinidad and British Guiana until at least the mid-twentieth century. Animal sacrifice was abhorred by colonists as well, and was looked down upon by Brahmans and other Hindus, too; however, this still continues in the Caribbean as part of non-orthodox observances.

Apart from occasional celebrations or temple-based activity, it was the ordinary, daily practices which formed what could be considered the core of Hindu religiosity in the early years of Caribbean settlement. Sacred plants, vessels and implements used in worship, and images of deities were brought from India,[40] Hindu scriptures were imported and sold, and wandering Brahmans and sadhus gathered Hindus, told tales and expounded beliefs. All these elements contributed to the construction of a religiously affirmative environment. The domestic sphere was perhaps of greatest importance, since it was where the most common beliefs and modes of worship were perpetuated by the migrants and taught to their offspring. Household shrines, personal prayers and small acts performed by various family members constitute the essential ingredients of Hinduism in any of its forms or traditions, and these were carried out in the colonies among plantation barracks and homes in the early villages. Invoking images of village life in North India itself, Kingsley provided a print of a Hindu performing morning oblation outside of a thatched house in Trinidad, while Bronkhurst observed that in British Guiana,

> Before a Coolie eats, he places a small quantity of the prepared food before the idol or god of the house to propitiate his favour.... Rising at dawn, the Hindu goes to the trench, or takes the water into his own yard, and there, with religious care, he cleanses his teeth, performs his sacred ablutions, imprints the emblems of

> his faith upon his forehead, arm, and breast, visits the idol of the house, or faces the rising sun, before which he falls down... (1883; pp. 257–8).

However normal such basic religious practices became in the nineteenth-century Caribbean, though, the fact remained that Hinduism was a minority religion – considered 'heathen' and even demonic by members of the ruling community – within highly pluralistic societies. This situation had the effect of stimulating self-consciousness about religious beliefs and practices, which subsequently entailed perhaps deeper reflections on choice in religious belief and practice, more attempts to justify ideas and activities, and more sharpened skills at defending religious tenets than would have been the case in villages of India. Exacerbating these circumstances were missionary activities directed primarily at Hindus, especially by Methodists and Anglicans in British Guiana, Moravians in Surinam, and Presbyterians in Trinidad.[41] While these missions were not without considerable success (some 10 per cent of Indians in British Guiana and Trinidad were Christian by 1911),[42] many Brahman pundits became quite adept at verbal combat with Christians, and through such channels, Hinduism came to be portrayed more and more as a unitary religion on social and doctrinal par with any other in the colonies. In time, formal Hindu organizations were established with the expressed goal of standardizing and promulgating such an opinion.

The growth of 'official' Hinduism in the Caribbean

Probably the most significant socio-religious change that occurred among Hindus in the Caribbean, and one which was a prerequisite for the rise of an institutionalized and all-embracing Hindu orthodoxy, was the attenuation of the caste system. Space does not permit a full treatment of the whys and wherefores of this process as it occurred in the Caribbean.[43] In the Caribbean, specific caste *identities* were often retained through the years (particularly in terms of *varna*, and to a much more limited extent, of *jat*, and only effectively called into play in the arrangement of marriages or sometimes with regard to claims of public status). Yet caste could never be transplanted as a *system* (as it was in India, simultaneously being a hierarchy and social relationships, a network of economic interdependence, an order of reciprocal ritual duties, and a conceptual continuum of ontological states according to notions of purity and pollution). This inability for reconstruction occurred because the caste system is a highly localized phenomenon in villages of India; it had no chance of being maintained through historical conditions in which individual members of diverse caste groups (many unheard of from one region to another) were plucked out of local hierarchies throughout North and South India and placed together in contexts where their proximity and commensality, economic activities, and social relationships were managed by non-Indians on estates and, after indenture, altered by wholly alien socio-economic circumstances. For most practical purposes, this resulted in a new kind of egalitarianism among Hindus in the Caribbean.

Yet Brahmans retained a special religious role, albeit different from that in India. 'As pandits', van der Burg and van der Veer point out, 'they monopolized the sacred knowledge of rituals and Sanskrit texts, so that ritual knowledge replaced purity as the legitimation of the Brahaman's status.'[44] In the new context of the Caribbean, Brahmans gained clients for their ritual services by offering to all – regardless of caste background – the beliefs and practices previously within their own exclusive preserve (that is, the features characterized by some as being of the 'Great Tradition' of Hinduism). The 'Brahmanization' of Hinduism thus occurred in the Caribbean, whereby throughout each Hindu community, a core of Brahmanic ritual directed towards Sanskritic gods came into ascendency.

These Brahman-dominated practices, which became the routine features of Hinduism in all three Caribbean territories, included the performance of formal *puja* (involving Sanskrit formulae governing sixteen offerings, or *shodasopachara*, made to various deities – though Hanuman *puja* was by far the most popular in all three contexts under consideration), *samskaras* (rites of passage marking key life-stages), *kathas* (routinized recitals of sacred lore, particularly a text devoted to Satyanarayan), weddings (though only the climatic formal rites were overseen by Brahmans), funerals (involving a host of ceremonies over a period of at least ten days), a *bhagwats* or *yagnas* (remarkable socio-religious activities centred on the reading of a sacred text – usually the Shrimad Bhagavata Purana – spanning seven, nine, or fourteen days and involving a variety of rites, massive communal meals [indicative of caste's demise], and much social interaction among possibly hundreds of participants). These have continued through to the present, often in vibrant and uniquely modified forms.

Organizational development of this 'Brahmanized' Hinduism was marginal for some time before undergoing a rapid acceleration. In Trinidad, for instance, a Sanatan Dharma Association was said to have existed since 1881,[45] though it is not known for having accomplished much in terms of influence or activity. By the 1920s, other small, Brahman-led groups were in existence (such as the Prabartakh Sabha of Debe and the San Fernando Hindu Sabha), but their endeavours were modest and essentially of local scope. Also, during the early decades of the century, a loose kind of pundits' *parishad* or council was said to have existed between Brahman priests in Trinidad, Surinam and British Guiana, such that their communication – though more through an informal network than through official channels – did much to standardize practices within the region. Such communication, including trips to perform rites, was most frequent between pundits in British Guiana and Surinam, owing to their common border. (It was even common for individuals from one country to have a Brahman 'godfather' [*guru*] in the other.)

In all three contexts, the undoubtable catalyst for the national organization of a unitary, standardized Brahmanic Hinduism was the introduction of the Arya Samaj into the Caribbean. The Arya Samaj, a reformist movement calling for a Vedic purification of Hindu belief and practice, was established in the Punjab by Swami Dayanand Saraswati in 1875. This radical movement had tremendous impact across North India, where it forced many Hindus to reflect on and articulate what it was they themselves believed. The result was a conservative backlash, part of which involved the creation of formal bodies to promote a formulated, 'official' orthodoxy deemed 'Sanatan Dharma' ('the eternal duty or order' – though 'dharma', here, came to mean something more like 'religion' in its Western sense). The Arya Samaj sent well-trained missionaries from India to Hindu communities throughout the diaspora, where they had identical effects.

A succession of Arya Samaji missionaries undertook prolonged visits to three Caribbean colonies. The first arrived in British Guiana in 1910, travelling that same year to Trinidad. Surinam received its first representative from the Samaj in 1912. Visits turned into sustained presence by the 1930s, highlighted by the charismatic personalities of Mehta Jaimani and Ayodhya Prasad. The Arya Samajis caused much consternation within Hindu communities through their staunch and knowledgeable advocacy of fundamental reforms in doctrine (especially by way of promoting their exclusive, Vedic-centred monotheism and rejection of idols) and in social structure (including efforts to upgrade the status of women and to criticize the Brahmans' self-ascribed authority). In each country, great debates were waged between Arya Samaji and 'Sanatanist' camps, some even ending in violent clashes.[46]

Just as in India, the forces of Brahmanism came together in each Caribbean country to create a sustained front against the Arya Samaj and to quell the air of doubt which the reformists had sent rippling through the Hindu population. This involved moves to tighten and structure their own ranks through organizational effort. In 1927, a Pundits' Council was formed in British Guiana to act as the sole authority concerning matters of doctrine and ritual, along with the Sanatan Dharma Sabha, created to act as a national representative body for Hindus in British Guiana. In Surinam, the

Sanatan Dharma (sic) was founded in 1929 to fullfil a similar role. In Trinidad, the dormant Sanatan Dharma Association was revitalized and incorporated in 1932, the same year a rival Brahmanic body was formed, the Sanatan Dharma Board of Control. And in 1934, the Sanatan Dharma Maha Sabha was established as the most prominent Hindu organization in British Guiana. (Meanwhile, the Arya Samajis had followed suit by instituting formal bodies, too: the Arya Dewaker in Surinam in 1930 and the Arya Samaj Association – later called the Arya Pritinidhi Sabha – in Trinidad in 1934.) Most of these Caribbean Hindu organizations forged links with kindred associations in India, thereby declaring further justification for the 'official' forms of Hinduism which they propagated. The unitary and Brahmanic thrust of these is exemplified by Trinidad's Sanatan Dharma Board of Control, which stated:

> The registration of this society is regarded by the Hindu community as being an important step in the direction of the unification of Hindu interests... and it is laid down as a definite policy that the Board of Control shall always be predominantly composed of orthodox, practicing pundits.[47]

These 'Sanatanist' organizations consolidated much support, especially from rural Hindus who preferred conservative modes of worship. They thereby far eclipsed the Arya Samaj, whose supporters tended to be well-educated, middle-class Hindus. In each country, the 'Sanatanist' groups achieved other important gains during the 1930s and 1940s when – after years of difficult campaigning – they succeeded in obtaining, from the respective colonial governments, legal recognition of Hindu marriages and permission to perform cremations. But perhaps the most effective organizational developments were those of Trinidad's Sanatan Dharma Maha Sabha, the body created in 1952 by Bhadase Sagan Maraj after he united the country's two previously rival Sanatanist organizations. In addition to obtaining the affiliation of dozens of temple congregations throughout the island (coordinated by the Maha Sabha's Pundits' *parishad*), Maraj oversaw the construction of no less than thirty-one Hindu schools between 1952 and 1956.

With such schools, temples, publications, collective celebrations, and the participation of almost every Brahman pundit, these highly centralized Hindu bodies culminated the long processes of standardizing and routinizing Hindu belief and practice in Trinidad, Surinam and British Guiana. In each context, the national organizations dominated Hinduism in ways akin to those which Smith described regarding the Sanatan Dharma Maha Sabha in British Guiana during the 1950s and early 1960s:

> This form of Hinduism [promulgated by the Maha Sabha] has gradually replaced all the lower-caste cults and special practices which used to exist among the immigrants, and it claims the affiliation of practically all the temples in the country. With its sister organisation, the British Guiana Pundits' Council, it may be said to control orthodox Hinduism (or the nearest Guianese equivalent to it), in British Guiana, and has come to constitute a 'church' in the technical sense.[48]

The 'official' Hindu bodies became so predominant, in fact, that they became major political forces. The Brahman leaders of Sanatan Dharm in Surinam established their own, short-lived Surinamese Hindoe Partij in the late 1940s; they later merged with other Indian parties to form the Verenigde Hindostaanse Partij, but continued to play a central part in this party's endeavours.[49] In Trinidad, under the strongarm tactics of Bhadase Maraj, the leadership and support of the People's Democratic Party (later becoming the Democratic Labour Party) was virtually indistinguishable from that of the Maha Sabha.[50] And in British Guiana, though the Indian-backed party was Cheddi Jagan's explicitly Marxist People's Progressive Party, it, too, was comprised of many Maha Sabha leaders.[51] Thus Hinduism had not only been 'Brahmanized' and 'officially' standardized, it had now become 'politicized'. This was particularly the case in the years immediately preceding each nation's independence (Trinidad 1962, Guyana 1966, Surinam 1975), when there were fears of political repression under Creole-backed parties – fears which have been subsequently justified.

Though the central 'Sanatanist' bodies have continued to hold much financial and organizational power, their popularity with average Hindus has greatly dwindled. This is especially so in Trinidad and Guyana. Many Hindus cite the Maha Sabhas' lack of assistance toward affiliated schools and temples, along with the arrogance of associated pundits, as reasons for this. But perhaps most damage was done in Guyana in the late 1960s and early 1970s, when the ruling, Creole-backed People's National Congress successfully gained sway over the Maha Sabha leadership, an intolerable occurrence in the eyes of average Hindus. Similarly, Trinidad's Maha Sabha suffered a crisis in leadership following the death of Maraj in 1971; much of the Hindu community grew dismayed with the Maha Sabha due to the ensuing political infighting and allegations of misconduct and corruption – made worse by its eventual leader's public support for the Creole-backed government of the People's National Movement.

Instead, new, alternative Hindu organizations have been created. While still advocating the same type of essentially Brahmanic, Sanskritic Hinduism, these have become more popular by demonstrating more grassroots activity and, importantly, more attention to the interests of young people, than the centralized organizations. These include the Nav Yuvak Sabha in Surinam, the Gandhi Youth Organisation in Guyana, the Hindu Seva Sangh in Trinidad, a number of other groups operating locally through mutually supportive networks.

Today a great deal of Hindu socio-religious activity in Surinam, Trinidad and Guyana takes place under the formal direction of the national bodies and the alternative groups. Yet much occurs outside of these auspices as well. The current range of all types of practice can be described with reference to their degree of institutionalization (that is, very basically, the extent to which activities are arranged and managed by set individuals performing specific roles) – in other words, from most 'official' to most 'popular' modes of religion.

Contemporary Caribbean Hinduism

The following list provides a classification of the most common contemporary Hindu practices in Surinam, Trinidad and Guyana. The sequence of listed items is according to the degree of ordered, collective activity (or, again, extent of institutionalization) undertaken in each type of practice.

A. Official forms

This rubric concerns those activities directly undertaken by the central, national organization (Maha Sabha) in each country. These include: weekly rites and *Kathas* held at temples; large-scale celebrations of annual holy days (particularly Divali, Phagua, Ramnaumi, Shivratri, and Krishna Janashtami – though affiliated temples also celebrate, on local levels, Navratri, Ganesh jyanti, Katik nahan, and Vasant panchmi); publications (including prayer books) and radio programmes; religious curricula in affiliated schools; contests (for Hindi language skills, debating, *chautal* singing [particular to Phagua season] and other arts); and, importantly, the pundits' *parishad* whereby doctrine and procedure is monitored.

B. Alternative official forms

Concerning most of the same activities listed above, these are only undertaken by organizations other than the Maha Sabhas, including practices in non-Maha Sabha-affiliated temples. Small-scale committees or groups (*goles* and *mandals*) also exist in villages for the specific purpose of holding *yagnas* and Ramayan *satsangs* (local meetings in which Tulsidas' epic is recited). Such alternative bodies have also creatively established practices aimed at Hindu youth, such as summer camps, marches, fund-raising bazaars, sports clubs and theatre groups.

A wholly different set of 'alternative official' Hindu phenomena is that centred on Kali worship (generally known as Kali Mai Puja), which has been gaining support in Guyana from a wide segment of the Hindu community (and among some Creoles) for many years.[52] More recently it has been reinstituted in Trinidad.[53] The tradition has developed from Shakti-oriented practices observed among the so-called 'Madrassis' in Guyana since the middle of the nineteenth century. These routinely involved animal sacrifice, possession (altered states of consciousness), and the worship of deities characteristic of South Indian Hinduism (such as Katheri, Munishwaran, Madraviran and Mariamma – the latter often identified with Kali). Such non-Brahmanic practices have long been castigated by pundits and others advocating a Sanskritic, 'Sanatanist' Hindu religion in the colonies. In Surinam, the tradition never really existed since the colony lacked South Indian practitioners; in Trinidad, it remained only in isolated pockets where 'Madrassis' had settled in number, but in Guiana, Kali Mai Puja became an active religious tradition (particularly in Demerara, which is home to a large proportion of South Indian descendants). Its mode of worship became increasingly standardized in the 1920s and 1930s under the direction of Kistima Naidoo, apparently waned in attendance during the 1940s and 1950s and has undergone a prominent renewal under James Naidoo since the 1960s. There are now estimated to be some one-hundred Kali 'churches' (*koeloos*) throughout Guyana, exhibiting numerous variations from the core set of rites long associated with the tradition. There are presently formal bodies representing this form of Hinduism, such as the Guyana Maha Kali Religious Organization.

There are also other formally organized Hindu traditions, regarded as 'non-Sanatanist', which are present in the Caribbean, including those of Kabir Panthis, Sieunarinis (Swaminarayanis), Arya Samajis, devotees of Satya Sai Baba, 'Hare Krishnas' (members of the International Society for Krishna Consciousness) and followers of various Hindu-derived yoga and meditation groups. These are quite small in membership, and moreover, their members quite often participate in 'Sanatanist' activities with little dissidence.

C. Collective forms

These are religious activities self-organized by groups of people (especially networks of extended kin and/or co-villagers). They include annual festivals marking important periods of the Hindu calendar, such as celebrations for Divali (plays, Lakshmi Puja, and the building of elaborate lighting displays) and Phagua (*chautal* singing, the construction and burning of a *Holika* bonfire, and traditional forms of playing with red dye), the staging of Ram Lila or Krishna Lila plays, and the cooperative management of *yagnas* and *satsangs* sponsored by individuals. Weddings and funerals are usually fairly large events organized *ad hoc* by groups of family and friends who systematically undertake a considerable number of chores in order to perform successfully the elaborate complex of accompanying rites. Also considered under this heading are the last vestiges of caste-specific rites: namely, sacrifices of hogs to the goddess Parmeshwari, still performed privately only by a few Chamar families.

D. Domestic forms

Religious activities conducted in the home by members of Hindu families include: *pujas* (sponsored annually or for special occasions – such as birthdays or anniversaries – in which a pundit is hired to perform the necessary Sanskritic rites; this is ideally undertaken over a weekend period, with Fridays reserved for Hanuman Puja, Saturday for Satyanarayan *Katha*, and Sunday for Suruj Narayan Puja); *samskaras* (naturally held at the appropriate times of children's lives – though presently, perhaps only three to five of the prescribed 16 rites are actually performed for most Caribbean Hindus); daily rites (usually performed by children or grandparents, involving prayers and the lighting of incense and lamps at an indoor shrine and/or outside in a little sanctum at the base of the house's *jhandi*,[54] or coloured flags erected on occasion of *pujas*); and infrequent pilgrimages (to rivers or the sea [representative of the Ganges in all three countries] or to special sites such as in Trinidad, where one small temple has an allegedly growing stone [regarded as a Shiva *linga*] and a Catholic church has a reportedly miraculous statue of the Virgin Mary [regarded by many Hindus as a manifestation of the one great Goddess]).

E. Individual forms

It is harder to list religious phenomena in this category, since they are by definition idiosyncratic. These features generally involve a person's *ishtdevata*, or form of god chosen for personal worship (such as Hanuman, Krishna, Durga or Shiva), and individual mode of worship (such as paying devotion to special images or symbols, reciting certain prayers at particular times, fasting on specific days of the week or periods of the year, making votive offerings and fulfilling promises to the god in given manners, and so on). Also of an essentially individual nature is the *mantra* (Sanskrit sound or prayer) imparted to a person by their Brahman 'godfather' on occasion of *gurumukh*, the 'christening' *samskara*.

F. 'Amorphous' or peripheral forms

Because a considerable set of beliefs and practices fall far outside the 'official' forms of Hinduism, as these have come to be constructed in the Caribbean contexts, they have often been maintained in a rather clandestine and unformulated, often quite vague, manner by a decreasing minority. These are usually directed toward therapeutic or protective ends, and include: beliefs and precautions regarding the evil eye (*najar* or *malja*), *jharay* and *phukay* (the use of specific *mantras* and motions to cure various afflictions), *tabij* (talismans) and *totka* (specific acts to undo the work of malevolent forces or omens), *ojha* (black magic, often blended with Creole forms, called *obeah*), exorcism of ill-meaning spirits, and offerings to minor deities (especially Dih, originally a guardian village godling, and 'the seven sisters' – which, though few can actually name them, are conceived to be manifestations of the Goddess).

Conclusion: ongoing trends and debates

The transformation of Hinduism in Surinam, Trinidad and Guyana is by no means complete. The long process of 'Brahmanization' and standardization, which culminated in domination by centralized organizations, has begun to unravel. A kind of fragmentation has begun – yet not one which necessarily divides Hindus, but rather, one in which Hindus are again recognizing the viability of a diversity of devotional orientations and modes of worship. Thus a more 'ecumenical', rather than unitary, type of Hinduism may be developing.

The beliefs and practices of 'Sanatan Dharma' are still by far the most pervasive – particularly among older Hindus, but also among a considerable number of youths. Yet especially among the well-educated young people in each of these countries, interest is building in more philosophical and less sacerdotal forms of Hinduism (such as the teachings of Vivekananda and Aurobindo); this trend is fostered by some of the 'alternative' Hindu associations. Whatever the variety of approach taken by various groups and individuals, however, they are all being justified under the banner of *bhakti* (devotion to God) – even Kali Mai Puja, in which *bhakti* has been equated with *shakti* (such that the manifestation of divine energy is a sign of true devotion).

But the trend toward acceptable heterogeneity is not proving smooth, and several issues are presently being debated. These include: the questions as to whether only Brahmans can serve as priests, the place of Hindi and Sanskrit in Hinduism, which is a key part of the general quandary of Caribbean Hindus' relation to India, the role of women in Hinduism, and the problem of whether certain practices should be deemed 'low' and therefore undesirable.

Very much in contradiction to the statements of pessimistic observers during the 1960s, who predicted the religion's final demise in the Caribbean, Hinduism is thriving in Surinam, Trinidad and Guyana. The beliefs and practices which were drawn from throughout the subcontinent, merged and modified in new contexts, formulated and formally managed by purpose-made authoritative bodies, are now being maintained in a variety of ways, on a number of 'levels', in cities and villages of each nation.

Notes

1 Burghart, Richard, 'The Perpetuation of Hinduism in an alien cultural milieu', in *Hinduism in Great Britain*, Richard Burghart (ed.), (London, 1987), pp. 224–51.

2 Frykenberg, T. 'The emergence of modern "Hinduism" as a concept and as an institution', in *Hinduism Reconsidered*, H. Kulke and G. D. Sontheimer (eds), (Delhi, 1989).

3 Marriott, McKim, 'Little communities in an indigenous civilization', in *Village India*, McKim Marriott (ed.), (Chicago; 1955), pp. 171–223.

4 Leach, Edmund (ed.), *Dialectic in Practical Religion* (Cambridge, 1968).

5 Weightman, Simon, *Hinduism in the Village Setting* (Milton Keynes, 1978).

6 Pocock, David, *Mind, Body and Wealth* (Oxford, 1978), p. xiv.

7 Jayawardena, Chandra, 'Migration and social change: a survey of Indian communities overseas', *Geographical Review* 58, pp. 426–49.

8 Bharati, Agehananda, 'A social survey', in *Portrait of a Minority: Asians in East Africa*, Dharam P. Ghai and Yash P. Ghai (eds), (Nairobi, 1970), pp. 15–67.

9 Kuper, Hilda, 'An interpretation of Hindu marriage in Durban', *African Studies* 16, pp. 221–85.

10 Van der Burg, Corstian and Peter van der Veer, 'Pundits, power and profit: religious organization and the construction of identity among the Surinamese Hindus', *Ethnic and Racial Studies* Vol. 9, no. 4, pp. 514–28.

11 This is not the case among postwar Indian migrants to Western countries like Britain and the United States; instead, these migrants have often retained many sectarian, caste-based or regionally-specific Hindu traditions. Reasons for this include: migration and settlement in large group numbers (as opposed to indentured migrants' transplantation as individuals), allowing for the continued use of regional language (whereas these had been blended or attenuated in places like the Caribbean) and for the greater maintenance of caste identities (which have largely disappeared among the post-indenture descendants); also, recent migrants have been able to retain social and economic links with India.

12 Bellah, Robert, 'Epilogue: religion and progress in modern Asia', in *Religion and Progress in Modern Asia*, Robert N. Bellah (ed.), (New York, 1965), pp. 168–229.

13 Population figures of Surinam are especially difficult to estimate due to a mass emigration to the Netherlands (perhaps 80 000 or more, largely Indians) over the past fifteen or more years. Similarly, Indians have been leaving Guyana increasingly since the 1960s, and a

predominantly Indian exodus seems to be underway currently in Trinidad. All of these flights stem from worsening economic and political circumstances.

14 Lawrence, K. O., *Immigration into the West Indies in the 19th Century* (St Lawrence, Barbados, 1971), p. 57.

15 During these years, migration from Madras was sporadic due to restriction imposed following high mortality rates at sea and abroad. The scheme for indentured migration from Madras to the Caribbean was terminated completely in 1862, long before the commencement of Indian migration to Surinam (however, over 3000 South Indians were again shipped to Trinidad during 1905, 1910 and 1911, and a further 376 to British Guiana in 1913 and 1914; Govt of Madras, *Annual Reports* 1899–1916). Reasons for this termination included: strong competition from Mauritius in recruiting workers, lack of both a suitable depot and an active recruitment service in Madras, and colonial planters' dissatisfaction with the working and other habits of the so-called 'Madrassis' (generally attributed to the contemporary notion that these migrants were originally city dwellers, as opposed to the rurally-derived 'Calcuttans'; though this may have been true in some cases, some now suggest that many of the South Indian migrants were originally coastal fishermen, an occupation which many indeed took up in Guiana following their indentureship).

16 The reader should bear in mind that these figures are cumulative, and that migration from the various districts varied importantly over the years. For instance, migration from Bihar to all colonies was high in the 1880s, but dropped substantially by the turn of the century; conversely, migration from the Native States (and therefore, of tribals or *janglis*) and from Central India rose considerably after the turn of the century, especially to Trinidad. Variation over the years is attributable to many factors, such as local droughts and famines, recruitment strategies or government restrictions. Variation between colonies is due to the fact that different numbers were requisitioned by planters in each territory, and that British Guiana (Demerara), Trinidad and Surinam had separate recruiting agencies and depots based in Calcutta.

17 Grierson, G., *Bihar Peasant Life* (London, 1885), pp. 403–7.

18 Planalp, Jack M., *Religious Life and Values in a North Indian Village*, PhD Diss., Cornell University, 1956, pp. 159–61.

19 Crooke, William, *The Tribes and Castes of the North-Western Provinces and Oudh*, 4 vols (Calcutta, 1986), Vol. 1, p. vi.

20 Wood, Donald, *Trinidad in Transition* (London, 1968), p. 150.

21 Morton, S., *John Morton of Trinidad* (Toronto, 1916), p. 23.

22 Ibid., p. 52.

23 Bronkhurst, H. V. P., *The Colony of British Guiana and Its Labouring Population* (London, 1883), p. 226.

24 Gamble, W. H., *Trinidad; Historical and Descriptive* (London, 1866), p. 34.

25 Tinker, Hugh, *A New System of Slavery* (London, 1974), p. 208.

26 Durbin, Mridula Adenwala, 'Formal changes in Trinidad Hindi as a result of language adaptation', *American Anthropologist* 75, 1978, pp. 1290–1304.

27 Ramnarine, Tyran, *The Growth of the East Indian Community in British Guiana*, 1880–1920, PhD Diss., University of Sussex, 1977, p. 199.

28 Bronkhurst, H. V. P., *Among the Hindus and Creoles of British Guiana* (London, 1888), p. 17.

29 Arya, U., *Ritual Songs and Folksongs of the Hindus of Surinam* (Leiden, 1968), p. 35.

30 Comins, D. W., *Note on Emigration from India to Trinidad* (Calcutta, 1893).

31 Moore, Robert James, *East Indians and Negroes in British Guiana, 1833–1880* PhD Diss., University of Sussex, 1970, pp. 369–70.

32 Underhill, Edward Bean, *The West Indies: Their Social and Religious Condition* (London, 1862), p. 52.

33 Kingsley, Charles, *At Last, a Christmas in the West Indies* (London, 1905), p. 300.
34 Froude, James A., *The English in the West Indies* (London, 1888), pp. 75–6.
35 MacNeill, J. and C. Lal, *Report on the Condition of Indian Immigrants in the Four British Colonies: Trinidad, British Guiana or Demerara, Jamaica and Fiji and in the Dutch Colony of Surinam or Dutch Guiana* (Simla: Government Central Press, 1914), p. 73.
36 Oddie, G. A., 'Regional and other variations in popular religion in India: Hook-swinging in Bengal and Madras in the nineteenth century', *South Asia* 10, 1987, pp. 1–10.
37 Mangru, B., *Benevolent Neutrality* (London, 1987), pp. 170–1.
38 O'Malley L. S. S., *Popular Hinduism* (Cambridge, 1935), p. 160.
39 Collens, J. H., *A Guide to Trinidad* (London, 1888), p. 235.
40 Poynting, Jeremy, *Literature and Cultural Pluralism: The East Indian in the Caribbean* PhD Diss., University of Leeds, 1985, p. 327.
41 Samaroo Brinsley, 'Missionary methods and local responses: The Canadian Presbyterians and the East Indians in the Caribbean', in *East Indians in the Caribbean*, B. Brereton and W. Dookeran (eds), (London, 1982), pp. 93–115.
42 Singaravelou, *Les Indiens de la Caraïbe*, 3 vols, (Paris, 1987), Vol. 3, p. 69.
43 Clarke, Colin, 'Caste among Hindus in a town in Trinidad: San Fernando', in *Caste in Overseas Indian Communities*, Barton M. Schwartz (ed.), (San Francisco, 1967), pp. 165–99.
44 Van der Burg and van der Veer, 'Pundits, power and profit', p. 517.
45 Kirpalani, Murli *et al.*, *Indian Centenary Review* (Port of Spain, 1945), p. 61.
46 Speckman, Johan D., *Marriage and Kinship among Indians in Surinam* (Assen, 1965), p. 48.
47 Forbes, Richard H., *Arya Samaj in Trinidad: An Historical Study of Hindu Organisation Process in Acculturative Conditions*, PhD Diss., University of Miami, 1984, p. 60.
48 Smith, Raymond T., *British Guiana* (London, 1962), pp. 123–4.
49 Dew, Edward, *The Difficult Flowering of Surinam* (The Hague, 1978).
50 Ryan, Selwyn, *Race and Nationalism in Trinidad and Tobago* (University of the West Indies: Institute for Social and Economic Research, 1972).
51 Vasil, Raj K., *Politics in Bi-Racial Societies* (New Delhi, 1984).
52 Phillips, Leslie H. C., 'Kali-Mai puja', *Timehri* 11, 1960, pp. 136–46.
53 Vertovec, Steven, *Hinduism and Social Change in Village Trinidad*, D.Phil. thesis, University of Oxford, 1987, pp. 325–7.
54 The use of *jhandi* demonstrates one important source of difference between Hindu practices in the three countries: whereas only red (for Hanuman) and, less frequently, white (for Satyanarayan) flags tend to be erected following 'Sanatanist' *pujas* in Surinam and Guyana, a range of coloured flags are displayed by 'Sanatanist' Hindus in Trinidad (including pink for Lakshmi, dark blue for Shiva, yellow for Durga, orange for Ganesha, and more).

CHAPTER 6 Authenticity and authority in Surinamese Hindu ritual

Peter van der Veer

Introduction

As an epilogue to *The Enigma of Arrival* (1987), V. S. Naipaul describes the mortuary rites (*shraddha*) which were performed for his sister. It is a surprisingly mild and rather touching description for an often cynical observer of religion. Moreover, it highlights a few important aspects of modern Hinduism in the Caribbean. His sister had not been a believer, but her family had thought it necessary to perform the usual rites. Nevertheless, it may be noted in passing that, in fact, only these mortuary rites are literally said in Hinduism to arise from faith (*shraddha*). However, we do not have to be drawn into a tedious discussion of what 'belief' and 'faith' would mean in Hinduism, to be able to observe that it is the rite rather than professed dogma which is at issue here. A Hindu does not need the permission of a Church to be buried in sacred soil. Nothing resembles the soul-searching confession of sins and absolution by the priest of Roman Catholicism. Instead, the ritual by which the ghost of the deceased is transformed into benign ancestor has to be performed in the prescribed manner. The Brahman priest and his counterpart, the sacrificer (*jajman*), are entirely immersed in what Naipaul calls 'the physical side of the ceremony', in ritual practice. It has to be done correctly, 'this pressing together of balls of rice and then of balls of earth, this arranging of flowers and pouring of milk on heaps of this and that, this constant feeding of the sacred fire'.[1] Correct practice appears to be essential in Hinduism rather than correct belief.

This point should, however, not be exaggerated. There is and always has been a content, a semantics, to ritual action and this, again, is nicely brought out by Naipaul's description. His sister's husband asks whether his wife will return to earth and whether they will be together again, and the priest answers that in that case he would not be able to recognize her. This is a nice point of theology and such points are never far away from ritual practice. Nevertheless, Naipaul is right when he observes that, though the rituals had always been partly a mystery, his family could not anymore easily surrender to them. They had become self-aware by education, travel and history, transformed by wealth. A quest for 'personal experience and meaning' has to some extent been added to the earlier emphasis on 'correct procedure'. Despite the image of changelessness that rituals tend to project, Hindu ritual clearly acquires another significance when new social configurations arise.

Hinduism and Hindu ritual have long been interpreted as the ideology and practice of Indian society. India has, in general anthropological theory, become the locus of caste and hierarchy, just as Africa has become the locus of segmentary society and the lineage, and the Mediterranean societies of the honour-and-shame complex. Such concepts become hegemonic in a discipline, since they provide a shorthand for summarizing cultural complexities as well as a link between ethnographic reality and theoretical preoccupations.[2] While these concepts are related to places and tend to confine culture to its locality, they are not directly, inductively, derived from field-work, but may have a complex origin in anthropological theory. While native culture is confined to its locale, anthropological discourse is metropolitan and derives its inspiration from all places.

What makes the case of Surinamese Hinduism of such importance for anthropological theory of Hinduism, is exactly that it shows so clearly that 'native' culture is not all confined to one locality, since the 'natives' live all over the world. It thus provides an excellent critique of the sociological determinism which confines Hinduism to Indian society, seen as a whole. Hinduism is clearly not a local religion, though it is practised and understood in particular places and at particular moments. Its study has therefore to be contextualized.[3] Differences in the ways in which Hinduism has been elaborated in local contexts exist as much between India and Surinam as between Uttar Pradesh and Tamil Nadu. Certainly, nobody would think of arguing that Christians cease to be Christians when they leave Western Europe. Similarly, it would be ridiculous to say that the Hinduism of Hindustani in Surinam or of Gujarati in East Africa is not relevant to the anthropological discussion of Hinduism.

The social construction of religious and, for that matter, ethnic identities depends, to a great extent, on historical context. The authority of certain discourses and practices does not depend on what we as outsiders define as their trans-historical 'essence', but on the results of debates in localized arenas. This does not imply that I think that religion is simply a black box in which everything can be put according to the interests of the principal actors in a political arena. Religion is not an infinitely plastic resource for pursuing political interests. What I do want to argue is that to understand why some religious discourses and practices become authoritative, while others are rejected or stigmatized as inferior or 'wrong', we have to contextualize religious identity in terms of religious organisation and broader social configurations. However, it is not only historical context that is important. Social practice generates 'habitual dispositions' which are to a great extent unconscious.[4] These affective styles as well as the related practical skills and behaviour patterns are inscribed in the body during early childhood and define the rhythm of life. On the one hand, then, Hindu identity changes when its context changes, since new generations acquire it through socialization in these new contexts. On the other hand, however, Hindu identity defines the ways in which these new contexts are understood. Moreover, religious dispositions depend on ideologies which tend to deny change and history. That Hinduism is external and unchanging is the message of its ritual and theology. Surinamese Hinduism is thus a form of Hinduism which is understood and elaborated in Surinamese and Dutch contexts, but which in its ideology denies historical context.

The Surinamese case contradicts anthropological theory by showing us Hindus who have neither caste nor sect. As in the Indian case, however, Brahmans continue to play a dominant role in Surinamese Hinduism. They are still a relatively closed endogamous group of ritual specialists whose position, however, is based upon their ritual knowledge rather than upon their purity. They keep their knowledge and professional positions in hereditary possession and are in important respects the informal leaders of the Hindu community. Sects, organized around a nucleus of ascetic renouncers, are only of marginal interest in Surinamese Hinduism, which is a religion of priests, not of renouncers. The main bone of contention in Surinamese Hinduism is the question of whether the priest should be a Brahman or not. It is therefore not any of the traditional sects, but the anti-Brahman reform-movement of Arya Samaj which is the rival of Brahmanism in Surinamese Hinduism. Even for the reformers, however, the Brahmanical, Vedic ritual is the core of religious practice. The Arya Samaj propagates an even purer ritual than the Brahmans offer, but performed by non-Brahmans. For an understanding of Surinamese Hinduism, ritual and the position of the Brahman priest are clearly the heart of the matter.

Before we can discuss the ways Hindu ritual and the role of the priest are understood in the Dutch context, it is important to give some basic information about the Hindustani community in Surinam and the Netherlands.

A house divided

The Dutch had their own East India (later: Indonesia) and contract labourers from both Dutch and British East India were brought to Surinam. A distinction had thus to be made between (British) East Indians and (Dutch) East

Indians and this was done according to area of origin. The first were called Hindustani after Hindustan (present day Uttar Pradesh and Bihar), while the latter were called Javanese. A correct Dutch spelling of Hindustani is Hindoestani, but we find till the present day the spelling Hindustani. This may have been an accidental misspelling by Dutch administrators, but it has acquired an ideological salience, when used by the Hindustani themselves. They have the idea that Hindustani refers to the Hindu, not to the Muslim community. Hindus are in a great majority (76 per cent), while Muslims are a minority (20 per cent). To use the word Hindustani therefore means to emphasise the common origin of the ethnic group, while underplaying its religious diversity.

Despite important differences in religious identity among the Surinamese Hindustani, they clearly also share an ethnic identity which derives basically from their history of migration and from the competition with other Surinamese ethnic groups. Labour migration from Northern India to Surinam took place from 1873 to 1916. When this migration stopped after pressure from the Indian National Congress, the majority of the labourers chose to stay on in Surinam; in 1927 the Hindustani became Dutch citizens living in the Dutch colony (Surinam was known as Dutch Guiana until 1948). Most of them had lost contact with their families in Hindustan.

After the Second World War the Hindustani started in increasing numbers to leave the rural area and to compete with the Creoles for the same administrative and educational jobs. In this period ethnic identification beyond ideas of common origin and race became important for political and economic mobilization. In 1949 a Hindustani political party was formed as an alternative to the other major party in Surinam which was dominated by the Creoles. Ethnicity was a major factor in politics before the Surinamese independence of 1975. The elite of the Hindustani had already gone to the Netherlands at the beginning of the sixties, primarily for a limited period of higher education,[5] but at the beginning of the seventies a cross-section of the Surinamese population, including many Hindustani, escaped from a Surinamese society in which they did not expect to have a viable future, to what the Hindustani writer Bea Vianen called 'the Paradise of Oranje'. The popular idea that the Netherlands attracted the Surinamese because of its social security system, though often used in racist contexts, is less of a myth than a valid explanation of the migration in this period. Hindustani, however, present their migration often in terms of a flight from Creole oppression. Hindustani leaders had declared themselves against independence, since they were not represented in the government which negotiated the independence, despite the fact that the Hindustani had come to form the largest ethnic group (37 per cent of the population, 142 300 people in 1971) in Surinam.

Some 80 000 Hindustani came to live in the Netherlands in the seventies and the chance that at least a major part of them will return to Surinam in the near future has diminished since the military coup of 1980 and the establishment of a dictatorial regime afterwards. The Dutch government decided in 1974 and 1975 to implement a policy of dispersal, which resulted in the fact that Hindustani live in various small towns and villages all over the country. Despite this policy, however, a major section of the Hindustani (some 20 000 to 30 000) took up residence in the Hague, while there are also major communities in Amsterdam and Rotterdam.

At first glance there is thus reason enough to speak of a Hindustani community which is based on common history and shared language. However, religious identities divide the ethnic community radically. The most important of these divisions are those between Muslims and Hindus, while within the majority group of Hindus, a major distinction is made between 'orthodox' and 'reformists'. Hindu–Muslim relations in Surinam form a religious configuration which is always affected by developments in the Indian subcontinent or in the Islamic world. When Pakistan emerged as an Islamic state after the Second World War, relations between Hindus and Muslims in overseas countries also deteriorated. It is interesting to see in the Dutch situation that Hindustani Muslims try to emphasize their contacts with India. There is a continuous flow of religious personnel and articles between the Indian subcontinent and the Netherlands to cater for the needs of both Hindu and Muslim Hindustani.

As I have mentioned before, the dispute between reformists and orthodox hinges critically on the position of the Brahman priest. In 'orthodox Hinduism', Sanatan Dharm, Brahmans are a kind of ritual entrepreneur.[6] They inherit ritual purity and sacred knowledge and have to protect these qualities by remaining endogamous. In that way the Brahmans are the only 'caste'-like group in Hindustani community as a result of their successful attempt to monopolize certain ritual functions. The Brahmans are, as entrepreneurs, connected with networks of patrons (*jajmans*, 'sacrificers') who need their ritual services. A major development of Hinduism in Surinam has been the expansion of Brahman ritual activities even to areas of religious practice which had been in India the exclusive domain of lower castes, like ritual therapies and possession cults.

The position of the Brahman in religious networks is a major religious and political fact in both Surinam and the Netherlands. It has been subject to severe attack since the beginning of this century (c. 1912) when the Arya Samaj, a reformist group, started its missionary activities in Surinam. According to this group, which preached a fundamentalist return to the Vedas, the putative roots of Hinduism, every knowledgeable lay person can become priest, because it is not purity by birth, but knowledge of the sacred texts which is of major importance here. The Arya Samaj had been founded at the end of the nineteenth century in North India and can be seen as a reaction to the challenge of Western science and colonial power. As an ideological movement the Arya Samaj is quite clear about what it thinks Hinduism is and what should be done with it. It is, however, much less clear what the Hinduism of the Brahmans, their opponents, is. As Burghart argues,[7] Hindus describe their religion systematically in terms of the concept of dharma. There are numerous senses of this word, but one widespread meaning is 'the everpresent moral order of the universe' (*sanatan dharma*) for whom the members of the Brahman caste are the terrestrial spokesman. It is important to see that the Arya Samaj forced their opponents to explain this term in much more specific and ideological terms. This amounted to the 'ideolization' of Hindu discourses and practices, which resulted in the organization of a so-called 'orthodox' Hinduism, which was called Sanatan Dharm. The conflict between Aryas and Sanatani is to the present day one of the major dynamics in Surinamese Hinduism.

Ancient rituals

The correct performance of rituals is the core of Surinamese Hinduism. This performance depends critically on the competence of the ritualist who is called a pandit, 'the one who has knowledge'. The Surnamese pandits are temple priests (*pujari*), family priests (*kul-purohits*), ritual specialists (*karmakandin*), magic healers (*ojha*) and funeral priests (*mahapattra*) simultaneously. They are active in all fields of ritual practice, although they do make a distinction between lower and higher activities. This distinction, however, does not entail a division of labour among religious specialists, as in India, but only a division in front-stage and back-stage activities.[8] Since these pandits can be employed by anyone, there is a great deal of free competition among them. This competition is almost as ferocious as that among pilgrimage priests in Uttar Pradesh. The pandits are cynically perceived by the laity to be money-grabbers of low morality. Nevertheless, Hindus cannot do without their services. They are the ritual authorities who know how to perform the rituals.

In the Netherlands, even more than in Surinam, temple worship is marginal as compared to house rituals. The most important of these are the rites of passage (*samskaras*) which perfect the body and mind of the performers from birth to the final sacrifice (*antyesti*) of death. Other important rituals focus on the worship of particular deities, such as the Mother Goddesses at Nauratri or Krishna at Krishnasthami. An important place is given to a number of rituals to ward off the evil influence of planets and ghosts. These are performed to prevent or cure illness and death.

The performance of Hindu rituals in the Netherlands highlights what interests, expectations and assumptions are actively brought forward in interaction between performers, patrons and public. In a condensed form it shows some of the basic aspects of Hindu identity and its contradictions in the Dutch context. In two short case-studies I will try to focus on a few major aspects, namely 'the authenticity of Surinamese Hinduism', 'the authority of the Brahman priest' and 'the question of language'. The first case describes a house-ritual performed by a priest for a family. The second case describes a public meeting of Hindus who perform a fire-sacrifice and, afterwards, I will discuss the language of rituals.

Case 1: A Mul-shanti ritual in a flat in Zoetermeer

For every important action, such as marriage, or event, such as birth, the Hindu has to consult the almanac. Since the Hindu almanac is extremely complicated, he has to go to a knowledgeable pandit who will advise him about the influence of the planets (*grah*) and what to do about it. Next to the rites of passage, rites to pacify the evil influence of planets (*grah-shanti*) rank high on the ritual agenda of Hindus in the Netherlands. According to some informants the life of a human being can be influenced in three ways: (1) by *karma*, the retribution of past actions; (2) by the influence of the planets; (3) by external influences such as curses and magic.

Hindu astrology has it that the year can be divided into twelve *rashis* which can again be divided in nine sub-divisions (*charans*). Together these sub-divisions make up the sacred number 108, to which there is always much allusion in Hindu ritual. If one is born under the evil influence of one of these *charans*, called *Mul* or Scorpio, this has to be pacified by a *mul-shanti*. Readers of V. S. Naipaul's great novel, *A House for Mr Biswas* (1961), will remember the beautiful description of Mr Biswas's birth under an unlucky sign in the house of his maternal grandparents. His father is not allowed to see him for the first 21 days and then only in the reflection of oil in a brass plate. The ritual has as its side-effect that the separated parents are conciliated. What Naipaul described is part of the *Mul-shanti*.

I recently witnessed a *Mul-shanti* in an apartment in Zoetermeer, near The Hague. Because of the Dutch climate, rituals there have to be performed indoors, which poses specific technical problems. In some rituals a hole has to be dug and water-libations have to be poured into that hole. This is clearly not possible in a flat. Moreover, many ritual handbooks have the injunction that rituals should be performed in the open air. It is a recurrent complaint of my informants that the whole atmosphere of the ritual is changed, now they are performed indoors, and they wonder about differences in outcome. A critical difference with rituals as they were performed in Surinam is their isolation. There is no gathering of the neighbourhood.

Everything is confined within the four walls of a flat in a building, populated by indifferent or even hostile Dutchmen. Hostility can be a result of the inevitable noise of the ritual, the beating of gongs and the blowing of the conch. Dutch neighbours do not have to be openly racist to complain of the oppressive and threatening strangeness of smells (of Indian food) and noises. Hindu ritual space is therefore in Holland an embattled space.

Part of the floor of the apartment is prepared for the ritual. Plastic garbage bags are put on the floor to catch the water from libations. Flour is thrown to purify (*pavitra*) the place. In my opinion an important part of the ritual has already been performed before the priest starts the performance. Days before the preparations begin, all kinds of ingredients have to be purchased or collected from sundry places. Expertise of older family-members has to be invoked to learn about the exact preparations. The family has to be alerted and invited. For a period the sacrificers (*jajmans*) should abstain from eating meat and fish as well as from drinking alcohol. The embarrassment of people who are invited to help in ritual activities and know that they have transgressed these taboos is often great. They are afraid that evil will result from rituals in which they partake, and try to keep a distance.

The sacrificers and the pandit have to be 'Indianized' before the ritual starts. The pandit changes after his arrival into a *dhoti* and *kurta*. The father of the newly-born child also dons a *dhoti* and *kurta*; the pandit puts a sacred thread (*janeo*) round his shoulders. He is purified in a short initiation-ritual in which he has to touch the twelve parts of his body. The mother wears a sari and her husband puts *sindur* on the hair-parting as a sign that she is a married woman. Hindustani pandits have told me that young, unmarried couples often request them to perform a shortened marriage-ceremony, so that the women are saved the humiliation of being excluded from a role in family-rituals. What is striking in the ritual as a whole is that, as compared to the North Indian situation, women play a much larger role in it. In the Indian situation, the ritual has to be performed by the man, supported by his wife, while in Holland important parts are performed by the wife, supported by her husband. Some pandits explicitly divide rituals into male and female parts, so that, for example, women worship with red flowers female deities as the Ganges-water (rivers are female deities).

The actual ritual has three parts. The first part is the showing of the baby to the father. A brass tray (*thali*) with water is placed before the father and the mother. Her sister and her mother's sister stand behind the sitting couple and hold the baby over their shoulders, so that they can see its reflection. The fiction is that the father sees his child for the first time, which is evidently not the case, since he has in the modern Dutch fashion helped his wife during the delivery and has seen the child every day since. This fiction is mitigated by the fact that it is the couple which sees the reflection rather than the isolated father. Special water with five elements (*panchadhatu*) is thrown over the child and drips from its body on the couple that looks in the brass tray. The father cuts the hair of the child in three places on the correct side of its head (right side for boys, and left side for girls). This hair is caught in a flat bread, *roti*, by the child's aunt (mother's sister). She gets a sacrificial fee (*dakshina*) for her role in the performance. This covers her costs of coming to Zoetermeer from the North of Holland.

The second part of the ritual is the rite of shaving the baby's hair (*mundan samskar*). This is not done by a person of the barber caste, as in India, but by a cousin who gets a gift of uncooked food plus a fee of 50 Dutch guilders for his performance. There is some awareness of the dangers of this rite. The steel shaver is first worshipped; because of its dangerous connections with some planets, Tuesdays and Saturdays have to be avoided in this ritual.

The third part is the actual pacification of the planets. All kinds of deities are worshipped with the giving of food, fruits and flowers. Much attention is given, as in most rituals, to Hanuman, the monkey god. The pandit has brought a small image for the worship of Hanuman. The child is made pure by the pandit and gets a dot (*tilak*) on the forehead. After that a fire-sacrifice for the planets takes place. The fire is lighted in a pot which is commonly used in Holland for outdoor barbecues. The flat bread with the hair is offered in the fire. Then everyone stands to sing a devotional song for Vishnu, a fire-worship (*arati*) takes place accompanied by the blowing of the conch and beating of the gongs. The ritual proper ends with the giving of a part of the offered fruits and food as 'grace' (*prasad*) to the audience.

Before and during the ritual some of the women are already preparing the feast. This is certainly a major aspect of a ritual occasion. Without a meal the ritual would be meaningless to many of the participants. The men are served first by the women, who will only eat after the men have finished. The pandit eats together with the other men at the table. After the meal he is taken aside by the women who ask him to give the child a name. When he returns there is a moment of relaxed conversation on religious topics, such as the Ram story. In this case, the child's grandfather, a man in his seventies, shows a philosophical bent of mind and is in fact very knowledgeable on points of theology. Nevertheless the pandit is clearly always given final authority on these matters. When the pandit leaves, the occasion is over.

There are a few themes in the occasion which need some elucidation. In the first place, one of the main functions of the ritual is clearly to enhance the solidarity of a family. Family-members cannot be missed in crucial parts of the ritual. Often rituals are performed to highlight certain occasions such as birthdays of important family-members, and the success of rituals is always related to the attendance of significant others. What is striking is that the cousin plays the defiling role of barber and takes also the customary gift for his performance. The caste notion of pollution is in fact absent, but instead there is a notion that there is a danger involved in these activities. It would be hard to find someone outside the family willing to perform this role. Moreover, in the particular case described above, the pandit had to solve a quarrel between the child's father and his father. They had not seen each other for half a year, but the pandit had said that the ritual could not take place without participation of the grandfather. In this sense pandits play an important role in maintaining the relations between family-members. They also play a major part in arranging marriages, since they have good contacts in the community all over the country. Secondly, there is a question of the authenticity of the ritual. Hindustani Hindus in the Netherlands feel all kinds of uncertainties in their religious life. They fear that they have lost basic aspects of it in the process of migration and often feel that they do not understand their religion enough to explain it to outsiders. These outsiders have become more important in Holland, where Hindus are only a tiny, scattered minority.

The Dutch context imposes an anti-ritualistic discourse, heavily influenced by Calvinism, on Hindus, in which 'theological knowledge' and 'personal experience' are key-words. Basic instrumental aspects of the ritual, such as the warding off of evil and danger, have to be explained in devotional terms which are in fact only marginal to it. I have even the impression that devotional elements are imposed upon some rituals for this reason. All this is compounded by the fact that Hindus in the Netherlands have a very ambivalent relation with India. India is seen as the pure heartland of Hinduism, in which rituals are correctly performed and everyone knows what he is doing. Gurus are therefore brought from India to teach the lost souls what Hinduism really is and Hindustani people often go to India to see the 'real' thing. On the other hand, India is regarded as a totally corrupted society, mired in poverty. Its priests and gurus are often regarded as lecherous, money-grabbing people who are also extremely arrogant. This contradictory image of India as an object of admiration and disgust is produced by a major anxiety of Hindustani Hindus, that they have lost their religion's authenticity. This anxiety plays an important role in the Arya–Sanatani controversy about the 'true Hinduism'. It often boils down to the question of the ritual competence of Brahman priests who earn a living by their calling.

The authority of the Brahman priest is in various subtle ways brought to the fore in ritual performances. His knowledge of the Sanskrit verses, the *mantras*, and of the ritual actions create a difference between him and the sacrificer. The pandit is in control: he has to show what the sacrificer has to do and how he should do it. He can ridicule bad performance and order people around. The pandit has to be worshipped as a god on earth. At the same time, however, he depends for his livelihood on the payment of the sacrificer. Hindus often resent the power pandits have and especially resent having to pay them. As far as the pandit himself is concerned, if he is really knowledgeable, he may also feel some awkwardness in accepting gifts at some ritual occasions. In the ritual described above, the dangerous influence (*prabhav*) of the planet adheres to the gift given to the pandit. In this case the pandit was aware of that and said that he always asks on these occasions that money is given to the foundation for cancer research, so that he only takes a fee and not the dangerous gift. He told me that Brahmans in India were shocked when he informed them of the kinds of rituals in which he participated. The question of authenticity was important for him. He showed me a Sanskrit document from Benares in which he was accepted as a priest by a committee of Brahmans and asked me to translate it for him into Dutch.

Case 2: A discussion in The Hague

In 1987 a group of young Hindustani students founded a new cultural association with the aim of stimulating debate on cultural issues among representatives of different groups in the Hindustani community. In February 1988 it organized its first activity in the building of The Hague Hindustani welfare-association, Ekta Bhavan. The subject was 'Hinduism in the Netherlands' and speakers were asked to address the problem of religious education for the generation brought up in Holland. The event consisted of two parts, the first part being the performance of a fire-sacrifice (*hawan*) by a young Arya Samaj pandit; the second being short introductory talks on the second chapter of the *Bhagavad Gita* by the Arya Samaj pandit, by a Sanatani pandit and by a well-known high-school teacher of Sanatani persuasion, followed by a general discussion between these specialists and the audience. The audience of about a hundred people were welcomed by a young, confident girl in her twenties who pointed out that young Hindus had great difficulties in understanding their religion, because they did not have sufficient Hindi.

The first part was therefore an odd mixture between a ritual performance and a kind of ritual demonstration. The pandit performed the ritual on a platform with two members of the organizing committee as sacrificers. The audience watched it as in a theatre. The Pandit introduced himself as having studied in Delhi. He announced that he was going to explain as much as possible in Dutch, but that to explain everything would take too much time. He asked the audience to relax and concentrate on their breath.

Evidently, he had been influenced by the techniques of Transcendental Meditation if not by its theories. The Vedic *mantra* with which the ritual started was the famous one of 'This is not for me, but for Agni (the God of Fire).' The pandit interpreted it as meaning that the results of the sacrifice would accrue to the whole community. After he had finished the sacrifice he explained that there was no contradiction between ritual and science. Science had shown that many cells of the brain were practically unused and, secondly, that soundwaves had important effects on the brain. Vedic *mantras* and music had a great power. He compared this to a therapy for the removal of stones in the kidney by soundwaves which he had just undergone. As a real scientist he concluded that more research on all this had to be done. He also claimed that burning ghee had a salutary effect on body and mind.

After a break, in which *prasad* of the sacrifice was given to the audience, the second part started. The Arya pandit explained the Gita as an epic story with human heroes. The moral of the story could be found in the Vedas and the *Upanishads*. He was succeeded by the Sanatani pandit who addressed the audience in the typical traditional manner of exegesis (*katha*). He quoted various verses of the Sanskrit *Gita* and argued that its message was that one's duty is bound to one's position in society. He had, however, great difficulties with the Dutch language, so that much of his argument remained unclear. Finally, the teacher started in a patronizing way to address some of his former high-school students. According to him, we had to look at the life of Gandhi to understand the message of the *Gita*. This was followed by a discussion with an audience which was very eager to participate.

The first question came from an opponent of the Sanatani pandit who was the leader of a successful group of non-Brahman priests who had begun to perform Sanatani rituals in Holland. His aim clearly was to show that, though not a Brahman, he knew more than anyone else. He questioned the translations of crucial Sanskrit terms in Dutch, as given by the Arya and Sanatani pandits. Since there was no way to translate Sanskrit into Dutch, children had to learn Sanskrit and Hindi. Both pandits answered that Sanskrit had been translated into Hindi, so that there was no reason to assume that it could not be translated into Dutch. The only difficulty that they saw, however, was that the Sanskrit soundwaves were so powerful, that the ritual had to be done in Sanskrit with an explanation in Dutch. A lady in the audience who declared herself to be a regular patron of the Arya pandit commented on this point that the pandit would lose his concentration and the ritual its force, when everything had to be explained in Dutch. Without much of a transition a full-scale quarrel then arose about what kind of Hindi would be correct; the standard one of India or the Sarnami variant, spoken by Hindustanis. Everyone started accusing everyone else of linguistic incompetence till the chairman succeeded in by-passing the problem. Another point was raised by a member of the audience who asked why only Brahmans were thought to be able to perform the ritual correctly. The Arya pandit was of course happy with that question, but evaded an outright conflict with his Sanatani colleague who argued that the Hindustani were only a tiny minority of Hindus who were the bearers of a world civilization of which Brahmans all over the world were the principal leaders. The Sanatani pandit informed me in private after the meeting that Brahmans had power (*shakti*) and that even Aryas came to them when they were really ill.

The discussion continued with the interpretation of the *Gita*. A student of English argued that the *Gita* was a psychological novel and the high-school teacher agreed. He was, however, subsequently the object of a fierce attack, when someone commented that his hero Gandhi had been anti-Hindu. The Sanatani pandit opened the attack on the Aryas by submitting that the interpretation of the *Gita* by Dayanand, the founder of the Arya Samaj, had been entirely false. This again created an emotional atmosphere, so that the chairman had to intervene by closing the meeting. The role of the chairman was interesting. As a professional student leader he tried to force the speakers to come quickly to the point and intervened in what I considered to be an admirably direct way. The audience, however, objected that he was conducting the event as if he were a Dutchman. This was not the way Hindustanis should behave. It was absolutely unacceptable that such a young man dared to stop elder people when they, in an elaborate Hindustani manner, set out to state their point of view. This was a show of disrespect which also demonstrated how alienated these people were from their Hindustani background. This opinion was not only expressed by older people, but also by some of the young members of the audience.

The meeting left many people disappointed. The organizers felt that the specific problem of young Hindus who could not understand Hindi had not been addressed in a positive spirit and that all attention had been given to the old, disruptive issues of the community. The Aryas complained that they had been insulted. And the Sanatani pandit told the leader of the non-Brahman Sanatani priests that he was a son of a pig.

Conclusion

In the study of ritual we can distinguish between its content and its performance. Rituals convey cosmologies which classify human beings, nature and the supernatural. In that sense rituals have a meaning, or rather, meanings. These meanings are elaborated in theological speculations. It is evident that the *shraddha* and *Mul-shanti* rituals refer to complicated and often contradictory cosmologies. That these cannot always be explained by informants only shows that rituals are different from Platonic dialogues. Their meaning is, however, at some point always discussed, and at these occasions we see how changing contexts impinge on cosmological reflections. On the other hand, we should realize that rituals do not merely communicate cognitive meaning. They are performances which make use of various means of expression, such as music, dance and play. Ritual as performance evokes and channels the emotions of participants and has important effects on their bodies and minds. The interactions of performers, patrons and public as well as the larger social context produce the actual performances which differ from one another in important ways.

From the formal point of view rituals can be characterized by conventionality, condensation and repetition. These formal aspects make their continuity so tenacious. In Hindu ritual, as in many others, there is much emphasis on correct performance. Despite all the evidence of change and contingency, the performers try their hardest to exclude creative innovation. Rituals create an illusion of stable continuity and derive that from their authority.[9] Sanatan Dharm, the eternal religion, as well as its counterpart, the primeval religion of the Aryas, transcend history and individual vicissitudes. Changes in context are ideologically made irrelevant in relation to a ritual discourse about an authoritative, transcendental order of reality. The illusion of total fixedness is thus part of the message rituals try to convey and an effect of their formal aspects of conventionality and stereotype.

Ritual practice in the Dutch context produces a specific Hindu identity which differs from Hindu identity in North India, but also, to some extent, from the identity in Surinam. In Hindu ritual some understandings of that identity are catalysed and experienced. A major cultural problem which is constantly taken up in ritual performance is that of 'authenticity'. In the Dutch context this problem is strongly felt by Hindus who are constantly asked by their Dutch neighbours what kind of religion they practise. It has recently become even more pressing, since Hindus are trying to open separate elementary schools, so that they need to decide what picture of Hinduism they want to present in education. One way of addressing the problem is by taking India as a standard. India is nearer to Holland than is Surinam in some important respects. Hindus in Holland can more easily go to India on pilgrimage and see for themselves what they suppose to be 'authentic' Hinduism. They are also in contact with India, while staying in Holland, because they can bring Indian religious leaders to Holland. Indian gurus often make a tour to Europe in which they include Holland. The video boom has also made many Indian films with religious topics available for Hindustani consumption. The major problem in taking Indian Hinduism as a standard is, however, that this simple act does not solve the problem of which Indian Hinduism should provide the standards. Caste is not part of Hindustani social practice any more and it is ideologically rejected by everyone. Since religious practice in India is always in some way or another related to the rest of social practice, there is no way in which actual practice in India can be taken as a standard. The irony is that Surinamese Hinduism shows that Hindu culture is not confined to Indian society, while Surinamese Hindus keep referring to India as a standard. The ideology of the 'eternal religion' projects, as much as anthropological essentialism, an image of reality which transcends history and context. However, this ideology is not enforced by a Hindu church which centralizes and unifies discourses and practices, while defining the boundaries between true religion and heresy. The authority of Surinamese Hinduism rests on the competence of the Brahman priest who is the local standard of religious practice.

As we have seen, much of this authority rests on ritual competence and is reasserted in every ritual performance. According to many informants, there is a growing demand for effective ritual in Holland. Some Hindu rituals, such as the pacification of planets and Mother-Goddesses, have a clear instrumental aspect. Though I do not have economic details, there is some evidence that Hindu ritual has become big business in Holland. Again, lack of quantitive data means that we can only speculate about the reasons for such a development. Dutch society has specific rewards as well as problems for the Hindustani community. On the one hand there might be more money available for 'conspicuous consumption'; on the other hand, there might be the necessity to keep the dispersed family together through ritual occasions, or the emotional need to alleviate the anxieties imposed by the unfamiliar bureaucratic procedures of a society in which one belongs only to a tiny minority. Whatever the case might be, competent pandits are very much in demand.

The authority of the pandit is not without its ambiguities. As we have seen, it is under constant attack from the side of the Arya Samaj and in Holland this attack has been joined by non-Brahman priests of Sanatani persuasion. Moreover, they are constantly criticized for imputed low moral standards and rapacity. Hindus often have the feeling that they have to pay too much for the 'unseen results' of rituals. Pandits may also feel some uncertainties, when asked to perform the instrumental rituals for which they are paid so well. They are often at least to some extent aware of taking impure and dangerous substances with them, when accepting gifts in these rituals. Moreover, they do not always feel confident enough to perform the rituals which they are asked to perform. Some of them go to places in India, such as Benares, for special training by ritual experts, but are made even more uncomfortable than before because of the vast distance between the theories and practices which have become accepted as 'Sanathan Dharm' in the Caribbean, and the theories and practices prevalent in Benares. From this point of view they look at the growing demand for efficacious rituals with some apprehension. On the other hand, the severe competition among pandits on the ritual market makes it hard for anyone to refuse to perform rites which are much in demand.

Finally, the recent tendency among the laity to ask for straightforward theological elucidations of ritual practice often poses insurmountable problems for the theologically unsophisticated ritual specialists. Instrumental rituals have to be explained in devotional discourse. Otherwise they are considered to be 'crude' and 'backward'. Devotional discourse itself has to be translated into the Dutch language, of which the young Hindus often have a better grasp than the pandits. Every single statement of the authority is debatable and the debate is conducted in a way more and more unfamiliar to the pandit. Ritual performances have clearly become the battleground for newly emerging forms of Hinduism.

Notes

1 V. S. Naipaul, *The Enigma of Arrival* (London, 1987).

2 A. Appadurai, 'Theory in Anthropology: Centre and Periphery', in *Comparative Studies in Society and History*, Vol. 28, no. 2, 1986, pp. 356–61; A. Appadurai, 'Putting Hierarchy in its Place', in *Cultural Anthropology*, Vol. 3, no. 1, 1988, pp. 36–49.

3 P. van der Veer, 'Taming the ascetic: devotionalism in a Hindu ascetic order', in *Man* (NS), col. 22, no. 4, 1987, pp. 680–95.

4 G. Carter Bentley, 'Ethnicity and Practice', in *Comparative Studies in Society and History*, Vol. 29, no. 1, 1987, pp. 24–55.

5 H. Van Amersfoort, 'Hindostaanse Surinamese in Amsterdam', in *Miuwe West-Indische Gids*, Vol. 47, 1970, pp. 109–38.

6 C. Van der Burg and P. van de Veer, 'Pandits, Power and Profit', in *Ethnic and Racial Studies*, Vol. 9, no. 4, 1986, pp. 514–28.

7 R. Burghart, ed., *Hinduism in Great Britain* (London, 1987), pp. 201–24.

8 P. van der Veer, 'Religious therapies and their valuation among Surinamese Hindustani in The Netherlands', paper presented at the Conference on South Asian Communities Overseas, Oxford (Mansfield College), 26–28 March 1987.

9 M. Block, *From Blessing to Violence* (Cambridge, 1987).

Part III

Biography

CHAPTER 7 Cheddi Jagan: The writings of a visionary politician

Frank Birbalsingh

Cheddi Bharat Jagan was born on 22 March 1918, in Port Mourant, British Guiana. His parents had come as indentured labourers from India, and their meagre wages as sugar plantation workers provided funds to send their son, at the age of 18, to study dentistry in the United States. Young Jagan spent seven years in the US before returning home as a dentist and with his American wife Janet, who was to be a co-worker throughout his life. In 1947 he was elected to the Legislative Council, or Parliament of his homeland, where ultimate authority rested with the resident British governor. In 1953, under a new Constitution considered the most democratic in the history of Guiana up to that time, Dr Jagan's party – The People's Progressive Party (PPP) – won elections with a majority of 18 out of 24 seats. But after only 133 days, this PPP government was dismissed by the governor, and the Constitution suspended. Restrictions were placed on the movement of some PPP members, and Dr Jagan himself was jailed for six months when he broke his restriction order. Dr Jagan's PPP won fresh elections in 1957, and again in 1961. Finally, in 1964, the PPP lost elections held under a system of proportional representation. Between 1964 and 1992 they formed the official opposition in Guyana.

Dr Jagan's political activities, especially in 1953, earned him fame (or infamy) as a colonial politician. To many Asians and Africans, he was a champion of fellow colonized people, fighting for liberation from British imperialists. To some Western nations, he was a sinister, communist agitator. But Dr Jagan's activities as a politician tend to conceal the fact that he has also produced countless booklets, pamphlets, papers, articles and speeches, in addition to four books. This body of writing is notable for at least two reasons: it provides a record of Guianese political issues and events by someone who played a central role in them; and it reflects a Third World politician's vision of international affairs from the time of Nehru, Nasser and Kennedy to the present day.

Dr Jagan's first major publication, *Forbidden Freedom*,[1] deals with the circumstances of his government in 1953. The theme of the book is the freedom which was forbidden to the Guianese people when British troops were sent to enforce the removal of the popularly elected PPP government. *Forbidden Freedom* outlines the aims and policies of the PPP:

> The PPP is a broad alliance of all progressive forces that are struggling for the freedom and independence of British Guiana and the social and economic well being of its inhabitants.

This statement reflects the visionary idealism which inspired Dr Jagan and his party in the early 1950s. The PPP convinced most sections of the Guianese population that it offered the best hope in their fight against a common enemy – British imperialism; in the process, there emerged a degree of national unity which has never been attained in Guyana since.

Dr Jagan makes no secret of the fact that his government consciously set out to redress what it considered as abuses inherited by a former slave-owning, plantation society. Political reforms were sought in many areas: 'ordinary people' were to be appointed to government boards and committees; and the rights of tenant farmers were to be protected by law. In economic matters, the rentals paid by foreign mining companies were to be increased, and efforts made to re-impose on sugar planters taxes which the previous administration had repealed. A wide variety of other measures were also contemplated: the fees of government doctors were to be revised 'to help the poor'; 'people's scholarships' were initiated to make university-level education available to more young people; and the administration of schools by Christian denominations was to be changed to accommodate large sections of the population that were non-Christian.

But instead of being readily embraced as democratic, these and other measures of the PPP government were regarded with suspicion. Many people feared revolution, and they thought their fears justified by such actions of the government as the decision not to send representatives during the Queen's visit to Jamaica in 1953. It may be that this decision can be defended on grounds of saving money, as Dr Jagan says; but like many other similar actions, it was taken as proof that his government was anti-British, communist and subversive. This fear of communist subversion was given by Sir Alfred Savage, the governor, as his main reason for calling in British troops.

In *Forbidden Freedom*, Dr Jagan appears bewildered by the governor's reaction to his government's policies. After listing his government's programme of 'progressive' measures, he continues with an earnest, questioning tone of having well-intentioned plans mysteriously aborted:

> Look again at this programme. Is it not the kind of programme for which any progressive person in Britain would give his vote? Does it indicate bloodshed, arson, totalitarian rule? Or does it indicate a desire to help people who sorely need help?

> Some of its provisions have origins in the most 'respectable' of countries. Our local government reforms came from the United Kingdom, our Labour Relations Bill from the USA, our land law from Puerto Rico, an American colony.

Dr Jagan's tone of wrongful victimization is persuasive. At the same time, one wonders at the absence of any awareness that his 'progressive' measures could be misunderstood or misinterpreted. Dr Jagan is so convinced by the self-evident altruism of his policies, that he cannot imagine they would fail to convince others. Whether his conviction is the result of visionary idealism or naiveté, it is a curious approach for someone dealing with the complex and volatile reactions of an electorate experiencing universal adult suffrage for the first time.

Dr Jagan's next book, *The West On Trial*[2] describes the author's childhood, early education, studies abroad, and subsequent political career up to the end of his third administration. Most of the book is devoted to the period between 1945 and 1965, when Guiana was transformed from a nondescript British Caribbean colony to one which, soon after the successful Cuban revolution under Fidel Castro, began to attract the attention of the Kennedy administration in the US. Many factors contributed to this transformation. One factor, ironically, was Dr Jagan's contribution in raising the political awareness of his countrymen. In 1953, as we have seen, Dr Jagan's PPP had the support of the large majority of Guianese people. In 1955, the party split into two factions, one led by Dr Jagan and the other by Mr L. F. S. Burnham.[3] This split gave rise to a divisive and chaotic atmosphere which, during Dr Jagan's régime of 1961 to 1964, produced strikes, riots and much loss of life. It was at this point that the British introduced proportional representation, resulting in victory for a coalition government led by Mr Burnham and his faction of the PPP, which had been renamed the People's National Congress (PNC). *The West on Trial* recounts all these events within an international framework that divided the world into two spheres, one of free enterprise capitalism led by the US, and the other socialism or communism led by the USSR. This is why President Kennedy feared the possibility of an independent communist Guyana, like Cuba, giving the USSR undue influence in a region traditionally regarded as the 'backyard' of America.

The West On Trial also considers the social and economic implications necessarily interwoven in the political affairs that it recounts. Dr Jagan untangles the web of corporate scheming by which foreign mining companies from Canada and the US exploited Guianese mineral and labour resources. He shows how these bauxite companies manipulated prices while enjoying low taxes and royalties that enabled them to make huge profits. Until 1961 all Guianese bauxite was shipped abroad for processing, and the Guianese bauxite worker was paid less than one-third the wages of his counterpart in the US. Dr Jagan summarizes the effect of such exploitation:

> The aluminium monopoly relegated to British Guiana the role of primary producer of the raw material, bauxite. It was only in 1961 that a small alumina plant was constructed. With a price structure of about $10 per ton for bauxite, $70 for alumina and $500 for aluminium in 1963 (expressed in round figures in US dollars) there was added more than a ten-fold increase in value in the reduction of bauxite into aluminium. All of this increased value accrued to persons and companies resident abroad in one form or another – wages, salaries, purchases, insurance, interest and profits.

Dr Jagan's summary is supported by evidence drawn from a variety of sources including scholarly works, journalistic reports and government records. These sources are admittedly selective, for Dr Jagan does not pretend to be objective. He has an ideological axe to grind. No wonder his writing is imbued with an urgent sense of mission, and a passionate commitment to confront abuses, redress wrongs, and promote what he regards as greater justice.

Most of the second half of *The West On Trial* is taken up by an account of the circumstances leading to the failure of the PPP in the 1964 elections. This part of the book illustrates one of the central themes of Dr Jagan's writing: that the gradual decline of British colonial power and the corresponding rise of American influence, following the Second World War, meant the hardline imposition of a world-wide, anti-communist American foreign policy that entailed the active 'containment' or repression of radical, revolutionary, nationalist, socialist or reformist movements in the Caribbean, Latin America, and indeed all over the world. Dr Jagan argues that it was the collusion of local and international forces, fostered by this hysterical atmosphere of anti-communism in the US, that engineered the imposition of proportional representation in 1964, with the intention of bringing together two Guianese parties, whose joint numbers would defeat the PPP. The theory was that the ostensibly democratic socialist PNC, led by Forbes Burnham, and the capitalist United Force (UF), led by Peter d'Aguiar,[4] could form a coalition government that would be non-communist, and keep the allegedly communist PPP from power. By Dr Jagan's account, the plan achieved total success.

According to Dr Jagan, the actions (real and imaginary) of his 1953 administration had alienated the support, not only of the conservative British government of Sir Winston Churchill, but of the British Labour Party and Trades Union Congress which were regarded as natural allies of a young socialist party like the PPP. More than that, their 1953 débâcle made the PPP lose the support of fellow West Indian leaders in Jamaica, Barbados and Trinidad. It is also claimed that some Afro-Caribbean leaders showed a preference for Mr Burnham over Dr Jagan. To these foreign 'enemies' must be added Mr Burnham's PNC, Mr D'Aguiar's UF, the entrenched colonial establishment in Guiana, the Manpower Citizen's Association,[5] and other social or religious groups like the Catholic Church. The disturbances encounterd by Dr Jagan's régime, between 1961 and 1964, are presented as the combined result of all these factors orchestrated by the devilish machinations of the American Central Intelligence Agency.

Despite its somewhat paranoiac flavour of victimization through conspiracy, Dr Jagan's story appears generally plausible, for example, his account of why Harold Wilson disagreed with proportional representation for Guiana when he was leader of the British Opposition in 1963, then supported it after the Labour Party came to power in 1964. Dr Jagan's explanation is that the British government was under strong pressure from the US not to grant independence to Guiana while he was in power. Hence the 1963 conference which was expected to set a date for Guianese independence, simply put the matter off, because of Dr Jagan's presence as leader of the government. But once Mr Burnham was safely installed as Prime Minister, in 1964, independence for Guyana followed.

In *The West On Trial* Dr Jagan justifies his policies by unwavering commitment to the cause he represents:

> In my early political career (1945–1953) I had taken a radical stand – pro-working class and pro-socialist. Had it not been for this militant radicalism, distinct from the moderate line of the Labour Party, the racist line of the League of Coloured People and the East Indian Association, there would have been neither the raised political understanding of the Guianese people nor in such a short time our remarkable 1953 electoral victory. Having preached to the workers the gospel of scientific socialism, I could not somersault. The 'art' of deception is a 'quality' I find detestable and difficult to practise. Had I taken this path, I have no doubt the workers would regard it as a betrayal of trust and treat me with the same contempt their one-time supporters came to feel for Leigh Richardson of British Honduras, Norman Manley of Jamaica, Grantley Adams of Barbados and Albert Gomes of Trinidad. (pp. 395–6)

This is the language of a visionary or mystic expressing unshakeable doctrinal belief. The cause of the workers is sacred, and Dr Jagan brings to it the righteous zeal and commitment of a missionary.

Dr Jagan's commitment, however, is not an unmixed blessing. Although morally admirable, it seems to invite self-victimization. The example of Harold Wilson's *volte-face* has already been mentioned. There was a similar incident earlier with the Guianese lawyer P. A. Cummings. When Cummings charged striking Canadian seamen high fees on the grounds that their union was wealthy, Dr Jagan lost his temper because he 'could not understand how anyone purporting to be a labour leader could take such an attitude' (p. 131). Again, Dr Jagan could not understand Mr Burnham's objections to the PPP budget of 1962, when the budget benefited the urban working class that supported Mr Burnham's party. The fact that Mr Burnham might be motivated by selfish political gain, or Mr Cummings by selfish financial gain, and Harold Wilson by the unsentimental demands of Realpolitik runs against the grain of Dr Jagan's missionary commitment. He is inhibited from anticipating the nimble manoeuvrings and expedient shifts of most of the politicians with whom he has to deal. The result is that he only comes to recognise their devious plots, subterfuges and alliances after the fact. This is one reason why, since 1964, his writing appears as one long record of disappointment, betrayal, failure and victimization.

Dr Jagan's attitude may be better understood if we remember that it originates in a mid-century context, when Cold War strategies dominated the international scene, and a process of decolonization was bringing former colonies mainly from Asia, Africa and the Caribbean into the calculations of Cold War strategists. At the same time, leaders from the former colonies, for example, Prime Minister Nehru of India, President Nasser of Egypt, and President Sukarno of Indonesia sought to resist entanglement in the diplomatic web of the Cold War by espousing neutrality. But even in those early days, when the post-colonial world was just emerging into international focus, there were signs that strict neutrality was impossible, that the decline of European imperialism was an illusion, and that formal imperial withdrawal did not entail a parallel dismantling of economic and other structures that, for more than four centuries, had sustained Western empires in Asia, Africa, the Caribbean and the Americas. It is evident from his writing that Dr Jagan's political awareness was nurtured in this context of the international shift from colonialism to neo-colonialism, and the experiences of leaders like Dr Mossadegh of Iran, and President Nasser of Egypt, whose efforts to assert post-colonial nationalism were crushed by imperial overlords, who had given up their former titles, but not their power. The similarity between the career of Dr Jagan and leaders like Dr Mossadegh and President Nasser derives from a rather innocent post-colonial optimism which inspired such leaders in the 1950s, before the full working of the Western neo-colonial apparatus became well enough known to expose the futility of their innocent faith in the effectiveness of Western parliamentary traditions in post-colonial affairs.

Dr Jagan's third book, *The Caribbean Revolution*,[6] illustrates the working of this apparatus through speeches made between the 1940s and 1970s. Subjects include the controversy over West Indian Federation in the 1950s, issues of the Caribbean Free Trade Agreement (CARIFTA) and the Caribbean Common Market (CARICOM), the February revolt in Trinidad, and strategies of global imperialism in Third World countries. Whatever their subject, Dr Jagan's speeches illustrate common themes and a common outlook: the problems of Guyana and the whole Caribbean are caused by colonialism and imperialism, for which the best solution is the gospel of 'scientific socialism' or Marxism-Leninism. These problems are presented within an international context, implying a world-view that is catholic and principled, neither self-serving nor petty. This is seen in 'February Revolt', for example, which discusses the revolt by a regiment of soldiers in Trinidad on 29 April 1970. The revolt was eventually put down with help from Venezuela, the US and Britain; but Dr Jagan's examination of its historical background and possible causes takes in the interests of peoples in the whole Caribbean region. While blame is squarely levelled against policies of the Trinidad Prime Minister, Dr Eric Williams,[7] Dr Jagan links the causes of the revolt to similar conditions in the Dominican Republic, Anguilla, Antigua, Curaçao, Surinam, Montserrat, Jamaica, Guadeloupe and Guyana. Thus, the author's opinion of Dr Williams is not based on narrow, petty, or self-serving grounds. He praises Dr Williams for his scholarly work as an historian, but implies that he succumbed to 'the impermanence of racism as a political tool' (p. 122), a charge which he also levels against 'Burnham's racist neo-colonialist régime'. At the same time, Mr Burnham is paid the dubious compliment of possessing 'greater demagogic skill' (p. 122) than Dr Williams, and the ability to employ 'leftist phraseology' (p. 122) with ease.

Dr Jagan's reference to Dr Williams and Mr Burnham invites comparison with the careers and writing of two politicians who were his exact contemporaries. Dr Williams and Mr Burnham both had university training in the arts or humanities. Dr Williams did his PhD at Oxford University, and is respected for his scholarly works on West Indian history, while Mr Burnham earned academic and legal qualifications before entering practice as a lawyer, and winning admiration for his oratorical skills. By contrast, Dr Jagan trained as a dentist, and is a complete autodidact so far as his knowledge of history, economics and politics is concerned. His self-education began in the US during the Second World War when he was a dental student, and when he read the works of colonial leaders like Gandhi and Nehru, and the writings of Karl Marx. From then on, Dr Jagan read informally what he could. His writings reflect these varied sources and their informal and popular, rather than academic origins. His books, speeches and essays derive from the interest of someone who, inspired by pure faith, spends a lifetime restlessly collecting and assimilating information, quotations, references, and arguments which justify his faith.

Mr Burnham, with advantages of a better educational background and natural oratorical gifts, scarely wrote anything during a political career that lasted for more than thirty years. Such were Mr Burnham's skills as a speaker, that he appears to have left few written versions of his speeches. In *A Destiny to Mould*[8] a collection of speeches, statements and broadcasts compiled by two of Mr Burnham's followers, the compilers state

> Prime Minister Forbes Burnham very seldom writes out his speeches and as a result a great many of his speeches have to be culled from tape recordings. (p. XXXV)

This may explain why the writing in *A Destiny to Mould* exhibits oratorical grace, dramatic flair, and smooth phrasing, which give an impression of polish, dexterously applied, to conceal lack of real substance. By contrast, Dr Jagan saturates the reader with facts which may be less palatable than Mr Burnham's smooth speeches, but are more substantial and convincing.

On the whole, Dr Williams's writing consists of scholarly works of formal history, rather than the free-ranging, topical commentaries and confessional memoirs that we get from Dr Jagan. Dr Williams's *Inward Hunger*, however, tackles the genre of political autobiography, as exemplified in *The West on Trial*. There is much in *Inward Hunger* that comes from the pen of the professional historian; for example, the ease and scope of reference to works of history, philosophy and literature, often written in languages other than English. However, *Inward Hunger* contains surprising examples of colloquial idiom, as when Dr Williams describes the efforts of the Caribbean Commission to keep him out of Trinidad before the start of his political career:

> Then they tried to keep me away from Trinidad. Now that I was back in Trinidad they tried to get me back to Washington. What was I, a blasted football of the commission? Who the bloody hell were the Commission anyway? I let them have it. (132)

This idiom is sometimes combined with a recurring note of personal assertiveness, as in Chapter 32, where Dr Williams describes himself as the only person who could write a history of his homeland. When he claims to have written *The History of the People of Trinidad and Tobago* in only one month, his boastful self-congratulation is in direct contrast to the earnest and sympathy-winning record of selfless service that is found in *The West on Trial*.

In the end, sympathy is probably the chief response evoked by Dr Jagan's writing. This is reinforced by his fourth book, *The Caribbean – Whose Backyard?*[9] which sums up the views and opinions of his previous writings, and places them within a coherent, general argument about global imperialism being managed and orchestrated principally by the US. After a brief, historical outline which establishes a pattern of US imperialistic domination of Latin America and the Caribbean, Dr Jagan shows how this imperialism, at first restricted to a region believed to be the American 'backyard', spreads out after the Second World War, when the US took over the 'responsibility' for former European empires, in order to 'contain' the perceived threat of communism all over the world. One cannot help being awed by the variety of information Dr Jagan amasses. The details, facts, figures, names and statistics which he has gathered, stored, organized and expressed in the thirteen chapters of *The Caribbean – Whose Backyard?* represent a lifetime's accumulation, encyclopaedic in proportion, of material assiduously collected from books, journals, official documents, newspapers and other publications.

From the enunciation of President Monroe's (in)famous 'doctrine' on 2 December 1823, to the Truman doctrine, Dr Jagan argues that American foreign policy in the Caribbean has always been intensely chauvinistic and imperialistic. In support, he cites examples of US imperialism during the time he has been active in politics:

> From aid to the fascists in Greece and Turkey it was a 'short' step to aid for Chiang Kai-Chek (*sic*) in China, the French in Indochina, the British in Malaya (now Malaysia) and the Dutch in Indonesia; intervention in Korea in 1950; the overthrow of the Romulo Gallegos government in Venezuela (1948), the Mossadegh government in Iran (1953), the PPP government in British Guiana (1953), the Arbenz government in Guatemala (1954), the attempted overthrow of the Nasser government in Egypt (1956); the Bay of Pigs invasion of Cuba (1961), the overthrow of the Patrice Lumumba government in Congo in 1961, the removal of the Goulart government of Brazil and the PPP government of British Guiana (1964) and in Vietnam (1965–1973); the overthrow of the Sukarno government of Indonesia (1965), the Nkrumah government of Ghana (1966), the Allende government in Chile (1973), the Makarios government of Cyprus (1974) and others. (p. 52)

The list illustrates Dr Jagan's method of marshalling superabundant details, often in voluminous lists, that win the reader's conviction by sheer saturation. Critical exactness is less important to this method than undiscriminating volume. But Dr Jagan's method makes American imperialism too uniformly successful, and Caribbean victimization correspondingly too convenient.

It is not that one disagrees with Dr Jagan. His documentation, for example, of CIA efforts to install Mr Burnham as winner of the 1964 elections is persuasive. Using plausible journalistic evidence, he shows how President Kennedy forced Mr Macmillan, the British Prime Minister at the time, to refuse independence to Guiana during the 1961–64 period. At the same time, he quotes a special assistant[10] to President Kennedy who advises the President that

> an independent British Guiana under Burnham (if Burnham will commit himself to a multi-racial policy) would cause us many fewer problems than an independent British Guiana under Jagan. (*Backyard*, p. 83)

He also links American activities in Guiana in 1962–64 with the pattern of destabilization of Chile in 1973, and in Jamaica in 1980. But these claims of successful American Machiavellianism, and the repeated failure of its victims, eventually become routine and mechanical, and the reader loses interest in ever-lengthening lists of traitors, opportunists, cynics and apparently wicked people who succeed not despite, but because of their wickedness. The suspicion therefore emerges that Dr Jagan's committed or 'moral' approach, within the real circumstances of twentieth-century Caribbean politics, may itself invite self-victimization.

It may be that Dr Jagan's own political nurturing in the Cold War years of bi-polar, superpower diplomacy, has left a Manichaean stamp on his political thinking. This is the consequence of operating within an inflexibly dualistic framework of capitalism versus communism, of bad versus good. His self-evaluation in *The West On Trial* appears to confirm this:

> It would seem therefore that the two courses open to politicians like myself are to move to the right or to the left. A movement to the right means a betrayal of the working class, confusion of the workers, loss of their confidence and ultimate rejection by them. A move to the left can mean overthrow by reactionary elements as has happened to such people as Romulo Gallegos, Arbenz, Quadros, Arosemena, Goulart, Bosch and myself. It seems that which ever way one moves, one is caught. But since there is a choice for me there is only one road – the road to the left. This is playing true to my own conscience, keeping faith with the future, and moving with the mainstream of history. (p. 401)

Dr Jagan's choice left him out of power for 28 years until his party was finally re-elected in October 1992.

So far as moral steadfastness and integrity are concerned, Dr Jagan certainly played true to his conscience, and his ensuing feat of regaining political power in Guiana after twenty-eight years is utterly without parallel in the Caribbean and rare anywhere. Its closest parallel is the achievement of Nelson Mandela who, during the almost identical period 1964 to 1990 suffered continuous imprisonment, yet maintained a lofty sense of idealism and integrity that steadfastly rejected compromise with his racist jailors. But whereas Mandela's integrity had a world-wide network of support that eventually helped in forcing his white South African jailors to capitulate, it is doubtful whether, without the collapse of the Soviet Union and the consequent disappearance of the American fear of communism, Dr Jagan and his party would have been re-elected. Even without the Soviet Union or the Cold War, it required a coalition of Dr Jagan's PPP with another political group – the Civic – and the supervisory role of the Carter Centre, including the active participation of ex-president Carter himself, to secure relatively free and fair elections. At any rate, Dr Jagan's superhuman integrity was finally vindicated when he became president of Guyana in 1992, and he is now in a position to revive his nation from the ravages of PNC mismanagement and corruption that reduced Guyana to a rank only above Haiti as the poorest country in the western hemisphere.

If anyone can revive Guyana it is he. Even his enemies acknowledge that, quite apart from political ideology, it requires something as potent and durable as Dr Jagan's integrity first to cleanse the Augean pollution that has clogged up the engines of Guyanese government and society under the PNC, before a national revival can materialize. In this respect, it is interesting that whereas, in 1953, Dr Jagan was inspired by Marxist ideology to unite the nation, he is playing down the more doctrinaire aspects of this ideology in his current programme of national revival. There is no doubt that the changed circumstances in Guyana and the world require fresh approaches to government, and there is also no doubt that these approaches will be nourished by the same integrity and patriotism that enabled Dr Jagan to persevere against all odds for nearly three decades and prevail in the end. This achievement as a political leader places him with Gandhi and Mandela in the very first rank of heroes who fought against colonialism in English-speaking territories during this century.

So far as Dr Jagan's writing is concerned, its relevance is assured by virtue of its closely observed, historical record of Guyanese, Caribbean and international affairs during the past four decades. If this record does not reflect the organized, critical analysis of original sources that we find, for example, in Dr Williams's *Capitalism and Slavery*[11] and in Walter Rodney's *A History of the Guyanese Working People*[12] it enlists a doggedly energetic, meticulously cataloguing intellect, and an encyclopaedic grasp of political affairs that is unmatched by any other politician in the English-speaking Caribbean. Among writers of the region, in fact, only C. L. R. James matches Dr Jagan's grasp of Caribbean and international politics since the Second World War. But James was not a politician. To some extent, therefore, the quality of Dr Jagan's writing has to be measured by its consistency with his own beliefs and policies as a practising politician. By this measurement it surely emerges as the work of a great man.

Dr Jagan's greatness is evident not only in his writing, but in his total achievement as a politician, writer and a man. As someone whose plantation origins offered no advantages by way of material comforts, educational opportunity, or general incentive, Dr Jagan did exceptionally well to qualify as a dentist, which could have enabled him to live in relative affluence as a member of the professional classes in Guyana. But his sense of the injustice suffered by his countrymen under British colonial rule drew him inexorably into a political career which turned him into a champion against American imperialism before fellow travellers such as Fidel Castro or Ho Chi Minh had scarcely made their first move against the same enemy. His first great political achievement is his valiant struggle between 1947 and 1953, when he single-handedly defied an entire colonial establishment in the Legislative Council of Guiana, and in 1953 provided the Guianese people with their first opportunity of demonstrating a united national will. But his crowning political achievement remains his unyielding resistance to PNC demagogy and corruption over 28 years and eventual triumph in October 1992.

The West on Trial remains Dr Jagan's best writing because it blends intimate, autobiographical details and an impassioned study of public affairs into a narrative of compelling authenticity, powerful conviction and reasonable hope. Dr Jagan's all-encompassing mastery of historical or international affairs, and his persuasive linking of Guyanese or Caribbean events to these affairs is another feature of his writing which may be seen, for example, in his comments on Indian indentureship:

> It was a hybrid of slavery and feudalism and was perhaps unique to British owned colonies. In fact, what was being witnessed was a swift transformation from slavery to capitalism in the Caribbean, particularly in the British territories. The Caribbean transformation from communism to slavery to semi-feudalism to capitalism was really a telescoped version of the socio-economic development and transformation of Europe which took place over a longer historical period. (*Backyard*, p. 20)

One will be hard put to find a description of Indian indenture that is more succinct and comprehensive than this.

Since all aspects of Dr Jagan's career are obviously interdependent, his greatness has more to do with his moral qualities than with his achievements in politics and writing. These qualities have sustained him, unbroken, despite the grievous and repeated disappointments that he describes in his writing. Perhaps his enemies will regard such steadfastness as mere stubbornness, a blind allegiance to rigidly dogmatic belief. But there is a difference between blind dogmatism that seeks power at all costs, and selfless devotion that risks everything out of high-minded principle. For it is moral principle, flawless in its altruism, that first enabled Dr Jagan to bring political maturity to Guyana, then energized his writing over forty years, as part of his struggle to restore democracy to his native land. And now that democracy has at last been achieved, it is moral principle that will again serve to cleanse pollution from the engines of the nation and set them working smoothly for the future.

Notes

In this chapter I am concerned with Dr Jagan as a *writer*, not as a politician. I have therefore not dealt with the complex issue of his Marxist politics.

1 London, 1954–55.

2 London, 1966. Revised and republished in Berlin, 1972, 1975, 1980.

3 L. F. S. Burnham (1923–85), of Creole extraction, was originally a member of Dr Jagan's PPP, and served as Minister of Education in the 1953 government. Mr Burnham was Prime Minister of Guyana from 1964 to his death.

4 Mr Peter d'Aguiar was a businessman of Portuguese extraction. His political career was short-lived.

5 The Man Power Citizen's Association was a Trade Union that represented sugar plantation workers from the 1920s. From Dr Jagan's point of view, this union became infiltrated by the interests of plantation owners. Dr Jagan supported a rival union, the Guyana Agricultural Worker's Union.

6 Prague, 1979.

7 Dr Eric Williams (1911–82) was Prime Minister of Trinidad and Tobago from 1956 to 1981. He is the author of *Capitalism and Slavery* (London, 1964), *History of the People of Trinidad and Tobago* (London, 1964) and *Inward Hunger: The Education of a Prime Minister* (London, 1969).

8 London, 1970.

9 Guyana, 1984.

10 According to Dr Jagan, Arthur J. Schlesinger, Jr. apologised for giving President Kennedy mistaken advice. This was years later, long after the Burnham or PNC regime had shown itself to be incompetent and corrupt.

11 See note 7.

12 W. Rodney, *A History of the Guianese Working People 1881–1905* (Baltimore, 1981).

Part IV

Early history

CHAPTER 8 Indian Government policy towards indentured labour migration to the sugar colonies

Basdeo Mangru

Indian Government policy during the eighty years of indentured emigration to the Caribbean (1838–1917) was influenced largely by the *laissez-faire* theory of administration then current in Europe. Its main features were minimum government interference in the pursuit of individual economic interests and few restrictions on the movement of goods, labour and capital. It was this belief in labour mobility and individual rights which permitted and sustained the export of indentured labour overseas for such a prolonged period. Until the beginning of the twentieth century the British administration in India saw no cogent economic reasons to prevent or curtail the free flow of labour to parts of the Empire where the demand seemed insatiable and wages comparatively higher. All the government needed to do was to ensure by legislative enactments that there were sufficient precautions to prevent fraud and coercion during recruitment, that depot accommodation and medical superintendence were satisfactory, that the physical conditions *en route* to the recipient colonies conformed to accepted safety and sanitary standards and that the interests of intending emigrants were protected against planter tyranny and neglect.

Once the authorities were satisfied that emigration arrangements in India were adequate and that colonial legislation provided, in theory at least, sufficient guarantees to labour, they were prepared to facilitate recruitment. The Bengal Government succinctly summarised these policies: 'So long as the Indian labourer fully understands the prospects before him, and the colonial authorities provide for his protection by proper legislation and efficient supervision, the Lieutenant-Governor will always be ready to insist on all due facilities being afforded to the colonial agents here for the discharge of their important duties.'[1]

Government policies on emigration were enforced largely by emigration acts promulgated from time to time by the central and provincial governments. Prior to 1837 the only control which the Government of India sought to exercise was the requirement that intending emigrants appear before a magistrate to satisfy him that they were leaving voluntarily, that they knew their destination and understood their contractual obligations. In 1837 a Law Commission which examined the question of the degree of protection which emigrants should enjoy made certain recommendations which formed the core of the Indian Emigration Act V of that year. Applied originally to Mauritius and British Guiana, the Act embodied regulations regarding recruitment, transportation and the determination of contracts. Between 1837 and 1864 when the laws and regulations were consolidated within a single framework, 21 acts were passed. They were concerned primarily with matters of administrative detail relating to labour protection during recruitment, depot accommodation and the voyage overseas.[2]

The act of 1864 was a comprehensive document geared to systematize recruiting operations in the *mufassal* (country districts), remedy existing defects, define the multifarious duties of the Protector and legalize the several colonial depots. The most important aspect of the Act was the circumscription of the recruiter's activities by confining him to a single agency and requiring him to wear a conspicuous badge naming in English and Indian languages the agency to which he was attached. The Act required him to obtain a recruiting licence and to appear with his recruits before the district magistrate, who would determine the circumstances of recruitment and explain the contractual terms.[3] These various enactments were again consolidated in 1883 following a spate of recruiting irregularities, particularly the enlisting of labour in one district and registering in another, which suggested that the protective provisions of the law were inadequate. Amendments to the 1883 Act were made from time to time and these were consolidated by Act XVII of 1908 but the government's emigration policy of benevolent neutrality remained largely unaltered. It was only in 1910 that a major policy change occurred when the Hardinge administration assumed power to prohibit emigration to any country where Indians did not receive satisfactory treatment. This significant step paved the way for the eventual abolition of indenture in 1920.

The Government of India could intervene directly in the emigration process at three levels, namely, if irregularities were detected during recruitment, if health and safety precautions in transit were persistently violated or ignored and if colonial legislation seemed to coerce labour or unilaterally discard contractual guarantees. The degree of government intervention was governed largely by experience and the persuasive force of planter pressure. I propose to examine first the effectiveness of policies designed to protect the interest of labour and the ways in which they were in practice obstructed during these three stages in the emigration process and secondly, to analyse the reasons for the change in emigration policy.

Government policies in relation to labour recruitment were designed to ensure that legitimate means were employed, that intending emigrants were not deceived or coerced, that they knew their destination and understood the contents of the contract. Once the emigrant knew his position, the notion was that he should act on a rational calculation of his own economic interests and if he did the system would function to the benefit of all. But as emigration progressed, government intervention became necessary, especially as the majority of emigrants were largely illiterate and needed protection. As specific abuses or major defects surfaced, the government correspondingly drafted rules and regulations, often on an *ad hoc* basis, to remedy them.

In the early period of colonial emigration when expatriate Calcutta firms enlisted labour, such irregularities as kidnapping, substitution, misrepresentation, secret embarkation and illegal confinement were prevalent. The active competition generated by the establishment of several West Indian colonial agencies in the late 1850s produced other abuses, especially the interception by rival agents of batches of intending emigrations *en route* to Calcutta and decoying them through bribes and deception to other agencies. Very often recruits were confined in private dwellings and secretly conveyed to the depot the evening before a vessel was scheduled to sail. The most prevalent abuse emerging from the mid-1870s and continually throughout the indenture period was the unlawful practice of recruiting labour in one district and registering it in an adjoining one. Intimidation of women, keeping then under *bandish* (forced detention), confiscating their jewellery and impairing their caste were other recruiting irregularities which were buttressed by the unlawful but customary practice of employing *arkatis* (unlicensed recruiters) to establish the first contact with unsophisticated villages.[4] This method of enlistment by unlicensed subordinates formed the backbone of recruiting operations and was the principal reason for the host of irregularities which permeated the system.

Despite systematic efforts (imprisonment of recruiters, cancellation of licences, heavy court fines) to rid the recruiting system of excrescences, there was hardly any substantial improvement during indenture. The Lord Sanderson Commission of 1910 found the recruiting system 'unsatisfactory', pointing out that barely 25 per cent of recruits could discriminate between the various importing colonies or had a reasonable idea of working and living conditions in them.[5] Socio-economic conditions in India posed a formidable obstacle to the enforcement of government policies on recruitment. Generally Indian villagers, largely poor and unsophisticated, were recruited in an unfamiliar environment and often in a hopeless economic condition, having been unable to find employment. It was at this psychological moment that they were entrapped with euphoric promises and money advances and threatened with confiscation of their personal possessions if they subsequently decided against emigration. Women in particular were vulnerable and often 'too bewildered and terrified to explain to the district magistrates the circumstances of their recruitment'.[6]

But it was the pressure exerted by the colonial plantocracy which provided the most effective obstacle to government policies. When their protests became vocal the Indian authorities tended to make concessions or even abandon vital legislation despite its acknowledged necessity, as evident in the Emigration Bill of 1883. The bill contained two vital provisions designed to suppress recruiting malpractices by fixing the salary of the sub-agent, which was linked to the numbers despatched to the colonies, and by circumscribing the movements of the recruiter so that his activities could be effectively monitored. The former was designed to bring the sub-agent under the purview of the law by subjecting him to penal sanctions for misconduct; the latter, to prevent the recruiter from escaping prosecution by merely shifting his operations elsewhere. These vital measures, which would have minimized irregularities, were stifled at birth as strong colonial opposition, principally on economic grounds, forced the Indian Government to abandon them.[7] The main explanation for this apparent contradiction in policy seemed to be that the Indian Government had recognized very early the economic benefits of a brief colonial sojourn and was thus disposed to grant concessions when legislation seemed to impede recruiting operations. An Indian Government Resolution of 1883 declared in unmistakable terms that 'it is bound in common honesty to the colonies, in consideration of the great expense they are put to in complying with the law, and their liberality towards the emigrant, to remove needless obstacles in the way of their obtaining Indian labour'.[8] Hence the difficulty in enforcing policies geared to safeguard the interests of emigrants. Consequently the recruiting system was never free from abuse.

The physical conditions under which emigrants were transported to the recipient colonies also came under government scrutiny. The rules and regulations promulgated from time to time were geared to ensure that colonial depots were in a healthy locality, that they were sanitary and commodious and equipped with necessary amenities, that emigrants were properly lodged and medically fit at embarkation and that their safety and comfort *en route* were promoted and mortality minimized.[9] Accordingly, the Government of India endeavoured to appoint experienced, qualified surgeons to ensure that emigrant vessels were seaworthy, that only good drinking water was in the receptacles, that medical and food supplies were adequate and that trained nurses were on board to minimize mortality. The government was less concerned with the physical capacity of the emigrants for strenuous plantation labour, which responsibility belonged solely to the colonial emigration agents.

These policies seemed to coincide with the interests of colonial employers, who wanted labourers to be physically fit on arrival so that the 'seasoning' or acclimatization period could be curtailed and expenses reduced. Heavy mortality on the voyage correspondingly meant economic loss to the planters. When mortality was excessive, both the planters and the Indian Government tended to institute a thorough investigation and adopt effective measures to prevent a recurrence. The innovations introduced into the system as a result of the initiative from both colonial and Indian Government officials were largely responsible for the progressively reduced mortality.[10]

The Government of India was particularly concerned with the contractual terms offered to intending emigrants and their socio-economic and political conditions in the several importing colonies. Accordingly it assumed the role of 'protector of the weak and ignorant, bound to supply their deficiencies with its own fuller knowledge, so that, as far as possible, they may be placed upon an equality with the more robust races of the West, and that in the bargains which they freely make with those who bid for their labour, they may not be worsted or imposed upon'.[11] Hence the Indian Government required that the wages and conditions of service were 'fully and clearly' stated in the contracts and that colonial legislation, in theory at any rate, provided 'efficient protection' against planter domination. Additionally, the colonies were expected to appoint an Immigration Agent and a corps of inspectors and to provide free housing and hospital accommodation, medical care and a free return passage at the termination of the contract.

Some of these policies seemed to conflict with the aims of colonial planters 'imbued with the putrid prejudices of slavery', particularly in the West Indies, with the result that the protection which legislation ostensibly offered hardly ever existed. Accustomed as they were to a mentality of coerced labour, the planters were mainly interested in acquiring effective control over labour to ensure it was readily available so as to boost production and maximise profits. With control they could use labour to depress wages or overcome any pressing emergency. Control was exercised through the plethora of laws and regulations which penalized workers for every minor infraction of the law, subjected them to arbitrary arrests and imprisonment, violated the sanctity of their homes, denied them redress at court and restricted their movements even during leisure. The laws even denied them legitimate access to the Immigration Department which stood *in loco parentis* to the immigrants. Indeed, the law was geared solely to chastize the immigrants as Stipendiary Magistrate William Des Voeux observed: 'The law had been so framed and its net, covering all possible offences, was woven so closely that not even the smallest peccadilloes could escape its meshes.'[12] The Government of India showed sporadic bouts of concern when abuses were discovered or major legislative amendments contemplated but generally it failed to take active measures to uphold the interests of its subjects in the colonies. It tended in fact to place the responsibility for good treatment on the Colonial Office. This did not mean that the Indian

Government did nothing to ameliorate the condition of Indian workers. In 1839 it imposed a ban on colonial emigration when the ever-vigilant Anti-Slavery Society highlighted the abuses of the system and the maltreatment of the 'Gladstone Coolies' in British Guiana.[13] By threatening to impose measures designed to restrict the flow overseas, the Indian Government forced the Guianese planters to legalize contracts made in India and guarantee a daily minimum wage.[14] Prior to 1872 contracts signed or attested to in India were very often repudiated in British Guiana.

But the defects and abuses unearthed by the Royal Commissioners who investigated the workings of the system in British Guiana and Mauritius emphasized the fact that however laudable colonial immigration laws might appear, they offered in effect 'no complete security' against ill-treatment.[15] Yet the Indian Government did not see the necessity, largely on the grounds of expense, for the appointment of an officer to visit the recipient colonies periodically to ascertain the true conditions in the 'coolie lines', although it admitted that the statistical data produced by the colonies were largely incomprehensible. It was forced to send out Surgeon-Major D. W. D. Comins (Protector of Emigrants at Calcutta) in 1891 when colonial planting interests were clamouring for the abolition of the return-passage entitlement. It was only in the terminal years of indenture, when the abolition campaign in India was reaching momentum, that the high-powered McNeill–Chiman Lal deputation was despatched to the four British colonies of Fiji, British Guiana, Trinidad, Jamaica and the Dutch colony of Surinam (Dutch Guiana).

The Colonial Office which from the outset supported immigration as a means of replenishing a depleted work force following emancipation, adopted the role of guardian of those unrepresented in the local legislature. The Colonial Office considered itself 'the only representative of the people, and in their present ignorance and helplessness, the only representative it is possible for the people to have.'[16] But this official pronouncement was honoured more in the breach than in the observance. While the planters used the labour and vagrancy laws to intimidate, coerce, underpay and brutalize the work force, the Colonial Office failed to establish adequate machinery for their protection. Workers' wages were stopped with increasing regularity, producing tremendous hardship in the immigrant camp. The Colonial Office seemed even to ignore the fact that theoretically the immigrant was not a slave and should never be debarred, in civil cases at least, from giving evidence in his own defence at court. Generally when the Colonial Office did intervene it was solely to protect the interests of sugar and the immigration system.

Consequently the indenture system in British Guiana and other recipient colonies replicated several of the features of African slavery. *The Times* (London) was convinced that indenture 'differs only in name'.[17] Joseph

Beaumont, Chief Justice of British Guiana in the 1860s, underlined the sense of helplessness and dependence experienced by the indentured workers.

> Practically an Immigrant is in the hands of the employer to whom he is bound. He cannot leave him; he cannot live without work; he can only get such work and on such terms as the employer chooses to set him; and all these necessities are enforced, not only by the inevitable influence of his isolated and dependent position, but by the terrors of imprisonment and the prospect of losing both favour and wages.[18]

Behind the façade of legislative protection the indentured worker was degraded and exploited between the levers of arbitrary wage stoppages and summary imprisonment. It seemed that in its endeavour to ensure the resuscitation of the sugar industry in the West Indies, the Colonial Office found it difficult to pursue any consistent policy on immigration. Policies were adjusted or shaped according to pressure and circumstance.

While on several emigration issues the Government of India tended to vacillate or succumb to pressure from the powerful planting interest, it never swerved from its *laissez-faire* policy throughout the nineteenth century. It was neither prepared to promote emigration directly or induce its officers to recruit labour even during periods of grave economic distress when emigration could provide requisite safety valves to a pent-up population. Although the government's official declaration of policy was made fairly late, it was in operation ever since indentured emigration became state-regulated in the mid-1840s.

In 1875 following a meeting at the India Office with the West India Committee, the planters' influential lobby at Whitehall, Lord Salisbury, Secretary of State for India, urged the Indian Government to encourage emigration actively. He underlined the economic benefits to Indians of an organized emigration scheme and suggested various ways of implementing it. Salisbury wanted the Indian Government to assume direct responsibility for the accuracy of information disseminated in the *mufassal* and for the performance of the terms of the contract. Officers appointed by the Indian Government but paid by the importing colonies would be stationed there to protect workers' interests and scrutinize colonial legislation. *Mufassal* magistrates would publicize the colonies and encourage emigration but during famines Indian Government officials would be directly involved in recruitment. In return, colonial authorities would guarantee good treatment, recognize the contract made in India and redress 'all reasonable complaints'.

Salisbury had no qualms about the treatment of Indians overseas.

> Above all things, we must confidently expect, as an indispensable condition of the proposed arrangements, that the colonial laws and their administration will be such that settlers who have completed the terms of service to which they agreed as the return for the expense of bringing them to the colonies will be in all respects free men, with privileges no whit inferior to those of any other class of Her Majesty's subjects resident in the colonies.[19]

This statement was undoubtedly true of Mauritius, Fiji and the British West Indian colonies, where racial origin as a qualification for political and civil rights did not matter. But in the white European settlements which enjoyed a measure of responsible government, or were aspiring to it, this promise was sheer verbiage as the political and civil disabilities of Indians in South Africa later showed.

Responding to Salisbury's proposals, the Government of India consulted the various provincial governments, the future pattern in all major emigration issues. Their replies opposed generally any active promotion of emigration on the grounds that there was an insatiable demand for labour in India, that vast tracts of land were yet undeveloped and that neighbouring Ceylon (Sri Lanka), Burma, the Straits Settlements and Mauritius offered greater inducements to labour. Direct government encouragement could very well be interpreted as promoting colonial interests at India's expense and could produce 'serious distrust and misconception'. Noting the strong opposition from several provincial governments and the 'infinitesimal effect' of colonial emigration on the pressures of population in heavily congested areas, the Government of India considered any material departure from the existing policy 'extremely impolitic'. In a carefully worded document the Government of India concluded:

> we do not think it possible to carry into effect in any material degree the suggestions which have been made in your Lordship's despatch for the further encouragement of emigration, and that, while we consider that all due faculties should be afforded to the Colonial Emigration Agents in conducting their operations, we are of the opinion that the success of those operations must depend almost entirely on the colonial employers. There are several respects in which it is desirable that our emigration law should be amended, but it seems to us that the general line of policy followed should be maintained.[20]

Lord Minto's despatch (10 December 1908) to the Secretary of State for India some thirty years later outlining Indian Government policy when the appointment of the high-powered Sanderson Commission was announced, continued to advocate a *laissez-faire* approach. The Governor-General emphasized that existing policies could be altered or modified only if the Imperial Government gave 'an absolute guarantee' that a change in the status of a recipient colony would not affect that of the Indian settlers. He cited the apparent unjust treatment of Indians in Natal and the Transvaal, and stressed that the Indian Government could not ignore the fact that similar action could be repeated when a colony became self-governing. The despatch expressed considerable alarm at the crisis in British East Africa where political recognition was denied to Indians, where they were reportedly despised and where certain areas, the fertile and beautiful highlands, were reserved exclusively for European settlement. Minto was apprehensive that when self-government was granted the antagonism between Indians and white traders would escalate, producing similar deplorable results as in South Africa. Since no such guarantees seemed forthcoming from the Imperial Government, the Government of India preferred not to abandon its existing policy, lest it discarded 'the lessons of experience'.[21]

The labour shortage in India seemed an additional factor. In 1905 a conference of the Indian Chamber of Commerce contended that the labour shortage was 'seriously restricting' the productive capacity of a sizeable section of the manufacturing concerns. As long as Indian industrialists continued to protest against an inadequate labour supply, the Indian Government considered judicious the continuation of its *laissez-faire* policy. Any fundamental change would expose the government to accusations of 'subordinating the acknowledged needs of the community to the problematic requirements of the Colonies in response to pressure from the Imperial Government'.[22] Nor was the government convinced that active promotion of emigration would elicit less suspicion than formerly. It was apprehensive that certain sections of the Indian press would seize the opportunity to publish, without proper verification, stories purporting to show harsh treatment in the colonies. The motives of government could be easily misconstrued and this could lead to an explosive situation.

Minto attacked the indenture system in veiled but unmistakable terms but no departure in policy or orientation in the attitude of the Indian Government occurred. However, a *volte-face* occurred two years later when Indian nationalists attacked the discriminatory immigration, franchise, registration and municipal laws passed in Natal which seriously affected the rights and status of Indians resident there. They protested particularly against the administration of the Dealers' Licences Act of 1897 which invested 'unlimited powers' in the hands of licensing officers who, 'actuated by race and colour prejudice', refused to issue new licences to Indians or renew or transfer existing ones. These measures had correspondingly resulted in the progressive elimination of the Indian traders in Natal. They also deplored the hardships imposed by the £3 poll tax, and the

Municipal Vagrancy regulations, which required Indians to carry special permits to establish their identity after stipulated hours.[23]

The Indian Government, unable to sustain its neutral attitude, recognized the 'grave injustice' to the Indian traders and requested the Natal Government to introduce a Bill allowing appeals to the Supreme Court against the decisions of licensing boards. The Natal Government not only refused but introduced further restrictive measures which suspended the issuing of new licences to Indians and withdrew, after a specified date, existing ones. Consequently, the Government of India amended the Indian Emigration Act XIV of 1910, empowering it to suspend emigration to any country overseas for reasons other than the actual ill-treatment of Indian labourers. This legislative measure paved the way for Gopal Krishna Gokhale, the most determined opponent of indenture, to introduce on 25 February 1910 a motion in the Imperial Legislative Council which terminated indentured emigration to Natal. [24]

Indentured emigration to the remaining four British colonies of British Guiana, Trinidad, Jamaica, Fiji and the Dutch colony of Surinam (Dutch Guiana) soon came under intense criticism as Indian nationalist feeling became politically articulate. The Indian press, women's organizations, missionaries, itinerant sages, nationalist, religious and commercial organizations all mounted a vigorous anti-indenture campaign which was punctuated by speeches, propaganda, pamphlets, petitions, memorials, telegrams and resolutions. The Marwari Sahayat Samiti, composed of wealthy Marwaris (the banking class of India), not only helped relatives to rescue loved ones from the depots but used various tactics to delay embarkation. The Indenture Cooly Protection Society distributed pamphlets and delivered anti-indenture lectures throughout Bihar and the United Province. These pamphlets warned: 'Save yourself from depot wallas.... It is not service but pure deception.... Don't get enmeshed in their meshes, you will repent.'[25] These several organizations and individuals all rejected outright the conclusions of McNeill and Lal, who investigated the workings of the system in 1914, that 'its advantages have far outweighed its disadvantages'.[26]

But it was Lord Hardinge's despatch of 15 October 1915 to the Secretary of State for India which truly exposed the ineradicable evils of indenture, making its abolition imperative. Throughout his administration (1910–16), Hardinge conceived and strove for the evolution of a self-governing India, arguing pointedly that self-respect should be the basis for self-government. Hardinge accepted the Indian position that indenture branded the whole Indian population 'with the stigma of helotry'. He refuted the overworked contention that the economic advantages of emigration far outweighed the moral and social evils. Alluding to the rise in wages and standard of comfort among the labouring population in India, Hardinge contended that the much-proclaimed economic benefits of indenture had been 'too readily assumed'. Hardinge then underlined the most crucial issue.

> But whatever may be the extent of the economic advantage arising from the emigration of indentured labour the political aspect of the question is such that no-one, who has at heart the interests of British rule in India, can afford to neglect it. It is one of the most prominent subjects in Indian political life today: and its discussion arouses more bitterness, perhaps, than that of any other outstanding question. For Indian politicians, moderate and extreme alike, consider that the existence of this system which they do not hesitate to call by the name of slavery, brands their whole race in the eyes of the British Colonial Empire with the stigma of helotry. How, they ask, will a European colonial ever admit us into the fellowship of citizens of the Empire, when he knows that men of our country and colour can be purchased for five years for five shillings a week?[27]

The despatch denounced the inherent evils of indenture – an inordinately high death rate, an appalling incidence of suicides, mounting planter prosecutions for breaches of the law, unsatisfactory recruiting practices. The startling suicide rate among the indentured population in the recipient colonies, which was six times higher than that in the major recruitment areas, attracted considerable attention and concern. What seemed the most explosive feature of the system was the 'indescribable' sexual immorality in the immigrant camp, particularly in Fiji, where Indian women 'by reasons of pecuniary temptation or official pressure, are at the free disposition of their fellow recruits and even of the subordinate managing staff'. The perception that Indian women were leading immoral lives in the colonies stirred Indian nationalist feeling against the continuation of the system.

Hardinge's indictment of the indenture system gave a tremendous boost to the anti-indenture campaign, for it was the first time that someone so eminent had openly proclaimed that the system was iniquitous and must be abolished. Austin Chamberlain, Secretary of State for India, noted the mounting opposition to indenture and emphasized that it would not be 'politically possible' for the Indian administration to continue to use its official majority to defeat recurring resolutions urging the end of the system. When in March 1916 the nationalist Madan Mohan Malaviya tabled his motion for the abolition of the system there was no dissenting voice.[28] On 20 March 1917, in response to the need for Indian labour in the military campaigns in Europe, the Indian Government temporarily suspended colonial recruitment. Three years later indenture was completely abolished. Attempts by the governments of British Guiana, Trinidad,

Jamaica and Fiji to introduce Indian workers under a colonization scheme did not reach fruition largely on account of financial considerations.

For the first sixty years of indentured emigration the issues which confronted the Government of India related largely to the methods employed in labour recruitment, the physical conditions on the voyage, wages and labour conditions on the plantations and the terms of settlement and repatriation offered by the recipient colonies. Its policy of non-intervention was in conformity with contemporary European ideas but it did very little to provide effective protection to labour. While the recruiting system was never free from abuse, indenture as it evolved and developed in British Guiana and elsewhere became synonymous with slavery. Moreover, it paid little attention to the social and psychological problems affecting the immigrants in their new environment, much to the chagrin of Indian nationalists. From the early twentieth century the social, political and civil disabilities of Indian settlers in South Africa and elsewhere became a matter of national concern and a burning issue in Indian politics. Indenture in the eyes of Indians conflicted with national honour and pride and 'so opposed to modern sentiments of justice and humanity' that no civilized country could tolerate it.[29] Its abolition stemmed from an intensive, vigorous campaign largely confined to India and spearheaded by an articulate section of the Indian population.

Notes

1 Government of Bengal to Protector (of Emigrants), No. 3159, 22 July 1872. Bengal Emigration Proceedings (hereinafter BEP), July 1872, No. 34.
2 PP 1874mXLVII, (314), pp. 2–15.
3 See Act XIII of 1864, articles 28–30, 41–3.
4 For details see B. Mangru, *Benevolent Neutrality* (London, 1987), Chapter 3.
5 'Report of the Committee on Emigration from India to the Crown Colonies and Protectorates', Pt 1 (London, 1910), p. 18.
6 C. Murdoch to F. Rogers, 27 April 1871. BEP December 1871, 10–11.
7 See India Emigration Proceedings (hereafter IEP), August 1883, 33.
8 Indian Government Resolution, 23 June 1883. IEP July 1883, 35.
9 Government of India to Secretary of State for India, No. 15, 3 May 1977. IEP September 1879, File 17.
10 CO 114/34. Immigration Agent General, British Guiana, Report for 1882.
11 Government of India to Secretary of State for India, No. 15, 3 May 1877. IEP September 1879, File 17.
12 W. Des Voeux, *Experiences of a Demerara Magistrate* (Georgetown, 1948), pp. 91–2.
13 See J. Scobie, *Hill Coolies* (London, 1839), pp. 12–21.
14 CO 111/390. Gov. J. Scott to Earl of Kimberley, No. 69, 22 May 1872.
15 Government of India to Secretary of State for India, No. 3, 26 January 1872. IEP January 1872, 26.
16 CO 884/1. West Indian No. XXII.
17 See the *Royal Gazette*, 28 November 1872.
18 J. Beaumont, *The New Slavery. An Account of the Indian and Chinese Immigrants in British Guiana* (London, 1871), p. 84.

19 Lord Salisbury to Government of India, No. 39, 24 March 1875. BEP November 1875, 10.
20 Government of India to Secretary of State for India, No. 15, May 1877. IEP September 1879, File 17.
21 Government of India to Secretary of State for India, No. 99, 10 December 1908. IEP March 1908, 8.
22 Ibid.
23 IEP, March 1910, No. 20.
24 Ibid., March 1910.
25 Ibid., December 1915.
26 See 'Report to the Government of India on the Conditions of Indian Immigrants in the Four British Colonies and Surinam', 1914, Pt 1, para. 322.
27 L/P&J/6/1412. Government of India to Secretary of State for India, No. 41, 15 October 1915.
28 See India Emigration Proceedings, July 1916, File 65. Resolution of Malaviya, 20 March 1916.
29 See Proceedings of the Council of the Government of India, 4 March 1912.

CHAPTER 9 The repatriates

Marianne Soares Ramesar

Introduction

First-hand accounts of repatriating Indian immigrants, and their return voyage to India, are unusual. This chapter reproduces one such account, and analyses it in the light of contemporary conditions.[1] Although only a fragment, it is a tape-recorded interview with an elderly Trinidadian of Irish descent, Linton Gibbon, who, as a boy of 15 or 16 years old, around the years 1902/1904, made the voyage to India on a sailing ship, which was conveying repatriates. The interview was conducted by his grand-daughter in 1976, when he was about 88 years old. Recorded during a festive occasion, the sounds of family and young children can be heard in the background. But the old man's concentration and memory were apparently good, and the grand-daughter understood the importance of capturing his reminiscences. Her patient, coaxing manner is rewarding, as she encourages him, despite spells of coughing and the rising background noises: 'Tell us about that trip you made to India, on the sailing ship, when you were young, grandpa,' she urges.

The narrative

'I was a little boy, about twelve years old, and supposed to be a cantankerous little fellow.... My father and mother thought the best thing was to give me a spell away from the family. (We were eight to ten children, always bickering.) I was taken from school, and put into a drug store, to learn medical dispensing. I stayed for about one year, which brought me to the age of thirteen.'

Nelson Island depot

'I was about thirteen or fourteen years old when I was sent to Nelson Island, one of the Five Islands off Port of Spain. There I found myself among a crowd of some 1200 East Indians, who had served their time in Trinidad under contract. Now this contract was in no form "slavery"', he assures us. They were contracted to work on the estates, for five years, during which time they must not run away and leave the estate.

Immigration policy

'If anything worried them or they were ill-treated by staff on the estate, they had great redress. My father and a Commander from the British Navy were two of the men appointed by Government to study any Indian's complaint. The Indian had perfect liberty to go to them at any time – the estate authorities could not prevent him – in order to lay his complaint. They [the Immigration officials] would visit the estate, and investigate. Invariably 90 per cent of the time, the Indian was put in the right, and the estate was put in the wrong.

'After serving for five years, the immigrant was entitled, with his family, to a free passage to Calcutta, as a gift.'

[Questioned by his grand-daughter, as to whether the period of service was not ten years, instead of five, Gibbon was insistent on the period being five years.][2]

Gibbon's job on Nelson Island, was to 'get food cooked' daily for some 1200 to 1400 Indians of all ages. 'Every morning there was a daily store of rice, flour and potatoes, sheep etc., enough food to last in order to provide two meals daily: breakfast in the morning, and dinner around 3–4 p.m. About 10 000 *chuppatis* were cooked. These were little "Johnny cakes", thin and round, like the round of a saucer, a little bit bigger. For a meal, ten of these were issued to each man, along with boiled, crushed pumpkin, or rice with curry, very tasty. I have eaten many of these (Johnny cakes) in my time,' he confides.

'I would be given a kerosene tin, full of Indian butter, which they called "ghee", made from cows in India, and specially imported for them. A woman [female immigrant] was on duty, and she dipped in her hand and smeared some ghee on each *chuppati*, plenty for any man to live on. As a result the immigrants could not have been said to be starved or ill-treated, 90 per cent of the time'.

Alternatives for time-expired immigrants

Gibbon informs us that Indians who had served their indentures could choose to remain in Trinidad, where the Government sold them any piece of land, virgin or forest, as 'much as 15–20 acres, with all the oil rights intact. That is why today you see many East Indian families.... very wealthy.[3] Indeed one man bought 15 acres, and sold it in a short number of years, when oil started to come in Trinidad. He sold it for $25 000. The minute he got the money, he got his death as well. This was old Partap. Unfortunately, poor fellow, he was murdered three weeks after this.'

The voyage to India

'While on Nelson Island, a sailing ship arrived, named the *Forth*. This was a three-masted, full-rigged sailing ship... with three masts. On board we were stocked with thousands of pumpkins and potatoes. We left Trinidad, I forget now, I believe it was around April of 1902... not too sure. So long ago now.... We sailed happily along in good and bad weather, until we reached the Doldrums. This is an area of the Atlantic with no air at all, and we never moved hardly a foot for two–three days, with all the sails hanging loose. We were drifting with the tide, but we didn't realize this ourselves. When the first breezes did arise, we arrived down towards the Antarctic region.

'By this time, unluckily, all our food on board – pumpkins, potatoes, set up an ungodly stench... they all putrefied. All I had left were about fifteen bags of split peas.

'We had arrived within a ten days' sail of Cape Town, but we had already passed by a few degrees of the Cape of Good Hope. The Captain had to change course and turn back up and try to get back into Cape Town, in order to obtain a fresh supply of food. In the meantime, a little riot broke out on board, as everyone, that is the migrants, thought that the crew had hidden the food for their own use, and that they were eating well in their cabins, while the Indians were starving.'

Punishment

'The ringleaders were punished and put into jail. Jail was a four-gallon water tank, and the captain and the doctor agreed to put the four ringleaders there, and left them there for about two days. After this, it was discovered that although we were talking to them, there was no reply. The tank was opened, and the men were found practically unconscious, probably from the heat and the confinement. Fortunately the doctor revived them.

'We neared Cape Town, where we took on board a new supply of food, including pumpkins. I have never seen pumpkins like these, in Trinidad. They were huge, about three feet high in the air, big round balls, and white. They were lovely. We also got potatoes, and only one or two bags of rice, which was kept for the little hospital, on board ship.'

The repatriates

'We entered the Indian Ocean, and were near to India, that is, to Calcutta. Although fifty miles from shore, there was no land in sight. At this point, all the Indians communicated that they did not want to set foot in India looking like Trinidadians [i.e. in dress]. They wished to look like Indians, like Hindus. So they were given all kind of cotton to make cotton *capras* [clothes]. They insisted on shaving their heads, leaving only a little top-knot or *churkee*. There was no one to shave them, and the Captain refused to let the Indians use the razors, of which there were some fifty on board. Instead the sailors were ordered to shave the Indians' heads. There were a few little "creepers" and this bothered the sailors a bit. The sailors were novices, unaccustomed to this "barbering" so they took a few days to finish the task, shaving a few heads per day of the 500–600 men (not the women). The sailors were only able to "zog" the heads, and they ended up with the blood running down. This was not done for wickedness, just the sailors' inexperience....'

Arrival in India

'At last we entered the Hooghly River, and made our way up to Calcutta. Along the banks of the river, I noticed great big piles of wood on which persons were being burnt up, or cremated. If a man was not sufficiently wealthy, there might not be enough wood for his funeral pyre, and the remains would be thrown in the river.... Many a crocodile had a little feast.

'The voyage had lasted four months and about one week, during which we never went ashore. (We were not allowed to land at Cape Town).'

Gibbon was paid off in cash, 'lots of gold sovereigns'. Now, not yet sixteen years old, he landed in India, 'knocked about', and saw many sights, among them the Taj Mahal in Agra, which he found too marvellous to describe.

Given a free return passage to Trinidad, Gibbon travelled on the British India ship *Gurkha*, a steamer, to London, passing through the Suez Canal. Here he saw miles of desert sand, with jackals and wild animals, forty to fifty feet away from the banks of the Canal. He then went on to visit Genoa in Italy, Spain and France. From England he went by steamer to 'Rossgard' [probably Rosslare]. Gibbon says that he went from a little port called Fishguard in England, to a little town on the south-east coast of Ireland – 'Rossgard' – and on by train to Cork and to Cork University, where he had a cousin studying law. The Principal was a Mr Harvey, an Englishman with an MA degree, apparently ignorant enough to enquire what train Gibbon had taken from Trinidad! By this time Gibbon, who had travelled some 15 000 miles by sea and had several eye-openers, including seeing white waitresses at work, and learning never to discuss religion in Ireland, felt quite superior. Gibbon was invited to join the University in Cork. He paid for one year's boarding among 40–50 other students. He went on to Belfast where he applied for articles to a shipbuilding firm, as an engineering trainee, but before he could finalize his arrangements, he got diphtheria, and nearly died. He also lost all his clothes, in a fire. On his father's instructions, he returned home to Trinidad. Here George Huggins (later Sir George) employed him as an overseer on his cocoa estate near Siparia.

The narrator

The narrator was Linton Gibbon, who was born in Trinidad in 1888. He was the son of Frank Gibbon, Senior Inspector of Immigrants at the time of Linton's voyage.

Frank Gibbon was an Irishman who had arrived in Trinidad in 1859, at the age of 17. He became a civil servant. (De Verteuil notes that many Irishmen came to Trinidad as civil servants: 'proportionately far larger numbers ... than the French Creoles').[4] He acted in several positions until March 1880 when he was officially appointed to the Service as 4th Clerk in the Customs Department, then 3rd Clerk and Statist. In 1893 he was made Senior Inspector of Immigrants, and during April–October 1898, he acted as Sub-Protector/Assistant Protector of Immigrants.[5] During 1909 he again acted as Protector.

Frank Gibbon had a liberal reputation during the 1890s. Then officials of the large Colonial Company attacked the Immigration Department, and Gibbon in particular, for presenting returns which revealed that a large number of immigrant labourers had very small earnings. The acting Protector of Immigrants, H. C. Stone, who favoured the planters, sought to transfer Gibbon, and to replace him by Thornton Warner, Warden of Tacarigua, and a wealthy landowner.

On this occasion, the colonial officials in London defended Gibbon, overruling even the Governor. Wingfield of the Colonial Office minuted that, if the proposed transfer was approved, 'a grave injustice may be done to a zealous and efficient officer, who has offended some of the most influential planters in the Colony... by standing up for the rights of the coolies'. Gibbon was described as a very courageous, firm and somewhat impulsive Irishman. He sometimes used hasty and indiscreet language, when insulted by estate managers, for instance George White, whose slanderous report to Messrs Tennant in 1893 had been completely refuted. Gibbon was directed to challenge the accusations of the estate officials.[6]

The Indians, too, had a good word for Gibbon. In evidence before the 1906 Labour Committee, Abdul Aziz of the East Indian National Association, testified that Mr Gibbon helped the (Indian) people.[7] Apparently Gibbon had a good knowledge of Hindi. In 1909 Protector Coombs stated that although his inspectors spoke some Hindi, 'I do not think they have studied it, except for the man who is acting for me now [i.e. Senior Inspector Gibbon]. He knows it well.'[8]

By this time, there had been great changes in the Immigration Department. Since 1896 Commander W. H. Coombs had replaced former Protector Charles Mitchell in a bid to 'tighten up' the Immigration administration. No doubt, Gibbon was affected. In 1903 we find a report of Gibbon obeying the law to the letter, when he fined protesting immigrants for leaving the estate in a body of more than five.[9]

In 1909 the Department came under attack by opponents of state-aided immigration from India, notably C. P. David, Member of the Trinidad Legislative Council, and British Member of Parliament Thomas Summerbell; and champions of the immigrants like George Fitzpatrick, who was to be the first Indian Member of the Trinidad Legislative Council. Gibbon, who was acting Protector, intervened and acted promptly and forcefully to see that three offending estate overseers were punished for ill-treatment of immigrants.[10]

In defence of the Immigration Department, Gibbon quoted three occasions during the 1890s when the Immigration Department had been criticized by officials, even the Governor, when it was doing its duty, on the immigrants' behalf.[11] But all the incidents quoted had occurred during the comparatively liberal regime of Charles Mitchell. Coombs had instituted a new regime. Gibbon was now older and in a senior position. He was connected by marriage to H. C. Stone, and had a large family. Although he personally continued to act fairly, he had little choice but to support the *status quo*, in a changed administration.

Immigration administration in Trinidad

Immigration affairs were administered locally under Legislative Council Ordinances, by an Immigration Department, headed by a Protector of Immigrants with extensive powers. He was *ex officio* member of the Legislative Council and Chairman of its Immigration Committee. Responsible to the Governor, his was the task of seeing that the provisions of the Ordinance were carried out. He was assisted by the Sub-Protector of Immigrants, based at the Immigration Office in Port of Spain, and by an Inspector in each of the North, Central and Southern divisions, with interpreters in each. Also appointed by the Governor, these inspectors were to pay regular visits to examine the estate books, hospitals and barracks, enquiring into complaints by or against the immigrants, helping the magistrate to estimate wages when these were in doubt, and instituting prosecutions. In theory, the Protector's title defined his role. The general welfare of the immigrant was his concern. He had the right of entry to all plantations employing indentured immigrants, with access to plantation books, hospitals and immigrants' quarters. He was expected to hear the immigrants' complaints, bring charges against delinquent employers and estate officials; in cases where the immigrant faced charges in court, the Protector was to watch the proceedings on behalf of the immigrant, acting as though he were the principal in the case.[12]

In fact, the character of the individual Protector was important, as was the pressure of planter opinion. Charles Mitchell tended to be forthright and paternalistic. Governor Broome described him, confidentially, in 1895 thus: 'Mr Mitchell is an independent and fearless officer, well versed in the business of his department. He has never been solicitous to cultivate the good opinion of the planting interest, but his endeavour has... always been simply to do his duty.'[13] Raising thorny issues of wage rates and earnings on behalf of the immigrants helped to cost him his job. Even then he continued to protest. Protector Coombs, his successor, as a retired naval officer with some experience of India, was intended to keep the indentureds under more systematic control. His early tendency to be lenient towards planters drew criticism from the newspapers, and was the subject of a Hindu *panchayat*.[14]

Linton Gibbon assumed wrongly that the immigrants enjoyed great redress for their grievances. Even near to the end of the indentured system, McNeill and Chimman Lal, visiting commissioners from India, deplored the lack of regular machinery for initiating enquiries, and hearing the immigrants' complaints and grievances. They declared that the willingness of the Protector and staff merely to carry out routine activities, however satisfactorily, was inadequate. While there were no legal difficulties in the way of prosecuting offending employers, the absence of even a register of complaints filed by labourers against their employers, and the rarity of cases against employers was enough to lead to suspicion on the labourers' part.[15]

The return ship

The official records available do not report the *SS Forth* sailing from Trinidad to Calcutta in 1902. Indeed the *Forth* arrived in Trinidad from Calcutta with new immigrants in November 1903. The Annual Report of the Protector of Immigrants for 1904–5 reports the *Forth* leaving Trinidad in 1904, as follows:

> The Return ship *Forth* (Captain T. Matzinger; Surgeon-Superintendent Dr. W. Kenny) left Trinidad for Calcutta, on 1st September, 1904. East Indians on board were: 413 men, 182 women, 58 boys, 57 girls, and 18 infants, in all 728 souls or $661\frac{1}{2}$ statute adults. Among these were twenty-eight certified by the District Medical Officer as absolutely 'unfit for service under indenture' (twenty-three of these had arrived by ship during the past twelve months). 15/60 convalescents in the Depot were repatriated. Many paupers had applied for repatriation, but there was no room after those entitled, and those who had paid their clothing account had been accommodated.
>
> Repatriates deposited with the purser £9,078.19/2 (TT$43,579) for transmission to them in India; and a further £204 (TT$979) was consigned to the Surgeon-Superintendent's care. [The Report noted that this total sum was about £100 (TT480) less than had been taken back during the previous year, although there were more people on this voyage. The explanation given was that a larger amount had been remitted to India by immigrants, during the year].[16]
>
> The *Forth* arrived at the Cape on 10th November 1904, and at Calcutta on 1st January, 1905, a journey of some 122 days. [Gibbon estimated a journey of about 129 days which is not such a difference to be mistaken about, after keeping this in memory for more than seventy years. It seems likely then that the 1904–5 voyage was the one which Gibbon undertook, along with the repatriates.]

The depot at Nelson Island

The Trinidad Immigration depot was housed on Nelson Island, off Port of

Spain. This depot was intended to relieve the congestion in Port of Spain – especially in the hospital – when several ships arrived. Here incoming ships from India landed with immigrants, and were met officially by the Protector of Immigrants, and Medical Officer, inspected and a report handed to the Governor. Healthy immigrants were despatched to the estates; sick immigrants were sent to the Colonial Hospital in Port of Spain. Usually 'convalescent' immigrants, i.e. those who were unfit for immediate service, but seemed likely to improve with rest and care, were housed temporarily in the depot. Those who remained unfit might be repatriated from the depot, from which return ships to India embarked with repatriates, supplies and so forth.

In 1902 the Immigration depot was improved and expanded with an upper storey to its barracks, to overcome the problem of overcrowding. A forty-bed hospital, built by the Government Public Works Department, faced the sea. Named the 'Marion' Hospital, it was intended to relieve the Colonial Hospital, and to provide inmates with pure air and healthy surroundings. When the *Forth* sailed, the Immigration Depot was kept open, because of a large number of immigrants under treatment. Dr Syed Ahmed Hossain, a native of India, was the Medical Officer in charge.[17]

Return ships from Trinidad

During the twentieth century, except for the war years 1914–15, a single return ship left Trinidad annually in September or October, with some 700 migrants.

Each year those wishing to claim their right to a return passage were required to register, so that a ship could be chartered.

Repatriates were sent by barge to the Immigration Depot on Nelson Island, to prepare for departure. Here all documents were prepared, remittances to India checked, passage money paid, and money deposited in the ship's treasury, certified. The Protector and the Government Medical Officer were required to inspect immigrants, ship and stores, listing the immigrants on board, certifying their number, condition and clothing for the journey. A roll-book was made up of all emigrants, with a list of paupers and invalids, who needed special care during the voyage.

Return ships regularly took a complement of 'unfit' persons, usually inmates of the House of Refuge in St James. Sometimes unsatisfactory workers were sent back. Later there were restrictions on the repatriation of lunatics and lepers.

Conditions for eligibility for repatriation changed over the years. Early immigrants were entitled to a free passage back to India after five years' service and residence in Trinidad. After 1854 they were obliged to complete five years' indentured service and then to serve a further five years' 'Industrial Residence', so Linton Gibbon's grand-daughter correctly suggested that the term for most immigrants in Trinidad was ten years.[18] Later those arriving after 1895 had to pay part of their passage: the men paid a quarter and the women a sixth, plus the cost of warm clothing for the voyage. Those arriving after 1897 paid an increased proportion: one-half for the men, and one-third for the women, plus clothing costs.

The 'coolie ship' traffic[19]

From the 1840s, there was an expansion in international shipping, which became engaged in carrying cargo from the China Trade with Europe, and migrants to the California Gold Rush. During the 1850s there was movement to and from the Crimean War area, and to Australia with migrants. Certain British shipowners, especially the firms of Sandbach, Tinne & Co. and of James Nourse, became involved, and soon cornered the business of transporting Indian and Chinese labourers.

Sandbach's involvement grew out of their interests in Demarara plantations since 1790, and as merchants trading mostly in sugar and tobacco with offices in Georgetown, and in Glasgow, Scotland. They used ships of small tonnage and shallow draft, in order to cross the bar of the Georgetown harbour.[20] In 1814, they invited the Hon. P. N. Tinne, Government Secretary for British Guiana, to join their Company. During the 1850s and 1860s, Sandbach, Tinne & Co. shared the 'coolie carrying trade' with other companies, using teak-built frigates. By the 1880s and 1890s, Sandbach, Tinne & Co. had acquired several fine iron clipper ships for this trade, which they now shared mainly with James Nourse.[21]

Nourse was born in Ireland around 1830, and went to sea at an early age. From his twenties, he apparently showed commercial ability as well as nautical skill, acquiring a financial interest in several small vessels. While a ship's master, he became a hustler, generating his own business, without consulting the owners of the ship, which he might keep out for two–three years, having arranged his own charters and freights, and offering quick turn-arounds, with no delays.[22] By 1860 he became a master–owner, and in 1861, he acquired the *Ganges*, a full-rigged iron ship. By 1867 he owned the *India*, *Jumna* and *Syria*, and his ships plied regularly into Garden Reach Harbour in Calcutta. Recognising the rapid growth of Indian emigration, he was soon building more ships, and engaging ships' masters to meet these special requirements, and competing successfully with other formidable and earlier-established rivals, like Sandbach, Tinne & Co. The latter also employed specially-built ships, notably the *Ailsa*, *Brenda*, *Godiva*, *Stronsa*, and *Jura*.[23] These two companies dominated all others, who became known as the 'outsiders' and took only occasional cargoes of 'coolies'.[24]

In Trinidad, the procedure was for Trinidad's Immigration Committee of the Legislative Council to agree annually on the number of migrants requested, and the expenditure for their introduction. The British Crown Agents then arranged contracts, usually with Nourse & Company, inspected and licensed ships. The 'coolie' clippers were specially developed to deal with the traffic. They were iron ships, with a big sail plan, and well-stayed masts. They had large crews, of 40–50 men. Cargoes were usually of salt to India, or rice to the West Indies.

The voyage to India

The voyage to India was not a light undertaking even for the dedicated migrant, and many would have been in two minds about the decision to repatriate. The distance between Trinidad and Calcutta was some 11 000 miles, and took some three to four months, or an average of 100 days. An outbreak of cholera or other contagious disease was also possible.

Disasters were known to have struck such vessels. It was known in Trinidad that in 1878, the *Pandora* had been wrecked off Port of Spain, with 500 repatriating Indians on board, as it entered Boca Huevos, and struck a reef. The Indians were transferred into boats, packed like sardines one on top of the other, helpless from fright. 240 of them were taken aboard the *Warrior*; the rest were put ashore. Apparently none died, but many decided not to resume the journey to India.[25]

Thus in 1885, John Morton described the mixed feelings, including apprehension, among the repatriates on a ship which he visited in Port of Spain to say farewell:

> October, 1885 On the first ult; a ship left this port for Calcutta, with 332 men, 138 women, 79 boys, 47 girls, and 18 infants, Indian immigrants returning to their country....
>
> ...The ship lay in the deep water, three miles out. Our Gulf steamer carried all out to the ship in one trip... I spent an hour aboard this steamer, while their names were being checked.
>
> Mothers counted their children, or gazed anxiously for grown-up sons, who had not yet turned up. Some wept for friends left in Trinidad; the faces of others were bright with vision of a long-awaited happiness drawing onto realization.... When the steamer moved off, a ringing cheer was raised, and in fifteen minutes we were alongside the ocean ship.
>
> The dispensary and hospital were on the main deck. On the next deck, a saloon – shall I call it? – 200 feet long by 40 feet at the widest part, was fitted up as night quarters for 600 souls.

> All through, the people behaved admirably. Fairly afloat, many of them seemed to realize the risks of a voyage of over four months, with so many on board. In passing round to say 'good-bye' and give a word of encouragement and advice, many a Hindoo and Mohammedan too, held my hand to say 'Till you hear we are safe at Calcutta, do not cease to pray God to be pitiful to us'.[26]

There was also the ordeal of the repatriation ship, *Mairi Bhan*. According to Lubbock, she was an 'outside ship', i.e. not a Sandbach, Tinne or Nourse ship, as none was available, but a ship chartered to take 800 repatriates from Trinidad to Calcutta. The ship had an experienced Surgeon-Superintendent, but a poor crew.

There was a long passage south, of 63 days, and they had to put into Bahia for provisions. The crew tried to mutiny. For three weeks the ship lay in Bahia, with a Brazilian guard on board, and the crew in irons. In trying to make up time after this, Captain McIntyre went too far south. Then, in the Indian Ocean, the Indians developed what seemed like cholera. Surgeon-Superintendent Booth-Clarkson coped, and there were few deaths. He gave credit to his Indian head *sirdar*, a Brahmin, whom he described (rather crudely) as working like a 'whole team of horses and a dog under the wagon'. In the face of an inefficient crew, and a threatened cyclone, the repatriates were said to have behaved splendidly, and often lent a hand to work on the ship. The ship's time from Trinidad to Calcutta was 196 days, or more than six months.[27]

On board ship, beriberi disease was frequent as a result of the diet of boiled rice, for instance on the *Moy*, a Nourse ship, sailing from Calcutta to British Guiana, with some 520 migrants. As a result of an outbreak, 46 (9 per cent) of the Indians died, and a further 88 (17 per cent) had to be hospitalized. Burials were held, with separate services for Hindus and Muslims.[28] On arrival in Guiana, the Governor ordered the Surgeon-Superintendent on that voyage to forfeit his gratuity of £480 (TT$2304).[29]

The crew

The crew was European and Indian. The most important officer was the Surgeon-Superintendent. From the United Kingdom he was sent out, with passage paid to India, usually on a P&O ship. His only superior was the Government Protector of Emigrants who appointed him and gave him instructions. His duties were: the medical inspection of the migrants, the inspection of the ship, the ventilation methods and cooking arrangements.

He also reported on the deck-house, which was set aside as a hospital. A good Surgeon-Superintendent was strict about ventilation, cleanliness, clothing, cooking and exercise. He gained his reputation for the good condition in which he landed his charges. Bad Surgeon-Superintendents were usually not rehired.[30]

The Surgeon-Superintendent's pay depended on the number of immigrants landed alive. At first this was 10/- per head, later increased to 21/- (about TT$2.50–$5.00). His pay could be forfeited, however, if his work was unsatisfactory. He could also cause the Captain to lose his gratuity if he gave a bad report.[31]

The Captain, or Ship's Master, and the Surgeon-Superintendent had joint jurisdiction over several areas of the voyage, and this called for tactful relations. However, since the Surgeon-Superintendent could be quite demanding on behalf of his charges, he often clashed with the Captain. For example, in hot weather, he might insist on the spreading of the awnings, and the working of the ventilators, for wind. For these duties, he demanded the work of the ship's watch. Sometimes he even insisted that the fast clipper-ship slow down, for the benefit of sick passengers.[32]

The Third Mate also held an important and responsible role towards the travelling migrants. He was the purser, taking charge of government stores provided for the Indians. (He was, therefore, in a position, if he chose, to slip a bag of rice, a hundredweight of potatoes, or a case of brandy, to the Captain.) In his supervisory role towards the migrants he was right-hand man to the Surgeon-Superintendent. He was responsible to the Captain for discipline among the migrants, and (apart from the Surgeon-Superintendent) only he had business in the migrants' quarters. He supervised the stewards, looked out for the migrants, and kept a sharp eye on activities below deck.

The Third Mate also received a *per capita* gratuity for every immigrant landed safely, so this was a lucrative job. He probably collected 2/6 (about 62 cents) per head (subject to the Surgeon-Superintendent's report). At the rate of some 500–800 migrants, this meant £63–£100 (TT$300 to $480) per voyage.[33]

The third ship's officer who held a responsible role on a migrant ship was the Engineer. He also worked under the Surgeon-Superintendent's orders. He had charge of the condensor, and this was essential for condensing the quantity of water needed daily, some 800 gallons, to provide steam for cooking. We are told that he had to rise early to get the fire going in the furnace, so as to provide enough steam by 5.30 a.m., to boil kedgerees for the morning meal.[34] The engineer received a small gratuity, once the Surgeon-Superintendent was satisfied with his performance, and recommended him.[35]

Other European crew

White tells us that the crews on sailing ships were mainly white. For a voyage to the West Indies and back, most of these would have been picked up in Calcutta. Under contemporary conditions, crimps were paid *per capita* to get scarce men, by the use of 'runners', using press-gang methods. Many recruits were British, Dutch and Scandinavian, of the worst kind. 'Sea lawyers' (argumentative, ringleader types) were to be avoided, also bad cooks, as their practices tended to stimulate mutiny. Many of the ships' carpenters were Chinese.[36]

In contrast, the crews of the later steamships, which became common from about 1904, comprised Indian *lascars* (sailors). These were considered better able to endure the heat of the stokehold, and the steamer's furnaces.[37]

Indian staff

Firstly, there were the *compounders* (Indian doctors) usually two per ship. These carried the honorific title of *Baboo*, and were important intermediaries between the Surgeon-Superintendent and the immigrants. Next were the *sirdars*, who were the chief Indian petty officers. (There was usually a Head Sirdar and four sirdars to every 100 Indians.) The sirdars were responsible for discipline among the Indians. They received and distributed the migrants' rations, and supervised the cooking. They were appointed by the Emigration Agent, but the Surgeon-Superintendent could 'dis-rate' or demote them for bad conduct.[38]

The *bhandarries* were the Indian cooks. Appointed at the Emigration Depot, they included a head *bhandarrie*. On the voyage they worked under the eye of the Surgeon and the Third Mate. Because of Hindu caste attitudes, the cooks were usually of high caste, Brahmins, if possible. One Surgeon-Superintendent gave the following advice on this question:

> Sometimes Brahmins and other high-caste Hindoos will come up and say that they cannot eat food prepared in the galley, and this, although they have been told, before embarking, that their food would be thus prepared. Often a man's prejudice (his caste has been broken by the mere fact of his having lived in the depot, even up-country) can be satisfied by putting him in the galley as a *bhandarrie*, or cook, if the complaint has not been made for that purpose, and there is a vacancy.[39]

On the other hand, the *topazes*, or 'sweepers' were of low caste. They were well paid for their demanding duties of cleaning the Indians' quarters, spending long periods in washing and drying, and sweeping both the main and the immigrants' decks. All these men operated under the Surgeon-Superintendent.[40]

The regime on board

Until the 1860s mortality rates on immigrant ships were often alarmingly high, leading to an official enquiry, and insistence on reformed conditions. Strict regulations of daily diet, cleansing and exercise were now considered vital in the confined space available on board during a lengthy voyage. No doubt the bonuses available to key officers for each immigrant landed alive induced the plan to keep these passengers healthy and busy. The daily routine included early rising, for the airing of clothes and bedding. There were weekly inspections of quarters by the Surgeon-Superintendent. Daily baths and weekly laundry were advised. There were two meals per day, around 9.00 a.m. and 4.00 p.m., on the upper deck, whenever possible. The dietary scale was laid down. The daily serving was to be supervised by the Surgeon-Superintendent, and formulae were laid down for the testing of food supplies, especially drinking water, lime juice, ghee, flour and rice. After each meal, the decks were to be swept, all cooking utensils cleared, and no stale food to be secreted or consumed by cooks or migrants.[41] Despite all this, the fruit and vegetables usually spoiled, before the end of the journey, as they did on Gibbon's ship.

We are told that the immigrants took their meals on board, 'in the traditional manner', squatting around big bowls of rice, piled high with curry.[42] For entertainment the Indians sang songs to the accompaniment of their drums. As for the journey from India, healthy migrants were, no doubt, encouraged to spend much of their time taking exercise, and amusing themselves in the fresh air of the upper deck. 'Noisy amusements', such as singing or playing drums, were restricted after a certain hour. Andrew Guyadeen who made a similar voyage *to* Trinidad as an immigrant in 1884, describes how on evenings 'we would assemble on deck, weather permitting, or in our dormitory below deck, to join in the group-singing accompanied by the sitar, sarangi and tabla'.[43]

Arrival in Calcutta

The entry into the harbour at Calcutta was very difficult. The channel was one hundred miles long, restricted and devious, with variable winds and shifting sand banks. There were the hazards of dropping wind, fog in winter and the mud banks. Because of these conditions, a ship would arrive at the Sandheads, and await the pilot's tugboat, which towed it in, for the last ninety miles. Towing in the River Hoogly was arduous and dangerous, with the ponderous hull of a 'coolie' ship, and towing charges were high. (During the 1880s, therefore, Nourse acquired for his company the tugboat *Hughli*, which was used especially for ships returning to India.) The ship then moved along the points of Diamond Harbour, e.g. Falta Point, to Garden Reach, where the Trinidad Emigration Depot was situated.[44]

The Indian Emigration Act of 1883 laid down a regular routine for ships returning with repatriates. On arrival in Diamond Harbour, the ship's Master was to telegraph the news, so that the Protector of Emigrants and Medical Officer could meet and inspect the immigrants, ship and stores, and receive the statements of the Master and the Surgeon-Superintendent, on the number and condition of the sick and helpless.[45]

Arthur Hill, a former Emigration Agent for British Guiana, described a scene which was vividly typical of migrants returning from the colonies:

> The Colony's Emigration Agent, with his staff of *babus* (clerks), *peons* (servants) and the Doctor *Babu*, board the ship, now rusty from its long voyage. They are greeted by the Ship's Surgeon, 'wreathed in smiles', since there has been no death during the voyage, and there are only two cases of illness in the ship's hospital. Around the ship are small boats waiting for fares, and salvaging the worn-out tin *lotas* (bowls), *thalis* (brass plates), and old clothes being thrown overboard.[46]

Lodged in the Emigration Depot, the return emigrants were to be fed, the sick treated, the paupers and destitutes returned to their home districts at the expense of the Colony's Agency, and provided with financial aid, where necessary. Those who had remitted money, or handed valuables to the Surgeon-Superintendent for safekeeping, were then to receive them. The personal effects of those who had died on the journey were to be handed over to the Emigration Agent, or banked, awaiting the heirs of the deceased who had to produce probate and documents, in order to claim sums of more than 300 rupees.

Hill pictures the scene the following morning, as the *peon* escorts paupers to the Howrah Station. The 'cheque-wallahs' (those who have received cheques), set out in hired *bandgharries* (horsed vehicles) to cash their cheques at the Bank of Bengal. By midnight, all are on trains bound for different parts of India, all expecting to pick up the old threads of their former life, some after forty years abroad.

The aftermath

This was not the end of the story, at least for some repatriates. Hill pictures the fortunes of some repatriates – a picture of severe dislocation. The scene takes place three weeks later: the Emigration Agent looks out to find an aged 'creole' group of repatriates under a tree in the Depot yard, begging to be allowed to re-indenture for the West Indies. They have spent all their savings, but are willing to borrow and repay. In their native village, they have found no old friends and relatives, and their Trinidad-born children do not speak the local Indian language. The agent is forced to refuse, as the people are old. For the young, he predicts that, when their savings have been spent, they will have to find work among the 'coolies' engaged in coaling ships at the Kidderpore Docks. Here they must get accustomed to the excessive heat, hard work, small wages (4–5 annas per day) and a 'monotonous' diet of *dhal-bhat* (split peas and rice) and *chuppaties*.[47]

While it is easy to dismiss Hill's account as the bias of an ex-Emigration Agent who was anxious to promote the benefits of migration for the colonies' sake, and even (in his paternalistic view) for the migrants', there is evidence from other sources that at least some repatriates had difficulty resettling in India.

Understandably, the question of repatriation was very complex, and some migrants' attitudes and reactions were ambivalent. Generally there was the intention to return home after one's indenture contract and period of compulsory residence was over. Certainly this was the spirit among Gibbon's migrant shipmates. Returning home may have been easier for the successful migrant – giving him the chance to return to his old village and to show off his gains and improved position. Indeed the repatriates' savings gave them some status: Marsden, the Trinidad Emigration Agent at Calcutta, reported in 1909 that, as long as the repatriate's money lasted, he was well received, and fêted in his native village. Some bought land and settled down, and were looked upon as *zemindars* (land-holders) in their native districts.[48] At the other extreme were the paupers and destitutes, who had been rounded up and put on the ship to make up numbers. No doubt they felt like failures in India, as in Trinidad.

Even for the financially successful, there were problems. Ironically, the repatriate's wealth made him vulnerable. Colonel Duncan Pitcher, who in 1882 had been appointed by the Government of India to enquire into the question of migration concerning the Northwest Provinces and Oudh, gave evidence to the Sanderson Committee in 1909, concerning repatriates from the colonies in general. Speaking from his several meetings with them, he reported that many, arriving in Calcutta with money, were robbed before they reached their homes. People lay in wait for them. He urged that the money should be received in the Treasury or Saving Bank, and then handed over to the repatriates in their homes.[49]

But some repatriates were wary of receiving their savings in their home villages, and with reason. William F. Bolton, Assistant Emigration Agent for Trinidad, Jamaica, Mauritius and Fiji, described a case in which a repatriate returned with a cheque for 8000 rupees (TT$2573 – admittedly an exceptional amount). Advised by Bolton not to take delivery of this amount in Calcutta, but to get the Emigration Agent to send it to the local treasury in Gorakhpur, the repatriate replied:

> if I have my money sent to the Gorakphur Treasury, the *babu* there will tell all the others, and none will be left for myself.[50]

Social dislocation

Newly-gained money was not the only reason for secrecy. Many of the repatriates would not disclose which colony they were returning from, because they did not wish their relatives to know that they had crossed the seas. This involved the important question of caste membership and regulations. Bolton noted that 'the priests and others wish them to buy themselves back into caste.... They are plundered in every direction.'[51]

There were reports that the repatriate who returned with money, having lost caste, would be harassed by his caste fellows, to give caste dinners in order to be readmitted into the caste. (This was one reason given for repatriates wishing to re-emigrate.) Inter-caste marriages, made in the West Indies, might not be tenable in India.[52] Earlier Surgeon-Major D. W. D. Comins had reported that inter-caste marriage acted as a deterrent to repatriation.

Some repatriates were disturbed enough to re-emigrate, even re-engaging as indentureds. In one case related by O. W. Warner, who had been Emigration Agent in Calcutta,

> because his relations, if he has plenty of money, will make him welcome; if he has none, he has lost his caste; as a rule, they are not kind to him. In fact I know; they have told me so.... They do not want to remain in India.[53]

Behind these simple statements, there must have been a great deal of heartache. Gillion notes, with reference to all the colonies, that one of the most pathetic features of indentured emigration was that some repatriates returned to India with no provision or preparation for finding a place in their old society. Some who had brought money, and had kept in touch with their relatives, were able to acquire land, and to settle down. Others were required to perform ceremonies of purification, or to undertake costly feasts in order to be received back into their former homes and villages. Still they might be humiliated by fellow-villagers, forbidden to touch the village well for fear of polluting it, and unable to find marriage partners for their children. (These difficulties, Gillion notes, were more likely in most parts of the United Provinces than in other parts of India.)[54]

These outcomes were not to be taken lightly. Similarly the Hindu migrant's original move to leave his ancestral society had meant a fundamental break with traditional supernatural powers (as well as defiance of the local officials who opposed the recruiting of migrants).

When the Hindu emigrant entered strange territories, he therefore took serious risks:

> once the wanderer leaves the hamlet where he was born, he enters the domain of new and unknown deities, who, being strangers, are of necessity hostile to him, and may resent his intrusion, by sending famine, disease or death upon the luckless stranger.[55]

But some returning migrants found that no propitiation was effective. One early repatriate who left Trinidad on the *Ganges* in October 1874 described the return to his native village, where no one recognized him, where they had forgotten his father's name, and when his money was spent, they drove him out as a *pariah* (outcaste), polluted forever.[56] One surviving pundit in Trinidad has recently described similar experiences, which caused him to return to Trinidad.[57]

In some cases, the repatriate himself had changed too much to fit into his native society. Some repatriates declared that they found Indian life, and the caste 'etiquette' intolerable, while their own 'unintelligible self-assertion irritated their seniors, and seduced their contemporaries'.[58] For the repatriate's attitude was likely to have changed, while he was away from home. As O. W. Warner told the Sanderson Committee.

> When a coolie is leaving India, as I stand on the gangway, you see him coming and touching my feet. When the coolie returns, he puts his hand out and says, 'How do you do? How are you? I know Mr. So-and-So in Trinidad; he told me to say "How do you do?" to you.' There is a difference between a coolie leaving India, and a coolie returning.[59]

So annually a number of repatriates returned to the colonies. Trinidad was the main choice of re-emigrating Indians up to about 1907, gaining 32 per cent of all returnees to European colonies during 1877–92; 40 per cent in 1905; and 34 per cent in 1907. The absolute numbers were not large – only 757 in the fifteen years 1877–92, that is, an average of only fifty per annum, compared with an annual average of 700 repatriates from Trinidad.[60]

From the 1890s, in Trinidad, there was a marked tightening of opposition to return-immigrants re-engaging as indentureds. Such return-immigrants were steadily unwelcome, and their return was deplored by both Protector and planters. In 1895, the Trinidad Immigration Committee passed a motion, instructing the Colony's Emigration Agent in India, not to recruit returnees, whether they had first served in Trinidad or any other colony. The Protector noted that he was not in favour of return-immigrants, since if there were no re-recruiting, the tendency to repatriate would decline. (There was no objection of course, to those few who could afford to pay their way to India, and to return to Trinidad, not under indenture.)

Trinidad's policy differed from colonies such as British Guiana. In 1902 we find the Trinidad Emigration Agent comparing the encouragement given to returnees in Guiana, where they were regarded as experienced and valuable workers. In contrast, the Trinidad Protector complained, year after year, that these were undesirable recruits, who knew too much, and no doubt were less docile, than the new indentureds. They allegedly gave 'bad advice' to shipmates and fellow workers, and instigated disturbances.[61]

Despite contrary advice from their Emigration Agents in India, who found it increasingly difficult to secure new recruits for emigration, Trinidad authorities maintained strong opposition to returnees. This policy probably resulted from the perceived failure of the Government land settlement scheme of 1869–90 to reduce the volume of repatriates. Immigrants who decided to settle in Trinidad were more likely to purchase land themselves, unlike many beneficiaries of the Government scheme. Also, re-emigrating Indians had preferable alternatives in Trinidad, to returning to labour on the sugar estates; unlike Guiana, where immigrants tended to remain as estate workers. They were able to influence inexperienced newcomers to seek outlets outside the estates, instead of completing their indentures. The influential planters, who were well-represented in the Trinidad Legislative Council, lobbied steadily against Government expenditure on returnees, on the grounds that they were unlikely to labour on the estates.

Eventually there was even a small number of time-expired immigrants who could afford to pay their own passage to visit India, and return to Trinidad. There is one such example in the ship's papers of the SS *Forth*, when it arrived in Port of Spain on 4 November 1903:

PASSENGER'S PASS
MAN

Trinidad Government Emigration Agency,
21 Garden Reach
Calcutta, the 16th July, 1903.

Passenger No. 1
for Ship '*Forth*', proceeding to Trinidad.

NAME:	Sitaram Singh, returnee of Trinidad
FATHER'S NAME:	Mausa Singh
AGE:	60
CASTE:	CHHATHI (sic)
NAME OF NEXT OF KIN:	Satnarain Singh, brother
NAME OF WIFE:	Sukhia, at Trinidad
DISTRICT:	Faizabad
THANA:	Bikapur
VILLAGE/TOWN/MAHALLA:	Sahsepur (?)
BODILY MARKS:	Scar on left side of ribs
OCCUPATION IN INDIA:	Labourer
HEIGHT:	5 feet, $2\frac{1}{2}$ inches

I have certified, examined and passed the above-named man, that he is free from all infections and contagious disease, and that he has been vaccinated.

(sgd) A. C. Stewart, Government
Emigration Agent for Trinidad

(sgd) Surgeon-Superintendent

Dated 15/7/1903

Those who did not return to India

The majority of Indian immigrants to Trinidad did not return home, i.e. some 110 645 of a total of 143 939, or 78 per cent.[62] Time-expired indentureds took advantage of opportunities to own land and pursue some independent economic activities like shopkeeping, milk-selling and transportation. A small group pursued education, and white-collar jobs as clerks or even teachers. Some slipped out illegally, some legally, to try their luck in the larger neighbouring country of Venezuela. Some stayed in Trinidad because they could not afford the increased costs of travel. Some had non-economic reasons, such as family ties, which kept them in Trinidad.

Apparently many who remained in Trinidad did not make a calculated decision to do so. Like V. S. Naipaul's old men who sat outside Hanuman House, talking of India, they had become accustomed to the 'familiar temporariness'.[63] In 1909 Arthur Marsden had described the stages by which immigrants developed an attachment to their adopted homes:

> when they leave India, it is with the intention of living abroad for a few years, and coming back with some money and being able to buy a little bit of land in India. But when they arrive in the Colony, and their indentures are over, then they have got to know a number of people in the Colony, and prospects are open to them of continuing there, and making more money than they would, when indentured.[64]

Rev. John Morton recommended that no time limit should be imposed on the immigrant's right to a return passage, as this would have the undesired effect of encouraging repatriation. Instead the Indians tended to follow a course which was natural and familiar among immigrants in general:

> in Trinidad the immigrants have simply drifted so long... and they have got more and more into the country, and the children will not go back... a great many never do go back. Sometimes an old man, when he is going to die, goes back to die in India, and leaves his family with us [i.e. the Canadian Mission], and his grandchildren, as I have known in several cases... the Christian element are not returning so much as the Hindu. As they are educated and brought up in the Island, they will return less.[65]

Morton's predictions seem to fit the case of young Francis Evelyn Mohammed Hosein, who gave evidence to the Sanderson Committee in London, where he had just been called to the English Bar, after completing his law studies. A son of Indian immigrants, he expressed pride in his and his family's achievements in Trinidad. Hosein conceded that large numbers of Indian immigrants returned to India, usually with a considerable amount of money, which showed that they had prospered. He didn't know how they fared there. No doubt they returned to India, not from any dissatisfaction, but because 'there's no place like home'. But for his part, none of his friends and relatives had repatriated. He even expressed a budding patriotism, when he declared that he would like to *visit* India, '*but certainly I do look upon Trinidad as my home*'.[66]

F. E. M. Hosein's attitude was probably quite unusual at the time, but it was likely to become more widespread among Indian immigrants and their descendants in Trinidad, in the future.

Appendix

Position of Indian repatriates at end of the immigration system

No. of India-born in Trinidad (1911 Census)	50 585
No. of India-born eligible for repatriation	50 000
Class 1 (arrived before 1895) entitled to free passage	9 882
Class 2 (arrived 1895–97) entitled to part cost of passage	4 806
Class 3 (arrived 1898–1917) entitled to part of passage	35 228
Total no. entitled (minus approx. no. deceased/ already repatriated)	49 916

Notes

(1) In Class 2, men had to pay one-quarter or TT$15.06; women to pay one-sixth or TT$10.04 each

(2) In Class 3, men had to pay half or TT$30.12; women to pay one-third or TT$20.08 each

Cost of repatriating those entitled to a return passage (at prewar prices of TT$60.24 per passage plus cost of clothing)

Class	*Number of immigrants*	*Amount to be paid by immigrants*		*Amount to be paid by government*	
1	9 882	–		£124 019	2/-
2	3 749 men	1/4=£ 11 762	9/9	£ 35 287	9/3
	1 057 women	1/6=£ 2 210	17/10	£ 11 054	
3	27 478 men	1/2=£172 424	9/10	£172 424	9/-
	7 750 women	1/3=£ 32 420	16/8	£ 68 841	13/4
Total:	49 916	£218 818	14/1	£411 626	13/7
		(TT$1 050 326 approx.)		(TT$1 975 805 approx.)	

Past record of repatriates

30 083 (30 per cent) of 99 438 (Class 1, introduced 1845–95) repatriated. (Plus an unknown number of 'ineffectives' from Classes 2 and 3 would have been repatriated as free paupers at an approximate rate of 100 per ship. Also children of parents entitled to a return passage would have been eligible to travel as dependants at an approximate rate of 100 per ship/16 per 100 adults.)

Source: CO 295/521, No. 146 Officer Administering (Trinidad) Government to Rt Hon. Viscount Milner, Secretary of State for the Colonies, 5 April 1919, enclosing Memo from F. C. Marriott, Acting Protector of Immigrants.

Notes

1 I am grateful to Mr and Mrs Patrick Gibbon for permission to use the recorded interview with his father.
2 After 1854, the period was a total of ten years.
3 This may refer to a short-lived scheme under which Indian immigrants were granted land in lieu of repatriation. In fact they were granted very poor, marginal lands.
4 De Verteuil, Anthony, *Sylvester Devenish and the Irish in Nineteenth Century Trinidad*, Port of Spain, Paria, 1986, p. 12.
5 *Trinidad Almanack*, 1891; *Trinidad Reviewer*, 1900; *Trinidad Blue Book*, 1904–5.
6 CO 384/192, Broome to Chamberlain, 26 November 1895, No. 445.
7 Report of the Special Committee appointed to consider matters relating to the Labour Question in Trinidad, 1905–6, CP 13/1906. Evidence of Abdul Aziz.
8 Report of the Committee on Emigration from India to the Crown Colonies and Protectorates, London 1910, Cd. 5192 (hereafter cited as Sanderson Report). Evidence of W. H. Coombs, p. 407.
9 *Creole Bitters*, 19 October 1903.
10 Sanderson Report, Appendix: Trinidad, Memo. No. 23. (2) enclosures 1 & 2. Minutes by the Acting Protector of Immigrants.
11 Sanderson Report, Appendix: Trinidad, Memo. No. 23 (5). Memo. by the Acting Protector of Immigrants on the evidence of Mr C. P. David.
12 Trinidad Ordinance No. 12 of 1897, sections 8; 16 (2); 20.
13 CO 384/92, Broome to Chamberlain, 9 November 1895. Confidential.
14 *Port of Spain Gazette*, 8 July 1897.
15 Report to the Government of India on the conditions of Indian immigrants in four British Colonies and Surinam, by Mr James McNeill, ICS, and Mr Chimman Lal. Part I, London, Cd. 7744, p. 39.
16 Annual Report of the Protector of Immigrants, CP 55/1905.
17 Ibid.
18 See Terms of Agreement in Comins, D. W. D., *Note on Emigration from India to Trinidad*, Calcutta, 1893, Appendix J, p. lxxxi.
19 Lubbock, Basil, *Coolie Ships and Oil Sailors*, Glasgow, Brown, Son & Ferguson, 1935, pp. 55, 70, 78, 84–5; White, L. G. W., *Ships, Coolies and Rice*, London, Sampson Low Marston & Co. Ltd., 1936, pp. 43, 92; (much of the information on the shipping of immigrants during this period comes from Lubbock and White).
20 Lubbock, *Coolie Ships*, p. 70.
21 Ibid.

22 Ibid., p. 84.
23 White, *Ships, Coolies and Rice*, p. 12.
24 Lubbock, *Coolie Ships*, p. 108.
25 Ibid., pp. 73–4.
26 Morton, Sarah E. (ed.), *John Morton of Trinidad ... Journals, Letters and Papers.* Toronto, 1916, pp. 272–3.
27 Lubbock, *Coolie Ships*, pp. 110–11.
28 White, *Ships, Coolies and Rice*, p. 20.
29 Lubbock, *Coolie Ships*, p. 96.
30 Ibid., pp. 55–6.
31 Ibid., p. 110.
32 Ibid., p. 55; White, *Ships, Coolies and Rice*, p. 19.
33 Lubbock, *Coolie Ships*, pp. 56–7.
34 *Kedgeree*, or *Kitcherrie* was an Indian dish (Hindi: *Kitchri*) of rice, cooked with butter or dhal, flavoured with shredded onion and spices.
35 Lubbock, *Coolie Ships*, p. 57.
36 White, *Ships, Coolies and Rice*, pp. 6–9.
37 Ibid., pp. 63–5.
38 Lubbock, *Coolie Ships*, pp. 57–8.
39 Laing, J. M., *Handbook for Surgeon-Superintendents of the Coolie Emigration Service*, quoted in K. L. Gillion, *Fiji's Indian Migrants: a History to the End of Indenture in 1920* (Melbourne: Oxford University Press, 1973), p. 62.
40 Lubbock, *Coolie Ships*, p. 58.
41 Indian Emigration Act XXI of 1883 (and modifications), Rules Nos. 171–5; 176–8; 180; 181; Section 91, Schedule D-Rules.
42 White, *Ships, Coolies and Rice*, p. 20.
43 Ibid., p. 101; Andrew Guyadeen's Notes, quoted in Ramesar, Marianne S., *Celebration: A Centenary History of Aramalaya Presbyterian Church, Tunapuna, Trinidad, 1881–1891*, Tunapuna, Aramalaya Presbyterian Church, 1988, p. 9.
44 Lubbock, *Coolie Ships*, p. 91; White, *Ships, Coolies and Rice*, pp. 33, 39, 42.
45 Indian Emigration Act, sections 191–5.
46 Hill, Arthur H., 'Emigration from India', *Timehri, Journal of the Royal Agricultural and Commercial Society of British Guiana* (3rd series), September 1919.
47 Ibid., pp. 50–1. (The value of the *anna* was 1 to $1\frac{1}{2}$ pennies, or 2–3 Trinidad cents. The standard wage in Trinidad was 25 cents per day, but the cost of living was higher than in India. The Indian immigrant's diet was likely to have become more varied in the West Indies, where he ate or produced unaccustomed ground provisions and vegetables. Likewise Indian food items were adopted by other residents of the West Indies.)
48 Sanderson Report, p. 181. Evidence of Arthur Marsden.
49 Ibid., p. 178. Evidence of Colonel Duncan G. Pitcher.
50 Ibid., p. 193. Evidence of William F. Bolton.
51 Ibid.
52 Ibid., pp. 94–5. Evidence of Sir Nevile Lubbock.
53 Ibid., pp. 29–30. Evidence of O. W. Warner.
54 Gillion, *Fiji's Indian Migrants*, p. 196.
55 Crooke, W., *The North-Western Provinces of India: their History, Ethnology and Administration* (London, 1897), quoted in Gillion, p. 40. Although Crooke exaggerated the immobile nature of Indian society, he did convey the idea that overseas migration involved super-rational risks.
56 Trinidad Emigration Agent's Report, CP 5/1876.
57 Interview conducted in 1988 on the occasion of the Indian Arrival Day commemoration.

58 Trinidad Agent General's Report, CP 16/1876.

59 Sanderson Report, pp. 29–30. Evidence of O. W. Warner.

60 Comins, *Note*, p. 25; Annual Report on Emigration from the Port of Calcutta to British and Foreign Colonies, by the Protector of Emigrants, passim.

61 Trinidad Emigration Agent to Secretary of State, CP 98/1902; Annual Report of the Protector of Immigrants for 1910–11, CP 143/1911; CO 571/1 (Confidential) 8 October 1913, minute by George Grindle.

62 Laurence, K. O., *Immigration into the West Indies in the 19th Century* (Barbados: Caribbean Universities Press, 1971), p. 57.

63 Naipaul, V. S., *A House for Mr Biswas* (London: André Deutsch, 1961), p. 174.

64 Sanderson Report, p. 181. Evidence of Arthur Marsden.

65 Ibid., p. 340. Evidence of Rev. J. Morton.

66 Ibid., pp. 311, 313. Evidence of F. E. M. Hosein. (Author's emphasis.)

CHAPTER 10 Early African and East Indian Muslims in Trinidad and Tobago

Brinsley Samaroo

The history of Islam in the Caribbean region is as complicated as it is interesting. The researcher is, however, assisted by the fact that the very distinctive philosophy of Islam, held together by an all-embracing system of belief and a host of rituals, marks out the Muslim from other members of the society. Wherever they went in the New World, the followers of Islam made no secret of their faith. They carried the Qu'ran either in their heads or in their pockets and used it as a constant point of reference. They wore the distinctive dress of the Muslim, male or female, ordained by their faith, learnt Arabic from an early age and often carried a charm or *Tabij* to ward off evil. As followers of a theocratic faith, that is, one in which there is no differentiation between religion and politics, their secular actions are always interpreted through theological spectacles. Wherever they went their Imams became both religious as well as secular leaders and their mosques could be used (as in Palestine today) as centres also for political activity. Finally their fight against oppression or wrong-doing of any sort has always taken on the dimension of a religious war or *jihad*. This holistic view of life where the separate parts of our existence are not compartmentalized, was of course the cause of considerable conflict between themselves and Christians, who sought to separate the affairs of State from those of the Church.

From the time of its founding by the Arabian prophet Muhammad in the seventh century, Islam or obedience to God's will, passed on to its followers a strict code of behaviour. All Muslims, for example, must believe in the Holy Qu'ran as Allah's final revelation. But this belief must, in its turn, be buttressed by other principles such as *Tawheed* (belief in one God), *Salat* (performance of five daily prayers), *Saum* (fasting in the month of Ramadan), *Zakat* (the payment of $2\frac{1}{2}$ per cent of one's annual saving to charity) and the *Hajj* or pilgrimage to Mecca once (at least) in one's lifetime.

In the second century of its birth the faith underwent its first major schism, which must be briefly discussed here, since it influenced the development of Islam in the Caribbean. Shortly after the death of the prophet, a serious conflict arose among his followers as to who should be the Caliph or supreme head of the faith. This was a most important position since the Caliph would be the one to uphold and apply the revealed and divine law. To defy the Caliph would be a crime as well as a sin. The majority of the followers were agreed on the principle that the Caliph should come from among his kin. But that was as far as agreement went. One group, the Sunnis, believed that the Caliph should be selected according to the custom or *sunna* which Muhammed and his companions had started, namely that the Caliphate should remain elective and that election thereto should be based on the merits of the various candidates. He who is finally chosen must be the most learned in the Holy Qu'ran and the divine law and must, by example, have earned the reverence and respect of most of the believers. The Caliphate would be decided by a college of electors, the electors themselves coming from the dignitaries and notables of the community. The opposing group, the Shi'ahs, argued that not only must the Caliph come from the Qu'raysh (the prophet's tribe), but soon narrowed this down to his clan, then his family and finally to the direct descendants of his daughter Fatima.[1] The Shi'ahs believed that the Caliph's was a divine appointment which would be made known by his predecessor and not through any election. From the very outset, upholders of these opposing views sought to resolve the matter through war. The prophet himself died in 661 and his grandsons, Hassan and Hosein, together with their Shi'ah followers, sought, by force or arms, to remove other pretenders. At the battle of Karbala in 680, the Shi'ah force (and thereby the Qu'raysh) was routed by the Umayyids who were supported by the Sunnis. The post-Karbala period witnessed the division of the Islamic Umma (Commonwealth) into these two major groups: Shi'ah and Sunni. Each year the Hosea (also known as 'Hussay') or Muharram festival is celebrated by Shi'ahs in commemoration of the 'martyrdom' of the grandsons of the prophet, Hassan and Hosein. When we come to look at the development of Islam in India we shall discuss another section which has relevance to the Caribbean, namely the birth of the Ahamadiyya movement.

From its beginnings in Arabia, the faith spread north and west to the Mediterranean world. But it was on the Iberian peninsula that it seemed to have been most influential. This was

> the most brilliant and fruitful contact between Islam and nascent European civilization developed over the course of seven centuries. Here, more than in any other Mediterranean land, the Arab settlement and the domination of their faith had time and means to infiltrate the pre-existent ethnic, social and cultural structure and, on their eventual withdrawal, to leave it greatly modified.[2]

This interaction between Islam and Roman Catholicism is of major importance in our study of Caribbean Islam because it was the Iberians who initiated the African slave trade to the New World – first to the Caribbean and later to Brazil. The ferocity with which the Spaniards sought to wipe out Islam among its slaves and to prevent its spread in the New World, stems to a large degree from the Iberian wars of the Reconquista, initiated shortly after the Moorish occupation of Iberia in the eighth century.

Another journey of the Islamic *jihad* against ignorance of its teachings was that from North to sub-Saharan Africa. Islam was spread to West Africa, from whence most of the Caribbean's slaves were derived, through the trans-Saharan trade in slaves, precious metals, salt, leather goods and palm oil. By the sixteenth century, the great Niger seat of learning at Timbuctoo had become well-established, and Islamic faith and practice, learning and ritual had become widespread in many of the nations who inhabited the great bulge of Africa. It was from these communities that the majority of African Muslims were drawn and transported to the Caribbean.

One researcher gives a panoramic view of the beginning of African Muslim migration to the New World. He points out that, starting with the Spaniards who brought Muslim slaves to their possessions in the New World, the other European nations followed. Thus by the eighteenth century there were black Muslims throughout the region holding their rites, teachings and ceremonies openly under the eyes of the Christians, undergoing intense persecution but steadfastly persisting in their faith.[3] In the case of Trinidad there is ample evidence to indicate the Muslim presence among those who came there as slaves.

Carl Campbell has documented the Mandingo Muslim presence in the Port of Spain area and in Central Trinidad from the start to the middle of the nineteenth century.[4] Jonas Mohammed Bath, who claimed that he was a Sultan in the Gambia, was well-versed in the Qu'ran, dressed as an Imam and was regarded as chief priest and patriarch of the Mandingos who set up their society in Port of Spain. Unlike many other Africans who were depressed by the harshness of slavery, these Mandingos of Bath's company were 'far from being psychologically crushed or culturally dehumanised. They were active, confident and successful.'[5] All of these Africans had a burning desire to return to the ancestral country. In one of their letters of longing to Lord Glenelg dated 12 January 1838, they claimed that one of their countrymen, Mohammed Houssa, had visited England in the previous year, had talked to the Queen and had been given the assurance that his group would be repatriated. Now they pleaded:

> That Your Memorialists, resolving to extricate themselves and others of their Nation, from the cruel and degraded state to which they had been reduced, formed themselves into a Society in this Island; and as the earnings of their honest industry accumulated, gradually redeemed themselves and their Countrymen from the

House of Bondage; hence on the memorable first day of August one thousand, eight hundred and thirty-four, a day which will always live in the Annals of Nations, and which will ever be remembered with feelings of the highest gratitude by the black man – Your Memorialists can safely, and with truth, assert, very few, if any of their tribe in the Island of Trinidad remained in Slavery to partake of the beneficent and humane achievement of the British Nation. – No! – Your Memorialists had long before unfettered themselves, their tribe and their families, by the fruits of their joint and industrious efforts.

That Your Memorialists have always behaved themselves as quiet and peaceable members of this Community; that they are proud of the name of British Subjects and feel grateful for the protection and benevolence which they have experienced from the Government.

That many generous and praiseworthy attempts have been made by the enlightened of Europe to introduce and establish civilization in Africa, but that such attempts have hitherto proved vain or but partially successful. That Your Memorialists feel confident that could they but reach the shores of the land that gave them birth, their efforts, as head of their tribe, would ensure success in propagating Civilization, the benefits of which they so deeply feel themselves, and would give them an opportunity of proclaiming to their Nation the liberality of the British Government.

That there are no means of direct communication between this Island and any of the British Settlements on the Coast of Africa, and if there were, the greater number of Your Memorialists have not the means to defray the necessary expenses attendant upon going there; besides which, Your Memorialists are greatly afraid, that if they were to venture upon the open sea, in any other than a British Armed vessel, they would be exposed to the imminent danger of being captured and again sold into the Iron Hands of bondage by the Nations that still carry on the Slave Trade.[6]

Whereas the petitioners of this group were not successful, another possibly more enterprising Muslim, Mohammedu Sisei, succeeded because of his persistence. Captured during a war in the Gambia in 1810, and brought to Trinidad in 1816, he was not only able to pay his way to England, but was finally successful in obtaining repatriation.[7]

The fierce, unrelenting spirit which Islam fosters among its adherents was accurately exemplified in the miserable story of an 85-year-old Mandingo Imam named Slamank, otherwise called Adam, who had been a slave on the Marli estate on the northern side of Port of Spain. In 1834 at age 84, he was told that he had been freed but that he was now an apprentice and had to learn the trade of 'digging cane', which he had in fact been doing for the past fifty years. When he protested against this he was imprisoned by the proprietress of the estate. In prison someone who saw him there indicated that 'he suffered so severely as to be unable to move on the second day of his confinement save on all fours like a quadruped'. Had it not been for the beneficence of his jailor, he would have 'expired from starvation'.[8] Slamank's petition to the island's Lieutenant Governor gives a good idea of the indignity of slavery. It also points to the fortitude of this old Imam. At 35 years of age, he claimed, he had been sold into slavery and 'notwithstanding his sacred profession, he had been forced to labour in the fields'. Now in his old age he had been separated from his family and had abandoned all hope of seeing the day of his redemption. If freed, he said, he would abandon all claim to compensation for fifty years of servitude, since the Mandingo Church in Port of Spain would support him.[9]

Even after slavery, many of the Mandingo Muslims tried to propagate their faith as they spread out from the town areas to the unexplored countryside. But this extension of 'heathenism' outside the centres where control could be exercised was a source of deep worry to ministers of religion as well as to the State. A Minister of the Anglican Church at Tacarigua noted, with deep regret, that the Africans who had moved to the far east of the island to Manzanilla and Turure, had been living completely without 'Clerical instruction, even the outward form of Christianity has almost disappeared among them!' The Minister further informed the Governor that 'many of them are nominally Mohammedans who are under the influence and guidance of five (so called) Mandingo priests by whom they are instructed in portions of the Koran; one only of this number can write, to whom they seem to look up with great reverence'.[10] The Minister then went on to indicate the methods which he was going to use to wipe out this heresy.

Evidence of the African Muslim presence, and of their religious fervour, is acknowledged by East Indians who arrived in Trinidad from 1845. In 1946 for example, an elder in the Indian Muslim community recalled that in his early boyhood he had been shown a copy of the Qu'ran in Arabic by someone whose father had received it as a gift from a Mandingo.[11] At the present time there is a Mandingo Road in South Trinidad, and it is not unusual to hear rural people refer to Muslims as 'Mandingas'.

By the middle of the nineteenth century, however, an effective, vibrant black Muslim presence in the Caribbean had disappeared. In the Spanish colonies (and Trinidad was a Spanish colony from 1494 to 1797), the victors of the Reconquista moved with vengeance against Muslims and all others who had failed to accept the Christian's one true God as saviour. Strangely enough, Roman Catholicism's religious fanaticism was strongly influenced by the fervour with which Islam socializes its own adherents. 'The central position which faith has in the soul of the Spaniard, individually and socially considered, is only comparable with that of Islam in the Muslim individual and in his society; and from this central position arise analogous consequences for both of these religious confessions.'[12] This explains the early introduction of the Inquisition in the New World, the Libris Indicis Prohibitorum and the burning of infidels.

In the non-Hispanic colonies the destruction of African Islam was ensured through subtle but effective means: the socialization of the African through Christian, Western education; laws that prohibited the practice of non-Christian cultural forms; rewards for those who abandoned their faiths and the denial of state patronage to those who did not.

Additionally, the break-up of the family and the non-recognition of African languages as proper means of communication all weakened the will and the capacity of the African to resist dominance. From 1845, for Trinidad, it was the East Indian Muslim's turn at the treadmill. As John Morton, pioneer Presbyterian missionary to the East Indians, contemplated the arrival of these new immigrants, half slave, half free, he rubbed his hands with glee as he saw a fresh challenge to his missionary zeal. 'This keen chilly wave from Hindusthan', he confided to his diary, was 'an adverse influence which has to be met and dealt with.'[13]

The Islamic 'invasion' of India was long (starting in the eighth century), continuous and three-pronged. Hence there were few areas of the subcontinent which did not feel the impact of Islam. Thus wherever the *arkatiyas* (recruiters) went to fetch indentured persons, Muslims were always present. From the ninth century, Arab merchants trading in the Indian Ocean had founded Muslim colonies along the south-western coast of India, particularly in the Malabar area. Even before that, there was the start of trading and proselytizing missions from Central Asia into Sind and later into the Punjab area. The third wave came through the north-eastern passes from Afghanistan in the tenth century and continued in the sixteenth century as the Mughals invaded.[14]

Through centuries of interaction, there was considerable merging of Hindu and Muslim practice and belief. Therefore, the Islam that came to the Caribbean from India was Indian Islam which differed in many ways from Middle-Eastern Islam. In modern-day Trinidad and Guyana where there are substantial Muslim populations, there is much confusion, often conflict, between these two types of Islam. While the majority of believers continue to follow this particular brand of Indian Islam, missionaries with Middle-Eastern training and assistance are doing their utmost to de-Indianize the faith. In India itself the syncretism that occurred with the meeting of Islam and Hinduism resulted in many new cultural creations. Out of the mixing of Persian and Hindi came Urdu and a new wave of literature which enriched thought on the sub-continent. Although most Indian Muslims were Sunnis, the Shi'ah observance of Hosea (Hussay) or Muharram came to be celebrated each year. But in India the elaborately decorated carriage (*tadjah*) used in symbolically transporting the tombs of Hassan and Hosein is clearly an imitation of the massive carriage used for transporting the deity Jagganath in the annual festival in praise of this God. This festival was transported in its Indian form to the Caribbean.

In like manner the Hindu caste system exercised considerable influence on the Muslim social order in India:

> In the social sphere the influence of Hinduism on Islam has nowhere left a more definite mark than in the creation of caste distinctions which indicate social status as clearly as they do in India.[15]

Additionally, Islamic monotheism had a strong influence on Hindu thought. This could be seen in the formation of new religious beliefs of the post-Muslim period, such as the Bhakti movement, Sikhism and much later the Arya Samaj movement. Each one of these was transported to the Caribbean to add to the cultural diversity of the region.

One further ideological stream of Indian Islam needs to be mentioned at this stage, because of its relevance to the Caribbean situation. This is the rise of the Ahmadiyya Movement in India during the late nineteenth century. This movement, also often called Qadiyani, because it was launched in the town of Qadiyan in East Punjab, has been regarded as being highly heretical by both Sunni and Shi'ah Muslims. The movement was founded in 1889 by Mirza Ghulam Ahmad (c. 1839–1908) who claimed that he was in fact the last of the prophets. In 1914 the movement split, one arm holding on to the view that Ahmad was in fact a full-fledged divinely inspired prophet; the smaller group preaching that Ahmad was no more than a reformer whose ideas on social reform surely merited attention. This second group set up its headquarters at Lahore under the leadership of Maulana Muhammad Ali and undertook, like the other group, missionary work in Pakistan, West Africa and the Caribbean. Conflict between Ahmadis and other Muslims, particularly the Sunnis, has always been intense. In 1973 the Government of Pakistan declared the movement unacceptable in the holistic Islamic sense. It was therefore banned in that country. The painful repercussions of this conflict, before and after 1973, have been strongly felt in the Caribbean.

On the very first ship that brought Indians to Trinidad, the *Fatel Rozack* on 30 May 1845, there was a number of Muslims among the 213 persons on board. Names such as Causmolle Khan, Furreed, Emambocus, Faize Buxo, Madar Buxo, Allar, Omrudee, Muhourun, Bahadur and Faizen all attest to the Muslim presence. Muslim Indians continued coming up to

1917, although not in the same numbers as the Hindus. Today they form about 6 per cent of the population of Trinidad and Tobago (total population: 1.2 million) whereas the Hindus constitute 25 per cent of the nation's population.

From the moment of their first arrival the Indian Muslims, like their African brethren before them, made proclamation of their faith. A nineteenth century English resident of Trinidad noted their observance of Salat:

> With regard to the first duty of prayer, and in fact, all the duties, Mussulmans in Trinidad soon grow lax and careless, but I have nevertheless frequently seen on an estate, a devout follower of the Prophet leave his work to face the rising sun, profoundly salaam, utter his formula and then proceed with his labour as though no interruption had occurred.[16]

As early as March 1868 John Morton recorded a visit to 'a Mohammedan house of worship – a nice little building with galvanized roof'.[17] His fellow missionary K. J. Grant, too, spoke of the persistence of the servants of Allah:

> The followers of Mohammed are not ashamed to declare their faith or offer their prayers wherever they may be. Vividly before my mind is the picture of a company of twelve or fifteen men, who had met together for prayer.... The scene was most impressive and yet it could be witnessed every Friday wherever there was a Mohammedan group.[18]

As will presently be shown, relationships between Hindus and Muslims were generally cordial, even during the intense conflict that took place on the sub-continent during partition. However, there was hardly the same cordiality between the Muslims and those whom they considered their oppressors: the British administration and the missionaries. This pattern of resistance had its roots on the Indian sub-continent. The Muslim response to British rule in India was at first not as receptive as that of the Hindus. It must be borne in mind that the British were seeking to displace a predominantly Muslim (rather than Hindu) regime in India. And the British, in their initial attempts to win support in India, favoured Hindus rather than Muslims from the time of the arrival there of the East India Company. Administratively, the Permanent Settlement of 1793 'reduced Muslim farmers and peasants to the level of agricultural labourers and created a class of Hindu landlords (*zamindars*) who thrived at the expense of the Muslim masses'.[19]

Instances of the transference of this conflict situation between Caribbean Muslims and the authorities are not hard to find. In British Guiana some planters resisted the recruitment of Indian Muslims on various grounds. They complained that Muslim holy men (*Fakirs*) were disrupting life on the plantations; some complained that they feared Hindu/Muslim tension on the plantations, while others claimed that the *Khanzadas* (that is, Rajputs who had become Muslims) were poor field labourers.[20] In 1884, in Trinidad, there was the confrontation between the Muslim-led Hosea celebrators and the State Police in which 16 persons were killed and about 100 injured. Again there is evidence of the British Government's fear of violence from the Indians after 1857 and of constant conflict between missionaries and Muslims in Trinidad.[21] During the twentieth century Muslims have played a leading role in the movement for independence and in the preservation of Islamic values.

What has been the nature of the relationship between the Muslims and the Hindus in Trinidad? Except for sporadic instances of conflict at the time of the partition, Hindu/Muslim relations have been remarkably free of most of the tensions that arose in the ancestral land. There are reasons for this. Most of the Indians who came to the Caribbean came from rural India, away from the power struggles which obtained at the higher levels of government. They were therefore insulated from the causes of tension and were in fact united by common poverty which impelled them to seek greener pastures abroad. The integration of Hindu practices with Islamic, and the partial merging of the cultures, aforementioned, served as cementing factors; the fellowship cemented by the camaraderie developed during the long journey from India was an additional consideration. This brotherhood of the boat (*jahaji bhai*) has persisted even among the descendants of the immigrants up to the present time. The common experience of indentureship and the shared initial alien-ness to the New World served as additional bonds. Indeed a prominent Maulana in Trinidad argues that Muslims have integrated not only with the Indian population but in the society as a whole, without losing their Islamic identity. 'In Trinidad, Muslims have so integrated themselves with peoples of other races and cultures and faiths without losing their identity, that in spite of being a minority group they have not enjoyed minority status, rather, they have enjoyed equality status.'[22]

The preservation of the Muslim identity has always been a matter of great concern for Muslims abroad, particularly in countries where they are in a minority. This indeed was the focus of a special conference convened by the Islamic Council of Europe, whose deliberations were published in 1980.[23] Interestingly enough, the concerns raised at that conference were very similar to those that were being raised by Caribbean Muslims more than a century before. The major question then, as now, was 'How do we preserve a Muslim identity in a predominantly non-Muslim state?'

In Trinidad there has always been a deliberate attempt by the Muslims to preserve and propagate their value system in a number of ways. By the middle of the nineteenth century they had established mosques in most of the areas where they settled. Side by side with these mosques were *maktabs* where children learnt Arabic and Urdu and were exposed to the teachings of the Qu'ran as well as the Hadith which is a collection of Islamic wisdom gleaned from the discussions of the Prophet and his companions. A number of the immigrants brought from India literary works by Urdu, Persian and Arabic writers. These were supplemented from the early twentieth century by regular importations from India. The musical works of well-known contemporary Indian (Muslim) composers were quite familiar among the settlers. Songs which recounted the life of the Prophet or the heroic exploits of his companions and descendants (Ghazals and Quaseedas) as well as their composers, Mirza Muhammad Rafi or Mirza Asadullah Khan Ghalib, were celebrated. The *marisya* (elegy) was very popular, as was one of its originators, Mir Babar Anis, whose fame arose out of his position as court composer to the Begum of Fyzabad, from whence many immigrants came. Based on the example of these *ustads* many local bards arose, taking their songs and poetry to all parts of the new land.

In seeking redress to the many grievances which they suffered as they sought to come to terms with the new environment, the early Indian Muslims frequently combined with the Hindus to make common representation to the authorities. Such early cooperation led to the formation of the Hindu/Muslim East Indian National Association in Princes Town in 1893, the East Indian National Congress in Couva and the Trinidad Indian League in Tunapuna. All of these organizations had a good intermixture of Hindu and Muslim leaders.[24] These early groups agitated for a wide range of reform. They wanted State recognition for Hindu and Muslim marriages, schools to be established where Hindus and Muslims would not feel threatened by Christian conversion; before the First World War they highlighted the wretched conditions of indentureship and they often joined hands in opposing missionary condemnation of their faiths. Newspaper reports indicate that the Muslims, like the Hindus, regularly celebrated their major festivals; they went on *Hajj*, starting as groups during the thirties of this century.[25] On occasion there were calls for Hindu–Muslim cooperation on common problems[26] which sometimes resulted in joint action. In 1930, for example, a Hindu–Muslim school was started in Chaguanas[27] and, when visiting dignitaries from the sub-continent were in the island, joint receptions were hosted. In September 1929, for example, the Rev. C. F. Andrews lectured to both groups on the ideals of Islam.[28]

While there is this early history of cooperation between these two religious groups, there is also much evidence of separate activity by both of them. From the early twentieth century both groups saw the necessity for the formation of separate Hindu or Muslim groups which would cater for specific needs. In the case of the Muslims, these groups sought to set up separate Muslim schools[29] to call meetings to discuss the question of Muslim unity[30] or to pay tribute to local or foreign persons of eminence.[31] In order to maintain contact with international Islam, the Trinidad Muslims maintained long contact with an Islamic Missionary group in the UK, in Woking, Surrey,[32] went on pilgrimage to Mecca and to India, sent some of their youths for Islamic training to the Indian sub-continent and sponsored continuous visits by Muslim missionaries. This has continued to the present time.[33]

The major preoccupation of the relatively small Muslim minority in Trinidad and Tobago has been that of their survival and the maintenance of their religious identity in a highly heterogeneous society. The foundations of their survival strategy were laid during the latter half of the last century by India-born immigrants who had transported that consciousness across the dark waters. The Muslims, like the Hindus and indeed the Africans before them, met a generally hostile new environment. This led, in the case of the Indian Muslims, to an accommodation with the Hindus on a wide range of matters and over a long period of time. There has been a relative absence of communal rivalry therefore, and their joint ventures did in fact yield positive results. The common experience of the crossing and of indentureship also served to cement the cordiality. At the same time, both Muslims and Hindus felt free to form separate organizations which catered for their distinct religious needs, as each group sought to maintain its identity in a world where Christianity appeared to reign supreme. The fact that the Indian Muslim came at a later period, when communications with the outside world were far better than in the time of Mohammedu Sisei, meant that Indian Islam could be nurtured constantly and continuously. Since the Indians came in frequent waves and in substantial numbers, there was a steady flow of believers who gave solidarity to existing numbers. In addition, by the early twentieth century Islamic missionary activity could successfully compete with Christian. Thus Christianity could be kept outside the door. Finally, the recency of the arrival of the Indian Muslim, compared with that of early African Muslims, kept the Islamic memory alive and has facilitated its growth into the present time.

Notes

1 B. Lewis, 'Politics and War', in J. Schact and C. E. Bosworth (ed.), *The Legacy of Islam* (Oxford, 1974), pp. 160–1.

2 F. Gabrieli, 'Islam in the Mediterranean World' in Schact and Bosworth, *The Legacy*, p. 81.

3 Clyde-Ahamad Winters, 'Muslims in Pluralistic Societies: The case of the West Indies,' *Al-Ittihad*, July 1978, pp. 39f.

4 Carl Campbell, 'Jonas Mohammed Bath and the Free Mandingo in Trinidad: The question of their repatriation to Africa 1831–1838', *Pan African Journal*, 7 (2) 1974, pp. 129–52.

5 Ibid., p. 145.

6 PRO State Papers. CO 295/12. Petition of Mandingo ex-slaves for return to their own country. There were twelve signatures in Arabic.

7 Carl Campbell, 'Mohammedu Sisei of Gambia and Trinidad, c. 1788–1839', *African Studies Association of the West Indies*, Bulletin No. 7, Dec. 1974, pp. 29–38.

8 Captain Studholme Hodgson, *Truths from the West Indies* (London, 1838), p. 151. Hodgson had served in Trinidad in the Queen's 19th Foot Regiment and was appalled at the cruelty of some of the island's slave-owners.

9 Hodgson, p. 358.

10 PRO State Papers, CO 295/134. Letter from Rev. J. H. Hamilton, Minister at Tacarigua to the Governor describing a tour of the Eastern settlements, 19 March 1841.

11 Syad Mohammed Hosein, 'Historical Sketch'. *Eid-ul-Fitr Brochure*, compiled by Unus Ali, Port of Spain, August 1948, p. 11.

12 Gabrieli, 'Islam', p. 90.

13 Sarah Morton, *John Morton of Trinidad* (Toronto, 1916), p. 420.

14 A. Ahamad, 'India', in Schact and Bosworth, *The Legacy*, p. 131.

15 M. T. Titus, *Islam in India and Pakistan* (Madras, 1959), p. 175.

16 J. H. Collens, *Guide to Trinidad* (London, 1986), pp. 188f.

17 Morton, *John Morton*, p. 53.

18 K. J. Grant, *My Missionary Memories* (Halifax, 1923), pp. 67f.

19 Ahamad, 'India', p. 138.

20 D. Bisnauth, 'The East Indian Migrant Society in British Guiana, 1891–1930', PhD History thesis UWI (Mona), 1977, pp. 97f.

21 See the author's study of 'Missionary Methods and Local Responses', in B. Brereton and W. Dookeran (ed), *East Indians in the Caribbean* (New York, 1982), pp. 96 and 100f.

22 Maulana M. K. Hydal, 'The Religious Experience of the Indians in Trinidad: the Muslim experience', in I. J. Bahadur Singh (ed.), *Indians in the Caribbean* (New Delhi, 1987), p. 191.

23 Islamic Council of Europe, *Muslim Communities in Non-Muslim States* (London, 1980).

24 See, for example, *The Mirror*, 8 and 15 Jan. 1913.

25 *East Indian Weekly*, 1 and 15 March 1930.

26 *The Mirror*, 1 October 1914. *East Indian Weekly*, 1 November 1930. Also, *East Indian Weekly*, 19 October 1929 for joint meeting to discuss educational problems.

27 *East Indian Weekly*, 15 November 1930.

28 *East Indian Weekly*, 14 September 1929.

29 *East Indian Weekly*, 2 May 1931.

30 *The Mirror*, 14 October 1914. *Port of Spain Gazette*, 21 August 1917.

31 See, for example, Grand reception for Maulana Abdul Aleem Siddiqui, reported in *Trinidad Guardian*, 5 March 1950.

32 *Eid-ul-Fitr Brochure*, compiled by Unus Ali, Port of Spain, 1948, p. 9.

33 The formation of Muslim groups and the visits of missionaries are discussed by the author in 'The Indian connection: the influence of Indian thought and ideas on East Indians in the Caribbean', D. Dabydeen and B. Samaroo (eds), *India in the Caribbean* (London, 1987), pp. 49f.

Select bibliography

Books and reports

Adamson, A., *Sugar without slaves: The political economy of British Guiana, 1838–1904* (Yale University Press, New Haven, 1968).

Arya, U., *Ritual Songs and Folk Songs in Surinam* (E. J. Brill, Leiden, 1968).

Bahadursingh, I. J. (ed.), *The Other India* (Arnold Heinemann, New Delhi, 1979).

—— (ed.), *Indians in the Caribbean* (Sterling Publishers, New Delhi, 1987).

Birbalsingh, F. (ed.), *Indenture and Exile* (TSAR, Toronto, 1989).

—— , *Indo-Caribbean Resistance* (TSAR, Toronto, 1993).

Bronkhurst, H. V. P., *British Guiana and its Labouring Population* (T. Woolmer, London, 1883).

—— , *Among the Hindus and Creoles of British Guiana* (T. Woolmer, London, 1888).

Clarke, C., *East Indians in a West Indian Town* (Allen and Unwin, Winchester: Mass., 1986).

Cumpston, M., *Indians Overseas in British Territories, 1934–54* (Oxford University Press, London, 1953).

Gangulee, N., *Indians in the Empire Overseas* (New India Publishing Co., London, 1947).

Gosine, M., *East Indians and Black Power in the Caribbean: The case of Trinidad* (Africana Publications, New York, 1986).

—— (ed.), *Dot-head Americans. The Silent Minority in the United States* (Windsor Press, New York, 1990).

—— (ed.), *The Coolie Connection: From the Orient to the Occident* (Windsor Press, New York, 1992).

James, C. L. R., *West Indians of East Indian Descent* (Ibis Publications, Trinidad, 1965).

Klass, M., *East Indians in Trinidad: A study in Cultural Persistence*. Reprint (Waveland Press, Illinois, 1988).

—— , *Singing with Sai Baba: The Politics of Revitalization in Trinidad* (Westview Press, Colorado, 1991).

Kondapi, C., *Indians Overseas, 1938–1948* (Indian Council For World Affairs, New Delhi, 1951).

La Guerre, J. (ed.), *Calcutta to Caroni*. 2nd Edition (University of the West Indies, Trinidad, 1993).

Look Lai, W., *Indentured Labour, Caribbean sugar: Chinese and Indian Immigrants to the British West Indies, 1838–1918* (Johns Hopkins, Baltimore, 1993).

Mangru, B., *Benevolent Neutrality: Indian Government policy and labour migration to British Guiana* (Hansib, London, 1987).

—— , *Indenture and Abolition. Sacrifice and Survival on the Guyanese Sugar Plantations* (TSAR, Toronto, 1993).

Nath, D., *A History of Indians in British Guiana* (Thomas Nelson, London, 1950).

Niehoff, A. & J., *East Indians in the West Indies* (Milwaukee Public Museum, Wisconsin, 1960).
Premdas, R. (ed.), *The Enigma of Ethnicity: An analysis of race in the Caribbean and in the world* (University of the West Indies, Trinidad, 1993).
Rajkumar, N. V., *Indians outside India* (All-India Congress Committee, New Delhi, 1950).
Rauf, N., *Indian Village in Guyana: A study of cultural change and ethnic identity* (E. J. Brill, Leiden, 1974).
Ruhoman, P., *Centenary History of East Indians in British Guiana, 1838–1938.* Reprint (Georgetown, 1988).
Saunders, K. (ed.), *Indentured Labour in the British Empire, 1834–1920* (Croom Helm, London, 1984).
Schwartz, B. M., *Caste in Overseas Indian Committees* (Chandler Publishing Co., San Francisco, 1967).
Seecharan, C., *India and the Shaping of the Indo-Guyanese Imagination, 1890s–1920s* (Peepal Tree Press/University of Warwick, Leeds and Coventry, 1993).
Singaravelou, *Les Indiens de la Caraibe.* 3 vols (Editions L'Harmattan, Paris, 1988).
Singh, K., *The Bloodstained Tombs: The Muharram Massacre in Trinidad, 1884* (Macmillan, London, 1988).
Silverman, M., *Rich People and Rice: Factional politics in rural Guyana* (E. J. Brill, Leiden, 1980).
Smith, M. G., *The Plural Society in the British West Indies* (University of California Press, Berkeley, 1965).
Speckermann, J. D., *Marriage and Kinship among the Indians in Surinam* (Van Gorcum, Assen, 1965).
Tinker, H., *A New System of Slavery: The export of Indian labour overseas, 1830–1920* (Oxford University Press, London, 1974).
——, *The Banyan Tree: Overseas emigrants from India, Pakistan and Bangladesh* (Oxford University Press, London, 1974).
Tyson, J. D., *Report on the Conditions of Indians in Jamaica, British Guiana and Trinidad* (Government of India Press, Simla, 1939).
Vertovec, S., *Hindu Trinidad* (Macmillan, London, 1992).
Weller, J. A., *The East Indian Indenture in Trinidad* (Institute of Caribbean Studies, Puerto Rico, 1969).

Articles

Emmer, P., 'Immigration into the Caribbean: The introduction of Chinese and East Indian labourers between 1838 and 1917', *Itinerario*, Netherlands, 1990, 14 (1).
——, 'Female indentured labourers in Suriname', *Boletin de Estudious Latinoamericanos y del Caribe*, Netherlands, 1987 (43).
Hoefte, R., 'Female indentured labour in Suriname: for better or worse', *Boletin*, 1987 (42).
——, 'The position of female British Indian and Javanese contract labourers in Suriname', *Boletin*, 1987 (13).
Jain, P., 'Exploitation and reproduction of immigrant Indian labour in colonial Guyana and Malaysia', *Journal of Contemporary Asia*, Philippines, 1988, 18 (2).
Jain, R., 'Overseas Indians in Malaysia and the Caribbean: Comparative notes', *Immigrants and Minorities*, Great Britain, 1988, 7 (1).

Jha, J., 'An Indian national "panchayat" of Trinidad, 1899', *Quarterly Review of Historical Studies*, India, 1984, 23 (4).

Mangru, B., 'Indian, Indentured Labour in British Guiana', *History Today*, Great Britain, 1986, 36 (April).

——, 'Abolishing the return passage entitlement under indenture', *Caribbean Quarterly*, Jamaica, 1986, 32 (3–4).

Miller, E., 'The rise of matriarchy in the Caribbean', *Caribbean Quarterly*, Jamaica, 1988, 34 (3–4).

Ryan, S., 'One love revisited: The persistence of race in the politics of Trinidad and Tobago', *Caribbean Affairs*, Trinidad, 1988, 1 (2).

Parboosingh, I., 'An Indo-Jamaican beginning: A fragment of an autobiography', *Jamaica Journal*, Jamaica, 1985, 18 (2).

Shepherd, V., 'From rural plantations to urban slums: The economic status and problems of East Indians in Kingston, Jamaica', *Immigrants and Minorities*, Great Britain, 1986, 5 (2).

——, 'Transients to Citizens: the development of a settled East Indian Community', *Jamaica Journal*, Jamaica, 1985, 18 (3).

——, 'Emancipation through servitude: Aspects of the condition of Indian women in Jamaica, 1845–1945', *Bulletin of the Society for the Study of Labour*, Great Britain, 1988, 53 (3).

Singh, K., 'The abolition of Indian indentureship and response of the planter class in Trinidad', *Journal of Caribbean History*, Barbados, 1987, 21 (1).

Sookdeo, A., 'Indian West-Indians and ethnic processes in Trinidad and Tobago with some reference to the Fiji Indians', *Journal of Ethnic Studies*, Great Britain, 1988, 16 (3).

Vertovec, S., 'Religion and ethnic ideology: The Hindu Youth Movement in Trinidad, *Ethnic and Racial Studies*, Great Britain, 1990, 13 (2).

Williams, B., *Stains on My Name, War in My Veins: Guyana and the politics of cultural struggle* (London: Duke University Press, 1991).

Index